Jewish Women Living the Challenge

A Hadassah Compendium

Jewish Women Living the Challenge

A Hadassah
Compendium
edited by
Carol Diament

Programming Ideas written and compiled by
Claudia Chernov and Leora Tanenbaum

HADASSAH
The Women's Zionist Organization of America, Inc.

Copyright © 1997, Hadassah
The Women's Zionist Organization of America, Inc.
All Rights Reserved

Published 1997 by Hadassah,
The Women's Zionist Organization of America, Inc.,
50 West 58th Street
New York, NY 10019

ISBN 1-889525-04-9

Designed by Tina R. Malaney
Illustrations by Susan Gross
Produced by the Creative Services Department of Hadassah

Manufactured in the United States of America

Printed on Recycled Paper

CONTENTS

CONTENTS

Unit 2: FAMILY AND HOME

Unit 3: WOMEN AND THE WORKPLACE

FOREWORD

The National Jewish Education Department of Hadassah has, over the past decade, anticipated and confronted the most crucial issues facing the Jewish community. We revealed the poisonous hatred between the Israeli Right and Left, exposing the division that led to the assassination of Prime Minister Yitzhak Rabin in 1995. We have explored the widening division between Israeli and American Jews. And we have analyzed the status of Jewish women through books, articles, seminars, educational retreats, and symposia. We therefore commend Hadassah's Strategic Planning Department for its commitment to understanding Jewish women's roles. Indeed, in 1995 Hadassah initiated the study that later developed into *Voices for Change: Future Directions for American Jewish Women*, and in 1997 Hadassah funded the International Research Institute on Jewish Women at Brandeis University.

In JEWISH WOMEN LIVING THE CHALLENGE, published jointly by the Education/Public Policy Division, the Center for Innovation, and the Marketing/Communications Division, we offer a retrospective of more than a decade of publications by the National Jewish Education Department, focusing on women's personal, social, political, and economic lives, in the United States and Israel. Many of our contributors observe that gender roles have changed dramatically over the past few decades—and so, we believe, must Judaism.

Why did we choose to re-examine the status of women in the family, the synagogue, and the Jewish community? Because problems in all of these spheres of Jewish life remain unresolved, despite the attainments of recent years.

Many Jewish women and men have found the marriage of Judaism and feminism to be wonderfully enriching. Yet others view this theoretical meeting ground as a battlefield. In the debate between feminism and Judaism, one side argues for the primacy of *halakhah* (Jewish law) and urges Jewish women to find satisfaction primarily in their traditional domestic role. This side asserts that different masculine and feminine roles are mandated by *halakhah*. However, traditionalists argue that in the divine perspective, the man's role of synagogue participation and religious leadership is equal in value to the woman's role of homemaking and childrearing.

The other side, however, rejects traditional sex-based roles for both men and women, and this side argues that *halakhah* can play no part in defining women's status. Since women have been excluded from the Jewish legal process in the past, they argue, the results of this process have no meaning for them. Most of the articles presented here tread a middle ground. The contributors treat Jewish law with respect, but many protest against specific legal rulings.

The articles in Unit 1, "Self," focus on physical and emotional well-being. What is the Jewish attitude toward medical care, preventive health care, and early detection of disease? Dr. Edie Gurewitsch writes that as Hadassah works to increase women's knowledge of medical issues, it fulfills a Jewish moral imperative. Other contributors focus on the meaning of female beauty, on aging, and on the experience of being a widow.

In Unit 2, "Family and Home," we consider some of the many challenges confronting today's Jewish families. Two complementary articles explore contemporary sexual behavior, an arena where the mores of Judaism and feminism collide. Feminists of all types have faced difficulty as they have faced and revised earlier moral and sexual norms. But Jewish feminists have had a unique task: how to live our lives according to feminist ideals and still follow Jewish traditions. Our two articles offer different responses to this question.

Also in "Family and Home," we examine the factors that make for a happy marriage. And we look into mother-daughter relationships, as we read of a trip to a *mikvah* (ritual bath) prior to marriage and then, in a short story, meet an Israeli mother who reconciles with her grown daughter.

Two articles in Unit 2 deal with two of the most disturbing problems in today's Jewish family: Jewish divorce law and domestic violence. The article on domestic violence differs from our other selections, because it was originally written for *The American Scene*, published by Hadassah's American Affairs/Domestic Policy Department.

Finally, "Family and Home" includes three essays on interfaith marriage. The National Jewish Education Department explored the rising rate of interfaith marriage several years before the Council of Jewish Federations issued its alarming report in 1990, and two of our early articles, both increasingly relevant today, are reprinted here, as is a more recent piece.

In Unit 3, "Women and the Workplace," we examine the contemporary working woman's "juggling act" as she balances job and home responsibilities. We note the changes in Jewish women's work force participation that have occurred in our lifetime. In the early years of this century, when American women were needed to fill factory jobs and supplement their parents' or husbands' income, women required and demanded a movement for equality. They sought higher education and political rights—and they won the vote. Yet by mid-century the American (and American Jewish) ideal was the wife whose husband provided her entire financial support. With a renascent feminism in the sixties and seventies, numbers of women began entering the work force, taking on jobs that their predecessors had only imagined. In an interview in this section, Judith Lichtman states: "The feminist revolution was really a revolution for both men and women." As more wives have accepted paid employment, more husbands have accepted family and household responsibilities. Nonetheless, Lichtman observes that, even as more and more women work for pay outside the home, caring for the house and children remains largely the woman's task. In this unit we also present a short piece of fiction that explores one of the unresolved problems of the workplace, sexual harassment.

Unit 4, "Social Action," opens with an article that presents Jewish women's earliest demand for equitable treatment under the law—the biblical story of the five daughters of Zelophehad. Jewish women's demands for social justice have been ongoing through history, reflected today by the many Jewish women who work for social justice throughout the world. Alice Shalvi's exploration of women's position in contemporary Israel is but one example.

Also in Unit 4, we explore the American debate on abortion from the framework of Jewish law. Though abortion is not an obviously Jewish issue, Hadassah, as a non-sectarian American organization concerned for the continued separation between church and state, seeks to preserve women's reproductive choice.

In addition to these issues, the Education/Public Policy Division has grappled with numerous social concerns over the past decade. The American Affairs/Domestic Policy Department has fought for increased awareness of domestic abuse, for health care reform, for expanded voter registration, and for greater funding for research into women's health. The Israel, Zionist, and International Affairs (IZAIA) Department has been an advocate for Israel. The Health Education Department has raised awareness and educated women about breast cancer and osteoporosis. Many of these social concerns are raised in Units 1 and 2, in the articles and the programming on women's health and on domestic violence.

In Unit 5, "Spirituality," we explore recent trends in women's religious experiences. Overall, how has feminism affected Jewish spiritual life in America today? We specifically explore women's prayer language, women's grieving, and new women's rituals.

Ultimately, all the articles in JEWISH WOMEN LIVING THE CHALLENGE lead to social action. Judaism works to mend and repair the world—*tikkun olam*. Feminism works to overthrow injustices against women. When Judaism and feminism are brought together, the vision of a better world becomes an attainable goal.

Programming

Each article is followed by suggested activities that are organized according to the five opportunities for participation outlined in *Building a Special Community for American Jewish Women: A Planning Guide for Local Hadassah Units*. These five opportunities for participation are: "At Home," "Interest/Study Groups" "Meetings," "Annual Events," and "Hands-On."

The programming for these five categories is actually very flexible. For example, many "At Home" suggestions can be easily adapted for use at meetings, as can many of the suggestions for annual events. Similarly, many of the suggestions for meetings could be used as sessions or workshops at an annual event.

Many of the "Hands-On" activities are equally appropriate for "At Home," particularly the suggestions for creating Jewish ceremonial objects. And the discussion questions listed for "Interest/Study Groups" could certainly provoke discussion and thought "At Home."

A special feature of the "At Home" programming is "Torah Table Talk." The model for this is the article "The Story of Zelophehad's Daughters" by David Epstein and Suzanne Singer Stutman (pages 201-204). Through reading this article, we learn some methods for holding a *talk* on *Torah*—perhaps at a Shabbat *table*. In other words, Epstein and Stutman's article is itself a Torah Table Talk. All other articles contain this special feature within the "At Home" programming. Each Torah Table Talk consists of a selection of Jewish text, taken from either the Bible, rabbinic writings, or recent Judaic scholarship, that corresponds to the article in JEWISH WOMEN LIVING THE CHALLENGE along with several questions to spur thought and conversation. Together with family and/or friends, perhaps at a Shabbat or holiday dinner table, read the selection together and, using the questions as a starting point, hold a discussion on Jewish thought and Jewish values.

The Torah Table Talk texts and questions would also be wonderful for study groups, adding depth to their discussions of the articles.

Because the Jewish texts vary in complexity and levels of difficulty, some of the Torah Table Talks might involve extensive intellectual conversations, and some might involve only a brief discussion. All of the texts are presented in English, and all can be approached by readers with little or no Jewish educational background. Indeed, the Jewish tradition encourages all, regardless of prior learning, to immerse themselves in the study of Torah and the Jewish tradition.

Furthermore, the articles and their programming ideas would be great follow-up materials for women's symposia participants who wish to further explore Jewish women's issues. The articles and programming ideas are also recommended for women's Rosh Hodesh groups that wish to incorporate study into their monthly *tefillah* (prayer) experience.

Finally, a rewarding opportunity to interact with like-minded women through the Internet is now in the offing. Check the Hadassah website at http://www.hadassah.org for details. A Jewish Education chat room will provide a place to further explore the issues raised in JEWISH WOMEN LIVING THE CHALLENGE.

Ordering Hadassah Materials

Many of the programming suggestions recommend the use of Hadassah materials—books, pamphlets, issue cards, etc.—and we have made every effort to include up-to-date ordering information. If this information is unclear, call the Hadassah National Order Department automated phone line at 1-800-880-9455 and request Hadassah's *Resource Catalogue*. This catalogue lists all available materials and all the necessary information on how to obtain them.

In some cases, Hadassah materials can be obtained through the National Hadassah department that produced them. In these cases, call the department directly to request assistance.

Barbara B. Spack
National Jewish Education Chair

Carol Diament, Ph.D.
Editor
National Jewish Education Director

ACKNOWLEDGMENTS

Because this is a decade-long retrospective of articles produced by the National Jewish Education Department on the changing status of Jewish women, we wish to acknowledge the foresight and vision of our past Jewish education chairs. They are representative of what is best and noblest in American Jewish leadership: Sue Mizrahi (1984-1988), Ruth G. Cole (1988-1992), and Belle H. Simon (1992-1993). We have always had the benefit of the devotion and expertise of our assistant director and production editor, Doris Oxenhorn. She has exerted an important influence upon the ultimate shape of the book by bringing it from manuscript form to the point of publication. We are indebted to our senior editor, Claudia Chernov, and associate editor, Leora Tanenbaum, for their outstanding editing and research. With pride, we note that they wrote and compiled the programming for JEWISH WOMEN LIVING THE CHALLENGE. And, we are grateful to Rachel Schwartz, our editorial assistant, for her work on all details of production, from typing manuscripts to researching Judaic sources, from copyediting to requesting reprint rights.

The programming is compiled from very many sources. We wish to express gratitude to the National Programming Department: Ruth Grossberg, chair; Linda Steigman, director; Randy Tunkel, administrator; and Danielle Lewis, administrative assistant for providing a list of program ideas which were then researched, expanded, and interspersed throughout the book. Special thanks to Linda for writing a number of programmatics for the subsection on intermarriage (see pages 134-135; 137-138; 149).

We are especially grateful to Ellen Singer, author of *A Companion Guide to Jewish Marital Status* (New York: Hadassah, 1989), from which we have borrowed or adapted discussion questions and programming suggestions.

We thank the staff and lay leaders of the Center for Innovation for their input during the planning process, for reading JEWISH WOMEN LIVING THE CHALLENGE and offering valuable insights, and for marketing the book to the widest possible audience: Karen Venezky, Division coordinator; Danielle Hilson, Division director; Phyllis Berlas, Pilots Department chair; Robin Bodner, Pilots Department director; Carole Curtis, Program Pilots chair; and Graham Austin, Pilots Department secretary. And we thank Ellen Hershkin, chair of Coordinated Training, for her willingness to use our materials in the coordinated training sessions and for developing training groups to pilot the use of our material.

We are grateful to the young women who sampled from a decade's worth of our publications, and offered suggestions on which to include in this retrospective: Leah Greengart of Strategic Planning; Suzy Burstein of Convention; and Marcy Felsenfeld of Israel, Zionist, and International Affairs.

Finally, we thank Michael Cohen, director of the Creative Services Department; Tina Malaney, who designed the book; and Susan Gross who illustrated it. Their work has made JEWISH WOMEN LIVING THE CHALLENGE attractive to our membership and to the broader Jewish community.

Responsibility for JEWISH WOMEN LIVING THE CHALLENGE is, of course, ours.

Barbara B. Spack
National Jewish Education Chair

Carol Diament, Ph.D.
Editor
National Jewish Education Director

SELF

The articles in this unit address our concerns as women about our physical and emotional well-being. Sue Mizrahi meditates on the meaning of feminine beauty in American society today and in the Jewish tradition. She writes of the never-ending conflict between the quest for physical perfection and the desire to abandon the quest. As Jewish women, we

regret that we don't mirror media images of female perfection. Furthermore, Jewish sources seem to equate feminine beauty with a woman's wisdom and morality. Mizrahi leaves us with a series of questions to ponder, as there are no answers.

In an essay on breast cancer, Dr. Edie Gurewitsch explains why breast cancer is a matter of importance to Jewish women. She notes that Jewish women may be particularly susceptible, and she explains the relationship between Judaism and medicine. From detection and risk factors to prevention and coping with the disease, Jewish tradition provides a sense of direction. Thus, Hadassah fulfills a Jewish moral decree as it educates Jewish women about breast cancer.

Sylvia Barack Fishman writes of aging in the Jewish tradition, and she implores us to look to the Bible for female role models. Her article demonstrates that Judaism is a rich resource as we enter middle age and beyond.

Finally, Gail Katz Meller reveals through prose and poetry how the death of a spouse has affected her. She describes the stages of her grief with candor and elegance, and she shows how others' perceptions and her own self-image altered over time.

The Beauty Myth— or the Mind/Body Problem, Revisited

Sue Mizrahi

On a videotape of Hebrew songs for pre-schoolers—wildly popular in Israel and the United States—a young man sings to a little girl:

> *You have such pretty eyes!*
> *You have such a pretty mouth!*
> *You have such pretty hair!*
> *How can you be sad?*
> *You're the prettiest one in the class!!*

Yes, of course, beauty is only skin deep. However, the skin is on the outside.

Yes, of course, beauty is in the eyes of the beholder. Does that mean the outside doesn't really matter, because everything depends on who is doing the beholding?

What if the beholder does not recognize beauty?

What if the beholder is the one *inside*?

Waitaminit—is this the mind/body problem?

Skin deep or soul deep, fleeting or forever, beauty is a long clause in the social contract. It helps to shape our sense of self and it colors our reactions to others. The politically correct stance today is to understand that the hunger for physical beauty, as well as the definition of that beauty, is greatly influenced, if not actually created, by the mass culture—by Hollywood and *Harper's*, by Madison Avenue and all its side streets. We understand as well that it's impossible to satisfy that hunger, but we keep feeding it ... sometimes from our own bodies.

"A pretty wife means a happy husband" (Yevamot 63b). "A wife should be chosen mainly for her beauty" (Ketubot 59b). The sequence seems simple: being beautiful gets a husband, staying beautiful keeps him.

But what about the rest of us?

Styles change, of course, but since the beginning of the beginning, the message has been clear: the race is to the gorgeous.

If beauty is in the eyes of the beholder, when did we put on the glasses that keep us from seeing ourselves as pretty *enough*, thin *enough*, blond *enough*?

And what about matters of the mind? "Clever" is OK, but "stunning" is better.

We understand that positive self-image goes beyond "how do I look?" and that "I feel pretty" is only one strand in the fabric of self-esteem, but the premium put on the physical seems to ensure that the starting point for our positive sense of self is all too often the mirror. We would probably be safe in saying that at every point in human history it has been considered important for a woman to be beautiful, but important for whom? Important for what?

The Jewish tradition genuinely values and reveres its women. Our matriarchs and biblical heroines are remembered for their words and their deeds, for their roles as wives, mothers, and leaders, for their place in our people's growth and history. We take note, then, that most of them—Sarah, Rebecca, and Rachel, for starters—are described as *beautiful*, if not in the Torah itself, then by the sages, who argued that Sarah was probably the most *beautiful*, even surpassing Eve.

Throughout history, cultural norms and expected patterns have been that men and women will marry. Marriage and family are the protected structures of a society's life, and being outside has never been safe—especially for a woman. It's been important for a woman to be beautiful, and it's been even more important to be married.

We might ask, again—important to whom? Important for what?

"Three things," the Talmud tells us, "improve a man's self-esteem: a beautiful home, beautiful clothes, and a beautiful wife" (*Berakhot* 57b).

"A man may not marry a woman he has not seen" (*Kiddushin* 41a). "A pretty wife means a happy husband" (*Yevamot* 63b). "A wife should be chosen mainly for her beauty" (*Ketubot* 59b). The sequence seems simple: being beautiful gets a husband, staying beautiful keeps him.

But what about the rest of us?

If we acknowledge that beauty is in the eyes of the beholder, we should certainly ask through what lens the beholder is looking.

The Rabbis were convinced that women had an innate instinct for jewelry and cosmetics, and permitted (or perhaps they encouraged?) women to bedeck themselves with all sorts of finery. Among the punishments prophesied by Isaiah against the "haughty daughters of Zion" would be the loss of pendants, bracelets, rings, veils, and sweet spices (Isaiah 3:16-24). Tradition says that God Himself braided Eve's hair before He presented her to Adam.

The pre-nuptial *mikvah* immersion takes place several days before the day of the wedding SO THE BRIDE'S MAKEUP DOESN'T GET RUINED.

The Talmud gives us permission to decorate or polish a piece of new merchandise in order to improve its market value, but cautions us not to deceive a potential buyer about the true condition of *used* merchandise. Such cosmetic improvements could apply to utensils, to animals, or, in the case of slaves, to people. The other side of "what is permitted" may be "what is expected"—or demanded. Rabbi Ishmael, we are told, was so concerned about helping women to appear beautiful that he arranged dental work for his niece to make her more attractive. (Dental work! In the second century?) Rashi reminds husbands that they are required to give their wives ten dinars as an allowance for cosmetics. (Whether they need them or not? Just kidding.)

Self-image or public image? Beauty in the soul or on the surface?
How much may we—must we—polish the merchandise?
A twentieth-century heir to Rabbi Ishmael, Rabbi David Halevi, the former Chief Rabbi of Tel Aviv and Jaffa, responds to a question about the *halakhah* of cosmetic rhinoplasty:

"Because you did not give me your first name I do not know if you are a man or a woman, so I will give you the ruling concerning both. Every operation has risks, but to risk one's life on looking better is strictly prohibited. A man may not risk his life on such trivial matters. He may, if he is embarrassed to show himself in public, have the operation under local anesthesia. However, *the case of a single woman who wants to improve her looks* is not a simple decision and should be looked at in a special light and with special consideration."

In order to change her status from *single*, a woman may *certainly* have her nose tailored to local specifications. She may, indeed, risk her life. But who does the specifying? How does a woman know that she is, or isn't, pretty? What are the rules, and WHO SAYS SHE'S PRETTY? Quite possibly, the groom's three dozen best friends.

Enters now the classic question: "How shall one dance before the bride?" (*Ketubot* 16b). Which means, "How shall we praise her if she's not really pretty?"

Well, to begin with, we might suggest complimenting her on her gown. Compliment her? Who said anything about *her*? The object here is to compliment the groom on his acquisition. Everyone is encouraged to look at the bride and tell her new husband how attractive she is. (Three things add to a man's self-esteem, we recall, and one is a beautiful wife.)

If she is ugly, according to Hillel a "white lie" is in order. The justification for the lie is the proof text for tact: all brides are beautiful in the eyes of their grooms anyway, and, more to the point, if a man made a bad purchase in the market and he can't return the goods, would you tell him he made a mistake?

The Torah does tell us "Keep far from a false matter" (Exodus 23:7), and Bet Shammai holds out for brutal truth, but in this case, as in so many others, the majority rules with Hillel.

The Talmud suggests that while men are greatly concerned with women's beauty, women do not care much about men's physical endowments. This news has not reached Tevye's household—"for me, well, I wouldn't holler if he were as handsome as anything"—or, for that matter, Calvin Klein.

But the imperative remains: Once safely married, stay attractive to your husband. Have we come back, then, to beauty in the eye of the beholder?

Of course, and we come back as well to the double messages and paradoxes of traditions old and new. "The beauty of a man is in his wisdom, the wisdom of a woman is in her beauty."[1] *There*'s the mind/body problem, all right!

In this judging of beauty, do we hear the voices of women? Do we see through the eyes of women? What, after all, *do* women want?

We want to find ways to satisfy the contradictory claims we make against ourselves, the impossible demands we make upon our lives.

We want to know—and to believe—that beauty is as much a state of mind and heart as it is a state of physical being, and that we can define it for ourselves.

We want to know—and to believe—that physical beauty will not determine joy, or satisfaction, or success, or love, or dignity, but we also want to know that should a woman choose cosmetic surgery the *halakhah* will permit the operation, even at the risk of her life if she is single.

We want to know—and to believe—that the beauty of youth and the beauty of health and the beauty of wholeness do not define a woman or a man.

We want to find the ways to teach ourselves, our daughters, and our granddaughters. We want to find the ways to learn, along with our sons and our grandsons, that life is not about being pretty and feeling pretty, but about cherishing and nourishing the soul and the spirit of every human being made in God's image. We want to listen to the sounds of our own voices.

From Textures, Hadassah National Jewish Studies Bulletin, *May 1994, vol. 12, no. 2.*

SUE MIZRAHI is Hadassah National Education/Public Policy Division Coordinator and immediate past National Secretary. She served as chair of the National Jewish Education Department from 1984-1988.

PROGRAMMING IDEAS

AT HOME

Torah Table Talk #1 A discussion of Jewish thought and values with your family and/or friends. The Talmud presents an argument between the followers of two Rabbis of the Second Temple period, Hillel and Shammai. In this case, as in most cases, the ruling is for the school of Hillel, who is considered the more lenient and humane of the two Rabbis. (The translation below is from *The Talmud: The Steinsaltz Edition*, volume 8 [New York: Random House, 1989], pages 27-28.) Arthur Kurzweil and Alan Zoldan explicate the terse language of the Talmud for readers today, and give a summation of later rabbinic commentary ("The Talmud—Timely and Timeless," *Textures*, January 1994).

Babylonian Talmud (compiled between 200 and 500), Ketubot 16b/17a

Our Rabbis taught: How do we dance before the bride? The Bet [*literally,* house of] Shammai school says: Each bride as she is. But the Bet Hillel school says: A beautiful and graceful bride. Bet Shammai said to Bet Hillel: If she was lame or blind, do we say about her, "A beautiful and graceful bride"? But the Torah (Exodus 23:7) states: "Keep far from a false matter!" Bet Hillel said to Bet Shammai: According to your words [if] someone has bought a bad purchase from the marketplace, should one praise it in the purchaser's eyes or criticize it in the purchaser's eyes? You must say: One should praise it in the purchaser's eyes. From here the sages said: A person's disposition toward people should always be congenial.

Arthur Kurzweil and Alan Zoldan, "Interpretation and Discussion"

The Talmud discusses what a person should say while dancing before a bride [that is, while celebrating the wedding]. The adherents of the school of Shammai argue that the words should be fitting to the bride "as she is"—that is, the dancers should sing about the good qualities with which the bride is endowed, avoiding anything negative. But the adherents of the more liberal Hillel school disagree and assert that we should treat every bride as if she is beautiful, saying: "A beautiful and graceful bride!"

The "as she is" advocates believe that this euphemism borders on dishonesty, and this school argues that calling a bride who is lame or blind "beautiful and graceful" violates the biblical prohibition against lying.

But the Rabbis ultimately rule against Bet Shammai. By pointedly avoiding the bride's defects, the wedding guests in fact remind her of them and cause her distress. From here, the Rabbis conclude that our disposition toward other people should always be congenial.

A significant ethical and spiritual question lies at the heart of this discussion: Are there any limits to telling the truth? According to the Talmud, there is just such a limit when we are in danger of hurting someone's feelings. Polite words, though they are sometimes not the absolute truth, are part of the structure of social relations. As we learn elsewhere in the Talmud (*Gittin 59b*), "The whole Torah exists only for the sake of peace." Peace among nations. Peace between us and our fellow human being. And peace within ourselves. Thoughtless remarks can all too easily destroy that fragile yet holy peace. This talmudic excerpt charmingly illustrates the principle of considerate speech. Even when we are praising the bride, we must be careful about what we say and how we say it.

Questions for Thought and Discussion

1. Why is the bride's physical appearance an issue of grave significance? What is at stake for the groom? Why is there no discussion of the groom's physical appearance?

2. The Rabbis discuss the "beautiful bride" as if there were one universally accepted idea of female beauty. (And perhaps in the rabbinic mind of the first century, there was agreement on the ideal type of beauty!) What might the followers of Shammai have said about a bride whom some considered "beautiful and graceful" but others considered "lame or blind"?

3. The Rabbis here place greater moral value on avoiding embarrassing or hurting others than on scrupulous honesty. Are there any instances in which you would make an exception?

Torah Table Talk #2   Rabbi David Halevi, the Chief Sephardi Rabbi of Tel Aviv-Jaffa, writes in response to a question, explaining what types of cosmetic surgery are permissible under Jewish law. His responsum was translated from the Hebrew by Barbara Harshav.

Rabbi David Halevi, Responsum on Cosmetic Surgery (c. 1985)

This is to acknowledge receipt of your letter pertaining to your question of whether anything in the law prevents plastic surgery of the nose to enhance its beauty.

Since you signed only the initials of your first name, I cannot determine if you are a man or a woman, hence I shall detail the particulars of the law in both cases.

First of all, every operation has some danger, hence even an operation that is medically necessary can be performed only if there is mortal danger or at least a severe interference with the smooth functioning of everyday life. Then it can be allowed. Therefore, how can an operation liable to endanger human life for reasons of beauty be allowed?

Some rabbis of our time have strictly forbidden cosmetic surgery for the reasons cited above. But with all due respect to modesty on my part, it would seem that the issue can be differentiated by types of operations as well as by cases and circumstances.

In my opinion, an operation in which the patient undergoes general anesthesia is strictly forbidden, since it is well known that general anesthesia is dangerous. But in an operation performed under local anesthesia solely of the operated area, the danger is quite minimal. Hence, for a man, all kinds of operations seem to be absolutely forbidden, for what does a man have to do with beauty, but it can be allowed in the case of a very prominent blemish that makes a person's face ugly. This is illustrated by Rabbi Moshe Isserles who wrote about the prohibition for a man to look in the mirror: for if he sees in the mirror that he has feathers in his hair or spots on his face and removes them so that he won't be disgraced among people, that is permitted since it is not his intention to embellish himself, but just to keep from being disgraced, etc. At the end of his remarks, he cites the Talmud: if there is no other grief than to be ashamed among people, it is allowed, for there is no greater grief than that, end of quote.

Hence, from the question of embellishment, it is permitted since the blemish makes him very ugly and ashamed to be with people, since his intention is not to make himself beautiful but to be saved from his shame. Hence, if the operation is not performed under general anesthesia and the danger is quite small, it may be permitted as stated above.

This applies even more to a woman who is allowed the above mentioned operation. But, concerning a woman, the above mentioned operation may be allowed (without general anesthesia) even if the blemish is not prominent and ugly, but overshadows her natural beauty and causes her grief, for a woman is allowed all kinds of beauty.

Thus far, it seems to me that the permission is clear. Furthermore, that is, if there is a need for an operation with a general anesthetic for the removal of a large blemish that causes ugliness and great grief, especially for a woman, and even more so for a maiden who wants to get married, it seems to me that every case must be decided individually, and a rabbi must be consulted in every case, for neither permission nor prohibition is simple.

Questions for Thought and Discussion

1. Rabbi Halevi permits cosmetic surgery when performed under local anesthesia; however, his reasoning differs depending on whether a woman or a man will have the operation. But how can we define the difference between feeling ashamed because of a blemish and feeling that a blemish overshadows

our natural beauty? Don't women feel ashamed because of blemishes? Don't men feel that a blemish overshadows the rest of their (acceptable) appearance? Is Rabbi Halevi actually differentiating according to the size or ugliness of the blemish? A man may correct only a large defect, while a woman may correct either a large or a small blemish?

2. Does Rabbi Halevi's ruling make sense to you in practical terms? In other words, considering how most men and most women feel about altering their appearance, is his ruling reasonable?

3. Rabbi Halevi writes that cosmetic surgery under general anesthesia might be permitted in certain cases for unmarried women seeking husbands, though each case would need to be judged individually by a rabbi. What might the rabbi's criteria be?

4. Do you feel that Rabbi Halevi is unfair in denying men permission for cosmetic surgery under general anesthesia? Why or why not?

5. Contrast Rabbi Halevi's attitude toward guarding one's health with attitudes currently popular in our society. Rabbi Halevi reasons that endangering one's own life is forbidden, and therefore general anesthesia poses too great a risk. However, most Americans today assume that they—and not religious law— should dictate whether or not to risk their lives. Discuss.

Additional At-Home Activities

❖ Keep a private "food journal" to record your feelings about eating, cooking, celebrating, and food—and its impact on your body image. Are you likely to overeat any one particular type of food? Do you eat differently on holidays? When you're with your parents? What is the connection between the way you eat, the way you feel about your physical appearance, and the way you feel about yourself in general? How do your feelings about food relate to your self-image as a Jewish woman? For example, in a *New York Times* article (March 20, 1997, page C6), a woman explains that she always keeps plenty of food on hand: "It's my Jewish upbringing. I've got to be able to feed 40 people at all times, even if they never show up." Based on the self-knowledge and confidence you gain through your journal, implement a food plan that will work for you! (For information on nutrition, call the Hadassah National Health Education Department at 212-303-8094.)

❖ With your family and/or friends, discuss how Jewish women are portrayed in the television shows that you watch or videotapes that you rent. Is there a prevailing "look"? Why is the Jewish woman in the media rarely, if ever, gorgeous? How are the Jewish woman's feelings about her body depicted? How do the other characters in the show or movie react to the Jewish woman? How does the depiction of Jewish women in the media differ from/conform to depictions of women of other ethnic groups?

❖ If you have an eating disorder, seek professional guidance. The National Eating Disorders Organization in Worthington, Ohio (918-481-4044), the

National Center for Overcoming Overeating in New York (212-875-0442), and the American Anorexia/Bulimia Association in New York (212-575-6200) are three potential rerources.

INTEREST/STUDY GROUPS

Hold a discussion based on the following questions:

1. Consider the verse from the children's Hebrew song quoted by Sue Mizrahi. How do we praise the beauty of our own daughters and granddaughters? What do we teach our own sons and grandsons about female beauty?

2. How would an article on beauty differ if it were written for and about Jewish men? Is there anything at all to say? (Can we conceive of reversing the sexes in the quotations from the Talmud?)

3. The Bible and later Jewish sources praise women for their "words and their deeds, for their roles as wives, mothers, and leaders, for their place in our people's growth and history." Note the Woman of Valor poem, from Proverbs 31:10-31 (see pages 182-183), in which "grace is deceptive, beauty is illusory; it is for her fear of the Eternal that a woman is to be praised." How have the different aspects of the Jewish female ideal been interwoven in your life? In the lives of Jewish women whom you admire?

4. Sue Mizrahi notes that the talmudic question *how to dance before the bride* is a euphemism for *how to praise the bride* "if she's not really pretty," and analyzes the rabbinic discussion. Read the excerpt from the Talmud in the "At Home" section, and reread Sue Mizrahi's analysis. Do you agree with this analysis? Why?

MEETINGS

❖ Organize a body image meeting. Sit in a circle and give each member the opportunity to speak about her actual physical appearance, her desired physical appearance, and the implications and consequences of low self-image. For conversation starters: How do women's attitudes toward their bodies change as they age? After they bear children? To what lengths do women go to improve their appearances? What factors affect women's self-acceptance? A husband's opinion? A mother's opinion? Media images of women? The appearances of friends? The goals of the meeting are to (1) give participants a safe place in which to hold a personal discussion; (2) improve the self-image of the participants; and (3) raise questions about American Jews' attitudes toward female beauty. Brainstorm together on what you as a group can do to raise your own and each other's self-esteem.

ANNUAL EVENTS

❖ Organize an Education Day based on women in the Bible, using the schedude below as a model. Invite a mental health professional who is knowledgeable on Judaism and a Judaic scholar. Make use of people in your community.

Biblical Images of Women

9:15-10:15 **Body Image: How We See Ourselves Today**
The ideal of the young, thin, smooth-skinned, blond-haired beauty sets an unrealistic standard for all women, so that nearly every American girl grows up believing that something is wrong with her. Women are constantly trying to change their bodies. For us, as Jewish women, our differences from a white, Anglo-Saxon standard can be debilitating. Many Jewish women, young and old, remember their parents pressuring them to conform to non-Jewish ideals of beauty in order to prove that the family had "made it" in America.

Though an unrealistic ideal of female beauty affects women of all ages, today's emphasis on youth is especially troubling for older women. In a society that often sees older people as non-people, and therefore asexual, what is the reality for older women? How might Jewish values work against negative views of older people and combat the American emphasis on youthful physical beauty?

10:30-11:30 **Leah and Rachel**
How is each woman presented and valued in the Genesis story? Why do many readers of the Bible think that Rachel is beautiful and Leah is unattractive? How are women pitted against each other in the narrative? How do they cooperate? What insights do the stories give us about sisters and sisterhood? (The book *Sarah's Daughters Sing: A Sampler of Poems by Jewish Women*, ed. Henny Wenkart [Hoboken, NJ: Ktav, 1990], pages 14-22, includes poetry written from the perspective of each sister.)

11:45-1:00 Lunch

1:15-2:15 **Female Wisdom**
Deborah is the only woman judge in the Bible and one of the few women who is not identified as a mother or by age (though as a respected legislator, she can't be young). Discuss her story, which is found in Judges 4:4-5:24. What model does she offer for us today?

2:20-3:30 **Female Sexuality**
Discuss Yael and her sexual deception of Sisera (Judges 4:1-17), along with Delilah and her sexual deception of Samson (Judges 14-16). What are the moral and feminist implications of using our sexual power in a deceptive manner? Discuss other instances of biblical sexuality, such as Ruth and Boaz, Tamar and Judah.

❖ As part of a Women's Symposium or an Education Day, hold one or two workshops on media images of Jewish women in America today. The following outline is adapted from an "icebreaker" presented by Bonnie Salmon at the Young Women/Young Leaders Institute of Hadassah's SUN Coop in 1997.

8 minutes	Name as many Jewish characters as you can from television. Who are the female role models for our daughters? The nanny? Are there any others? (Is their ethnicity clear, or is it implied?) Who are the male role models for our sons? Why is the love interest for TV's Jewish man almost invariably a non-Jewish woman?
8 minutes	Name as many Jewish characters as you can from movies released over the last ten years. Who are the Jewish women? What about the love interest in movies? Do we see Jewish men who love Jewish women? How have movie portrayals of Jews changed over time? How do antisemitic stereotypes persist?
8 minutes	Name today's famous Jewish actresses, actors, and other celebrities. Who besides Barbra Streisand? How do these actresses and actors portray Jewish characters—or *not* portray Jewish characters?
4 minutes	Tell Jewish jokes—Jews and money, JAPs, Jewish mothers, Jews and conspicuous consumption—and discuss. What do Jewish jokes say about the ways in which we see ourselves? How do stereotypes affect the ways in which single Jewish women and men see each other?
12 minutes	General discussion on media images, stereotypes, and our self-esteem. Discuss as well the prevalence of Jews in the television and film industries—as producers, writers, etc. Why do positive portrayals of Jewish women remain comparatively rare? Why are the Jewish women in movies and films so often variations on the JAP or the Jewish mother stereotype?

For a second workshop on media images of Jewish women, show excerpts from videotapes of films and television shows that include Jewish women characters, and then hold a follow-up discussion. Or, show one movie in its entirety. *The Heartbreak Kid* (1972; 106 minutes) contrasts a Jewish girl from Brooklyn with a Protestant girl from the mid-West, and is easily found in video rental outlets.

HANDS-ON

❖ Ask a friend to be your Body Image Buddy. If you hate how you look in a bathing suit, or if you're tempted to start a radical diet (like fasting), or if you've just eaten a pint of chocolate ice cream in one sitting, call your buddy for a pep-talk. Do the same for her when she calls you.

❖   Some women hate exercise, and some just need the motivation provided by companionship! Use the videotape *Live and Be Well—Get Movin' with Hadassah*, and gather friends for an exercise group. Play the video in a spacious room that is free of furniture and has a wooden or carpeted floor. Have participants take turns bringing water and a nutritious snack for the entire group. Each participant should wear comfortable clothes and sneakers or aerobic shoes, and should bring a towel. Call 212-303-8165 for information on ordering the video.

---

1. Bet Hamidrash, a medieval commentator, cited in Reuven Alcalay and Mordekhai Nurock, *Words of the Wise: An Anthology of Proverbs and Practical Axioms* (Jerusalem/Ramat Gan: Massada Press, 1970), page 262.

Your Body Is a Jewish Responsibility

Edie Diament Gurewitsch, M.D.

In 1995, Hadassah established the Health Education Department. Part of its mission was to broaden and promote the breast cancer awareness program, "Hadassah Cares," which had been initiated by Hadassah's Membership/Outreach Department. "Hadassah Cares" has a threefold purpose: to reach out to women by including programming on breast cancer at Hadassah meetings; to promote early detection through education on breast self-examination and through sponsorship of reduced-rate mammograms; and to increase federal, state, and local funding for research on prevention and treatment, through coordinated letter-writing efforts.

Hadassah's Involvement

Why is Hadassah involved with health education? Why has Hadassah committed itself to increasing breast cancer awareness? Hadassah's commitment to health care is certainly in keeping with its primary mission. That breast cancer is a women's issue is also clear (although men are subject to it, too). Furthermore, medical researchers have suggested that Jewish women are particularly susceptible.[1]

These reasons alone could justify our involvement. But are the principles of outreach, prevention, early detection, and treatment of disease Jewish issues? Are we as Jews to work for these ends? The answer is a resounding yes.

Medicine and religion have a unique relationship. Because God is the ultimate source of all healing, the first question from a religious standpoint is: Does human healing interfere with divine providence? And adherents of certain faiths believe that it does. Christian Scientists, for example, mandate reliance upon God alone. Similarly, the Karaite sect,[2] an offshoot of Judaism, narrowly interprets Exodus 15:26, "For I the Lord am your healer," and disallows all human healing. Normative, rabbinic Judaism, however, enjoins us to seek and provide medical assistance.

Leviticus 19:16 states, "Do not stand by the blood of your fellow." Maimonides explains this in *Mishneh Torah, Hilkhot Rotze'ah*: Whoever is able to save another, and does not, transgresses the commandment. The Torah, therefore, obligates us to heal the sick as a religious precept included in the category of saving a life.

Are the principles of outreach, prevention, early detection, and treatment of disease Jewish issues? Are we as Jews to work for these ends? The answer is a resounding yes.

Early Detection

Hadassah cannot stand by as breast cancer reaches epidemic proportions. Statisticians currently estimate that one in nine women will be affected by breast cancer during her lifetime. Promoting early detection is one way in which Hadassah saves lives—a Jewish religious injunction.

For humans, breasts are more than milk-producing organs; they symbolize femininity and play a role in sexual attraction, body image, and self-esteem.

Once a woman becomes aware of a lump, she faces possible suffering and death, as with any type of cancer, but she also faces mutilation, with all its psychological consequences. Despite public awareness of the incidence of breast cancer, between 20 and 60 percent of women invited to have mammography refuse it, and the number of women performing regular self-examination is small.

A reversal of this trend would be a monumental achievement. Hadassah's involvement thus fulfills a Jewish, moral imperative. Deuteronomy 4:9 says, "Take utmost care and watch yourselves scrupulously." Expanding on this, numerous passages of Talmud require an individual to obtain medical attention when sick. *Baba Kama* 46b states, "The person who is in pain visits a healer." Jewish medical ethics, however, go beyond caring for ourselves when sick. We are required to take preventative action. Rabbi Joseph Caro, in the *Shulhan Arukh, Orah Hayyim*, obligates us to take all possible measures to ensure health.

Maimonides enjoins us in *Mishneh Torah, Hilkhot De'ot* to "set your heart that your body should be healthy and strong in order that your soul be upright to know the Lord." In educating ourselves about breast cancer so that we can be vigilant in maintaining health, "Hadassah Cares" upholds these Jewish precepts.

Women themselves are responsible for the early detection of breast cancer. In the overwhelming majority of cases, the initial sign of breast cancer is a lump discovered by the patient. For this reason, self-examination is widely advocated. Hadassah's waterproof shower card contains step-by-step instructions. Hadassah has created the "Check It Out" program for high school youth and the "Buddy Check a Buddy" program for adult women; both programs emphasize the importance of monthly breast self-exams. Hadassah also promotes early detection through educational meetings and symposia and through community outreach programs, such as sporting events, fashion shows, health fairs, and business-community involvement.

Mammography is able to detect breast cancer at its earliest stages, and the American Cancer Society recommends screenings for all women above age 40. Hadassah's advocacy for affordable mammography reflects the highest concepts of *tzedakah*.

Coping with Breast Cancer

After a woman has detected a lump, there are two typical patterns of behavior. Many women seek immediate medical attention. Many others seem to be in denial and can wait several years before reporting the lump. Knowledge of the significance of a lump does not seem to explain who will delay, as most procrastinators report that fear of cancer caused the delay.

Outreach and dissemination of Jewish concepts of mercy and care for the sick could be a tool in combating this problem. Visiting the sick is a duty incumbent upon each of us. Just as God visits the sick—we must also. The sages of the Talmud interpret Exodus 18:20, "and make known to them the way they are to go," to refer to the duty of visiting the sick.

Jacob ben Asher, in the halakhic compendium *Yoreh De'ah*, states that it is a *mitzvah* to visit those who are ill and to help them in any way they require.

Once breast cancer has been diagnosed, uncertainty is replaced by fear of a life-threatening illness. And the negative consequences of treatment (a mutilating operation, radiation, and chemotherapy) result in a long catalogue of further psychological distress.

Recognition of the fears and difficulties by relatives, friends, and physicians can relieve some of the woman's stress. A husband's affection and intimacy play a key role, as does communal support. Hadassah meetings with candid discussion of breast cancer from both medical and personal perspectives allow women to share their fears, while promoting the Jewish ideal of maintaining health and preserving life.

Risk Factors and Prevention

Risk factors for breast cancer are classified as modifiable or non-modifiable. Sadly, most of the better documented risk factors are not modifiable—they are outside the individual's control. Nonetheless, knowledge of the risk factors should alert those at risk to the need for early detection. The non-modifiable factors are: (1) age—incidence increases sharply over age 30, and continues to increase with age; (2) family history of breast cancer—a woman with a first-degree relative (mother, sister, daughter) who had breast cancer is herself at greater risk; (3) early onset of menstruation; and (4) late onset of menopause.[3]

A recently identified risk factor is carrying specific mutations on the BRCA1 and BRCA2 genes. Carriers of these mutations may be predisposed to breast cancer (or ovarian cancer). These hereditary abnormalities are believed to account for five to ten percent of the breast and ovarian cancer in the Ashkenazi Jewish population, and genetic testing for the abnormalities is now possible. Critical features of this research were conducted by Dr. Tamar Peretz and Dr. Dvora Abeliovich of the Hadassah Medical Organization in Jerusalem, working together with the research team at the National Center for Human Genome Research in the United States.

Women in Western, developed countries are at greater risk than women in underdeveloped countries, suggesting a strong environmental predisposition to breast cancer.[4] Consequently, many researchers have examined the role of diet and nutrition. Obesity is associated with a higher risk of breast cancer, and a number of studies have also implicated high-fat diets. Cross-cultural studies have correlated a lower risk with both breast feeding and early first childbirth. Therefore, a woman who wishes to prevent breast cancer is advised to: (1) maintain her ideal body weight; (2) eat a low-fat diet; (3) breast feed; and (4) have children at a young age. (Breast feeding and age of first childbirth are obviously not modifiable for older women, nor for many younger women.)

Obesity deserves special mention, as it is a proven risk factor in several life-threatening conditions, notably heart disease. Maimonides states, "It is one's duty to avoid whatever is injurious to the body; therefore food should not be taken to repletion. One should not be a glutton.... Overeating is like a deadly poison to any constitution and is the principal cause of all diseases."[5]

The relationship between estrogen replacement therapy during menopause and breast cancer is not yet clear. One large American study found the number of breast cancer cases was the same among women who took estrogen and women who did not, but the size and severity of the tumors were larger among those taking the hormone.

Further research into breast cancer prevention is needed, and Hadassah actively pursues this goal, demanding political action on breast cancer research. The stakes are high and the quest is worthy.

From Textures, Hadassah National Jewish Studies Bulletin, *May 1994, vol. 12, no. 2.*

EDIE DIAMENT GUREWITSCH, M.D., is Assistant Professor of Gynecology and Obstetrics at The Johns Hopkins University School of Medicine.

PROGRAMMING IDEAS

AT HOME

Torah Table Talk A discussion of Jewish thought and values with your family and/or friends. The "Laws Relating to Moral Dispositions and Ethical Conduct" were written by Moses Maimonides (also known as the Rambam), the twelfth-century Spanish scholar, legal commentator, philosopher, and physician, in the *Mishneh Torah.* This 14-volume work is the first complete, systematic, and rational arrangement of Jewish law. The passages below are from the translation of Moses Hyamson (*Mishneh Torah, Book I* [Jerusalem: Boys Town Publishers, 1962]), reprinted in *A Maimonides Reader,* ed. Isadore Twersky (West Orange, NJ: Behrman, 1972), pages 57-58. The wording has been altered for gender neutrality.

Maimonides, Mishneh Torah, *Laws Relating to Moral Dispositions and Ethical Conduct 3:3, 4:1, 4:20, 4:23, 5:1*

Individuals who regulate their lives in accordance with the laws of hygiene, with the sole motive of maintaining a sound and vigorous physique and begetting children to do their work and labor for their benefit, are not following the right course. A person should aim to maintain physical health and vigor, in order that the soul may be upright, in a condition to know God. For it is impossible for anyone to understand sciences and meditate upon them when hungry or sick, or when any of one's limbs is aching. And in cohabitation, one should set one's heart on having a son who may become a sage and a great man in Israel. Whoever throughout life follows this course will be continually serving God, even while engaged in business and even during cohabitation, because one's purpose in every action will be to satisfy one's needs so as to have a sound body with which to serve God. Even when the individual sleeps and seeks repose, to calm the mind and rest the body, so as not to fall sick and be incapacitated from serving God, this sleep is service of the Almighty.

Since by keeping the body in health and vigor one walks in the way of God—it being impossible during [severe] sickness to have any understanding or knowledge of the Creator—it is each individual's duty to avoid whatever is injurious to the body, and cultivate habits conducive to health and vigor.

Those who live in accordance with the directions I have set forth have my assurance that they will never be sick until they grow old and die; they will not be in need of a physician, and will enjoy normal health as long as they live.

No scholar may live in a city that does not have the following ten officials and institutions: a physician, a surgeon, a bathhouse, a lavatory, a source of water supply such as a stream or spring, a synagogue, a schoolteacher, a scribe, a treasurer of charity funds for the poor, a court that has authority to punish with flogging and imprisonment.

Scholars will not be gluttons but will eat food conducive to health; and of such food they will not eat to excess. They will not be eager to fill their stomachs, like those who gorge themselves with food and drink till the body swells. Concerning such people, Scripture says, "I will spread dung on your faces" (Malachi 2:3). This text, our sages say, refers to those who eat and drink and spend all their days as if they were holidays. They are the people who exclaim, "Eat and drink for tomorrow we die" (Isaiah 22:13). This is how the wicked eat…. The wise, on the contrary, will only partake of one or two courses, of which they will consume as much as they need to sustain them.

Questions for Thought and Discussion

1. How does Maimonides explain the need to maintain physical health?

2. How is our health related to our observance of the laws of God? Don't we "walk in the ways of God" through religious observance, not through the amount we eat?

3. Analyze the list of officials and institutions mandated by Maimonides for every city in which a scholar lives, paying attention to the order of the list. What does Maimonides suggest about the mechanics of a city?

4. Why does Maimonides consider a glutton wicked?

5. Discuss the statement: "For it is impossible for anyone to understand sciences and meditate upon them when hungry or sick, or when any of one's limbs is aching." At what degree of sickness does understanding become impossible? Can one meditate upon science—and upon the humanities and upon the Torah—when a limb is aching? How badly?

6. Why are some of Maimonides's directions written for "scholars"? What is meant? Are all Jews scholars today?

Additional At-Home Activities

❖ Use the Breast Self-Examination cards produced by Hadassah's National Health Education Department. Call 212-303-8094 for information on ordering.

❖ Construct your medical family tree to track any inherited risk factors. Establish target charts for early detection and prevention. Consult *Our Health, Our Lives* by Eileen Hoffman (New York: Pocket, 1995) for information on risk factors, detection, and prevention.

❖ Act now to fulfill Maimonides' dictum to "maintain physical health and vigor," and to prevent heart disease, diabetes, and osteoporosis. Eat a calcium-rich diet that is low in fat and high in fruits, vegetables, and whole grains. Establish a regimen of regular exercise, including both aerobic and weight-bearing exercise in your regimen.

INTEREST/STUDY GROUPS

Hold a discussion based on the following questions:

1. What roles do family and friends play in the adjustment to breast cancer?

2. What is the Jewish viewpoint on seeking and providing medical assistance? Discuss the Jewish precepts and injunctions involved.

3. Dr. Gurewitsch states that "between 20 and 60 percent of women invited to have mammography refuse it, and the number of women performing regular self-examination is small." Why might women refuse mammograms? What might account for the small number performing self-exams?

MEETINGS

❖ Host a discussion on the BRCA1 and BRCA2 genes and how Jewish women of Ashkenazi descent are affected by mutations on these genes. Include two guest speakers: one on breast cancer, the other on genetic testing. What are the implications of genetic testing for the BRCA genes? What are the pros and cons of genetic testing in general? What sorts of choices are open at this time? How have women who know they carry a mutated BRCA1 or BRCA2 gene reacted? How has the knowledge affected their lives? How have health insurance carriers reacted to genetic testing? (See also the "Hands-On" section, pages 24-25.) What other sorts of discrimination do carriers of the mutated gene face? More information is available from the following National Hadassah Departments: American Affairs/Domestic Policy (212-303-8136), Health Education (212-303-8094), and Programming (212-303-8027).

❖ Invite a rabbi, hospice worker, and a representative from a cancer survivor support group to participate in a dialogue. Discuss how to help patients, families, and friends, both in and out of the hospital. What role can Judaism play in helping the cancer patient? Does prayer offer healing?

❖ Order the Hadassah Health Education booklet "Questions to Ask Your Primary Care Physician about Breast Cancer" to distribute at a health-related or other meeting. Call the Hadassah National Order Department,

1-800-880-9455. Order number: #R716. Available in packets of 25. Cost: $0.75 per booklet.

ANNUAL EVENTS

❖ Organize a health symposium. The schedule below is from a symposium held on November 24, 1996 at Congregation Rodeph Sholom in New York. The New York Chapter of Hadassah organized and co-sponsored the symposium together with the Sisterhood of Congregation Rodeph Sholom, the National Council on Women's Health, and the Lillian Wald Nurses Council. Hadassah's issue cards "Prevent Osteoporosis" and "Fight Breast Cancer" were available to spark participants' interest in membership. Use this schedule as a model, and adapt it to the expertise of health professionals in your community. (To order issue cards, call Hadassah's National Order Department, 1-800-880-9455. "Prevent Osteoporosis" order number: #R654f. "Fight Breast Cancer" order number: #R654e. Minimum order: 500 cards. Cost: $5.00 for 500. Available in packets of 100 per design.)

Hormones—The Key to a Woman's Health

From puberty to maturity, from teenage athletics to pleasure walking, every aspect of a woman's health is affected by hormones. Yet how can we— younger and older women alike—achieve healthy and more fulfilling lives? How can we glide gracefully through the changes our bodies are making? The answer is by understanding the role of hormones throughout our lives. This comprehensive health symposium offers a choice among twelve distinguished speakers, all experts in their fields, who will enhance our understanding of our reproductive systems, our bones, our heads, and our hearts. Join us, as we become empowered to make the best kind of personal health decision: an educated one.

8:30-9:00	Registration and continental breakfast
9:00-9:15	Welcome by Nansi Friedman, co-president of the Sisterhood of Congregation Rodeph Sholom, and Julie Hatterer, M.D., president of the National Council on Women's Health
9:15-9:40	**Overview of the Role of Hormones** *Susan C. Fox, M.D.*
9:40-10:00	**Intimate Moments: Sexuality, Gender Differences, and Hormones Throughout the Life Cycle** *Ruth Jacobowitz*
10:00-10:05	**Five-Minute Stretch** *Jane Katz, Ed.D.*

Select one workshop from each time period:

10:20-10:50   **A. Going for the Gold—Physical Fitness and Health**
Jane Katz, Ed.D., and Evelyn Hecht, P.T.

B. Women's Heart Disease—Different From Men's?
Niki E. Kantrowitz, M.D.

11:00-11:30   **A. Mood Swings—Can We Blame It All on Hormones?**
Jean Endicott, Ph.D.

B. Breast Disease and Hormones—A Safe Bet?
Jeanne A. Petrek, M.D.

11:40-12:10   **A. Infertility—When Nature Doesn't Take Its Course**
Satty Gill Keswani, M.D.

B. Breakthrough Therapies in Osteoporosis
Marjorie Luckey, M.D.

**C. Exercise for the Prevention and Management
of Osteoporosis**
Sandra Abramson, P.T.

12:20-12:50   **A. Coping with Endometriosis and Pelvic Pain**
Marcia A. Harris, M.D.

**B. Menopause and Hormone Replacement Therapy—
Options Your Mother Never Had**
Lila A. Wallis, M.D.

1:00-2:15   **Luncheon and Keynote Speaker**
Letty Cottin Pogrebin (author of Getting Over Getting Older*)*

2:15-2:45   **Book Signing**
Letty Cottin Pogrebin

(For assistance in organizing a Women's Symposium on health, call Hadassah's National Health Education Department at 212-303-8094 and National Jewish Education Department at 212-303-8132.)

❖ Create a day-long health fair. Instructions on how to organize a health fair are contained in the National Health Education Department's "Breast Health Awareness Kit." Call the Health Education Department (212-303-8094) for information on ordering.

HANDS-ON

❖ If someone you know suffers from cancer or other severe disease, say the *mi shebeirakh* ("may God Who blessed") prayer on Saturday morning at synagogue. This prayer, which originated in Europe in the Middle Ages, is recited on behalf of those in need of healing. The *mi shebeirakh* is said during the Torah reading on Shabbat and holidays. In some synagogues the names of all who are ill are recited publicly, while in other synagogues congregants silently say friends' and relatives' names at the appropriate time. It is traditional to state the Hebrew name of the person who is ill as well as her or his mother's Hebrew name. (If the words of the prayer are not meaningful to you, create your own prayer. Say it aloud at Shabbat services if your synagogue is receptive, or say it aloud at home.)

❖   Attend a healing service. These are offered by a number of synagogues as special, separate services, usually on a weeknight. Some congregations offer services of healing as part of their regular schedule, perhaps once monthly.

❖   Participate in Hadassah's "Buddy Call a Buddy" program. Call your buddy once a month to remind her to conduct her breast self-exam and call her once a year on her birthday to remind her about her annual mammogram. (Call the National Health Education Department at 212-303-8094.)

❖   Get involved in implementing Hadassah's "Check It Out!" program, a one-hour breast education and awareness program designed for 11th and 12th grade girls and presented in the school classroom. This program encourages adolescent girls to take responsibility for their own bodies and teaches them the skills needed to detect breast cancer early. The girls are asked to take information home and share it with their mothers and grandmothers. This has two important benefits—greater openness between generations, and giving mothers and grandmothers the impetus to seek professional advice on suspicious lumps. Hadassah needs volunteers to organize and publicize "Check It Out!" at the chapter and group levels. If you can implement the program at a local high school, contact the National Health Education Department at 212-303-8094.

❖   As genetic tests (for mutations on the BRCA and other genes) become more widely available, drawbacks have become increasingly apparent. One significant problem is that insurance companies and employers have used information from genetic testing to discriminate against individuals with particular test results. As a hypothetical example, a woman finds through a genetic test that she possesses a mutation that predisposes her to breast cancer. Though she may never develop the disease, when she tries to obtain health insurance, she finds that her rates are prohibitively expensive, because her insurance company has the genetic test results and has based her costs on those results. This is an instance of genetics-based health insurance discrimination. In a number of real-life cases, rates have been raised and health insurance coverage has been denied.

Hadassah's National American Affairs/Domestic Policy Department has launched an effort to prevent health insurance discrimination. Contact the Department (212-303-8136) for an "Action Alert," which contains information on contacting elected officials and urging them to support legislation that will prohibit genetics-based discrimination. Currently, a variety of legislative initiatives are underway, both at the federal and state levels. Become involved in working to pass this legislation through letter writing and lobbying your representatives.

For all members of your Hadassah chapter or group, make available the Hadassah issue card "Prevent Genetics-Based Insurance Discrimination." (Call Hadassah's National Order Department, 1-800-880-9455. Order number #R654i. Minimum order: 500 cards. Cost: $5.00 for 500.)

----

1. Studies to date are inconclusive.

2. The Karaite sect, which rejects rabbinic law, was founded in the eighth century. Today, approximately 7,000 Karaites live in Israel, and a few thousand live in the Near East or Europe. Both rabbinic and Karaite laws forbid marriage between Jews and Karaites, but the ability of the Karaite community to avoid assimilation in modern, multi-ethnic Israel is uncertain.

3. Age at onset of menstruation and of menopause are both dependent upon nutrition, so these factors are somewhat modifiable. However, the danger of inadequate nutrition, especially for pre-menstrual girls, is severe.

4. Studies in Israel are suggestive. For instance, the rate of breast cancer is much greater among Ashkenazim (whose customs derive from the industrialized European "first world") than among Sephardim; however, the incidence among Sephardim is rising, especially among those born in Israel.

5. Cited in Abraham S. Abraham, *Medical Halachah for Everyone: A Comprehensive Guide to Jewish Medical Law in Sickness and Health*, 2nd rev. ed. (Jerusalem/New York: Feldheim, 1984), pages 6-7.

The Way of Women: Finding Jewish Models of Aging

Sylvia Barack Fishman

Aging is a hot topic. In recently published books, Betty Friedan celebrates the accomplishments of talented older acquaintances, Germaine Greer grouses about menopause, Gail Sheehy urges a supportive movement among menopausal women, Carolyn Heilbrun argues that aging women experience unprecedented and exhilarating creativity, and Gloria Steinem promotes older women's self-esteem.

Some of these authors are Jewish, yet in their studies of aging, they almost never turn to Judaism's guidelines. *Pirkei Avot (Ethics of the Fathers)* provides a genealogy: at age 40 one arrives at the level of understanding; at 50, counsel; at 60, wisdom; at 70, white hair; at 80, the strength of age. The picture for later ages is less salutary: 90 brings the weight of years, and the person who reaches 100 is as if dead and removed from the world.

The Talmud (*Kiddushin*) details the respect that must be shown to elderly parents, despite any waning of their physical or mental powers. In the personal realm, rabbinic literature insists that elderly women be accorded respect and consideration. The Talmud recounts inspirational stories of men who cheerfully demean themselves to provide for their mothers' complete physical and mental comfort. However, in the public realm, detailed injunctions prescribe societal respect primarily for the older man. Jewish law and custom both urge that the utmost deference be shown to the white-haired man, especially if he is a scholar. Virtually absent is any notion that an elderly woman too might be a white-haired scholar—and thus deserving of public consideration!

The Bible, however, presents remarkable examples of powerful women—and the images of the older women's creativity and renewal are based almost exclusively on the maternal model. Sarah, the first Jewish mother, embarks on childbirth long after menopause. The narrator of Genesis informs the reader that Sarah has passed "the way of women." When Sarah overhears an angelic prediction that she will soon become a mother, she laughs and says to herself that she is elderly, well beyond the years of pleasure—and her husband is too old as well (Genesis 18:11-15). Rabbinic commentary interprets "pleasure" as either sexual pleasure or menstruation, both being associated with reproductive power. Nonetheless, Sarah is rewarded for her loyalty to God, and Isaac is born—surely the best-known post-menopausal birth on record.

Other aging women in biblical narratives have complicated roles, yet their stories are also interlaced with maternal imagery. Faced with developments that they recognize as contrary to God's plan, women such as Rebecca and Naomi—rather than the men or the young women around them—analyze the situation, plot, plan, and direct others in order to bring about the desired outcomes.

By responding forcefully and acting vigorously, the aging Rebecca and Naomi are very much within the Jewish ethos. The Bible seldom rewards a docile submission to an unfair fate. Rebecca and Naomi, rather than passively accepting their circumstances, act decisively, albeit behind the scenes, and change history. They succeed in their goals, and their progeny become the Israelite people's most respected leaders. These older women understand human motivations and are particularly able to seize their opportunity, thereby furthering the interests of Jewish peoplehood. As Tikva Frymer-Kensky points out,[1] their use of deception does not tarnish them. Within the moral structure of the Bible, they "do what they had to do, what was necessary for them to do, in order to achieve God's aims."

Rebecca's determination as an older mother is based on her earlier experience, when her two sons are in her womb and she feels them warring. Distraught, alone, and almost overwhelmed, she questions the purpose of her existence: "*Im ken, lamah zeh anokhi?*"—"If things are this way, why am I here?" (Genesis 25:22).

God answers Rebecca directly, "Two nations are in your womb, and two separate peoples will be separated from your innards, and one people will be stronger than the other people, and the older one will serve the younger one" (25:23). God grants Rebecca this painful understanding, and as her sons grow she perceives the spiritual chasm between them, seeing what Isaac does not. For example, both Isaac and Rebecca feel a "bitterness of spirit"—*morat ruah*—because of Esau's two foreign wives, yet Isaac still prepares to give the birthright to Esau (26:35). Rebecca, as an elderly and isolated woman, cannot directly confront the situation, because patriarchy and primogeniture are fixed structures within her society. But understanding that disaster will ensue if Abraham's spiritual heritage passes to Esau, the aging Rebecca finds the strength to act in defiance of conventional status considerations.

The power of the aging Naomi is also closely tied to childbirth and Jewish continuity. Almost from the beginning of the Book of Ruth, Naomi is the reference point. Her name appears early, in the same passage as that of her husband Elimelekh (Ruth 1:2) and by the third passage Elimelekh is identified as "Naomi's husband" (1:3). After Ruth's stirring declaration of loyalty to Naomi (1:16-17), Naomi returns to the center of the narrative. Surrounded by her old Israelite friends and acquaintances, she says, "Don't call me Naomi, call me Marah— Bitterness—for God has dealt very bitterly with me. I went out [of this place] full, and the Lord has brought me back empty. Why should you call me Naomi, since God has spoken against me and done evil to me" (1:20-21). At the age when she should be enjoying her grandchildren, she has been stripped of her husband and sons, of everything but her devoted daughter-in-law.

Each major character is identified through Naomi. The text states, "Naomi returned, and Ruth, the Moabitess, her daughter-in-law with her." When Boaz first glimpses Ruth, he is told that she is "a Moabite girl who came back with Naomi" (2:6).

Naomi, acting behind the scenes, directs the action throughout. At each step, Ruth tells Naomi what has transpired and follows Naomi's advice. When Naomi decides that Ruth must initiate action, she tells her, "Wash and perfume yourself, put on your cloak and go down to the threshing floor, but don't let Boaz know that you are there until he finishes eating and drinking. When he lies down, notice exactly where he is, then go into that place, lift up the covering at his feet, and lie down." This is certainly precarious advice, but Ruth answers unhesitatingly, "I will do whatever you tell me" (3:1-5).

Naomi—rather than Ruth—is restored as a mother in Israel when Ruth and Boaz are married and have a son. "Naomi took the child, and laid it in her bosom, and became a nurse to it. And the women, her neighbors, talked about it and said, 'There is a son born to Naomi'" (4:14-17).

Those Jewish women who feel renewed as grandmothers may well find sources for self-esteem within Naomi's triumphant surrogate motherhood. Moreover, the image of the older Jewish woman as the handmaiden of young romance is reinforced by popular films like Joan Micklin Silver's *Crossing Delancey*. Here romantic love—long the symbol of individual freedom—blossoms only when it accepts a *shadkhante* (female matchmaker) and a lovingly manipulative grandmother.

Today, however, many older American Jewish women are not grandmothers, and many who are do not wish to be defined by that relationship. Furthermore, few if any older women see their role as the manipulator of other people's lives. If we are not defined as grandmothers or as matriarchal manipulators, what guidance can we find in Jewish texts and traditions?

Some American Jewish women have responded to the question by creating new ceremonies to sanctify old age. Among a number of published celebrations are Irene Fine's *Midlife—A Rite of Passage* as well as her insightful *The Wise Woman: A Celebration*.[2] Such woman-centered initiatives are gaining importance among Jewish women today.

Biblical and rabbinic works, however, are far from devoid of inspirational value. More striking than the emphasis on physical motherhood is the valorization of the divinely maternal spirit. Judaism's sacred books pre-date Carol Gilligan in their belief that women have a unique moral vision. Biblical women—particularly older women—are blessed with a profound insight into people and actions. Women such as Rebecca and Naomi experience a crisis of belief and then, with the guidance of God, gain understanding and strength. Their insight, which grasps from the very beginning the potentials contained within a situation, prompts an extraordinary statement. One definition of an individual who has the wisdom to cleave to God's will, according to *Pirkei Avot*, is the person *asher ro'eh et hanolad*—"who sees the newborn."

Biblical women—particularly older women—are blessed with a profound insight into people and actions.

The metaphorical interpretation is that true wisdom is seeing a situation and understanding its possibilities. But in ancient civilizations, the actual newborn is first seen and assessed by the female midwife and the mother. The statement in *Pirkei Avot* thus elevates female experience to a primary condition for wisdom and piety.

Biblical scholar Claudia Camp notes that "mother in Israel" is "indicative of a complex of meanings associated with the mother," a role which "embodied the idea of the effective counsel of unity and *shalom*. The counsel of the mother was, metaphorically at least, Israelite counsel *par excellence*."[3]

This conception of female insight—and the appropriate use of such insight—illuminates Deborah's declaration. Deborah is a unique Jewish leader, judging her people and supervising the military activities of her general, Barak. Yet, when she chooses to praise herself, this woman of military acumen says, "I arose, a mother in Israel" (Judges 5:7). Deborah, the judge, sees herself in the tradition of Rebecca and Naomi, women who "see the newborn" and act on their extraordinary vision.

In the Bible, the absence or waning of reproductive abilities is accompanied by an increased capacity to see clearly and to respond to complex challenges. One of the great tasks facing older American Jewish women is reclaiming and revitalizing these positive images of the insightful and powerful aging woman.

From Textures, Hadassah National Jewish Studies Bulletin, *May 1994, vol. 12, no. 2.*

SYLVIA BARACK FISHMAN, Ph.D., is Assistant Professor of Contemporary Jewish Life and Associate Director of the new International Oral Research Institute on Jewish Women (sponsored by Hadassah) at Brandeis University. She is the author of A Breath of Life: Feminism in the American Jewish Community *and editor of* Follow My Footprints: Changing Images of Women in American Jewish Fiction.

PROGRAMMING IDEAS

AT HOME

Torah Table Talk   A discussion of Jewish thought and values with your family and/or friends. The obligation to care for elderly parents is discussed at great length by the sages of Jewish history. The excerpts below are from the Bible and later rabbinic commentary. They focus on some of the limits to the adult child's duty toward an elderly parent. The wording of certain passages has been altered to achieve gender neutrality.

Leviticus 19:32

Stand before a white-headed person and honor the face of an elderly person. And fear your God; I am *Adonai.*

Midrash, Pesikta Rabbati 23 (c. ninth century)

Rabbi Simeon ben Johai said: Great is the duty of honoring one's parents.... Whether you are a person of substance or not, you are obligated to "honor your father and your mother" (Exodus 20:12)—even if you have to beg from door to door.

Maimonides (1135-1204), Mishneh Torah, *Laws Relating to Rebels 6:3*

What does honoring parents imply? It means providing them with food and drink, clothing and covering, the expense to be borne by the parents. If the parents are poor and the child is in a position to take care of the parents, the child is compelled to do so. The parents must be supported in accordance with the child's means. The child must conduct the parents in and out, and perform for them such personal services as disciples perform for their teacher. The child rises before the parent, as the disciple rises before the teacher.

Joseph Caro (1488-1575), Shulhan Arukh, Yoreh De'ah 240:5

And if the child has no money, the child does not have to become a beggar to feed the parents.

Maimonides (1135-1204), Mishneh Torah, Laws Relating to Rebels 6:10

If the mind of one's father or mother is affected, the child should make every effort to indulge the vagaries of the stricken parent until God will have mercy on the afflicted. But if the condition of the parent has grown worse, and the child is no longer able to endure the strain, the child may leave the father or the mother, go elsewhere, and delegate others to give the parent proper care.

Rabad (Rabbi Abraham ben David of Posquires) (twelfth century)
(Commenting on Maimonides)

This is not a correct ruling! If the child goes and leaves them, who will attend to the needs of the parents and supervise their well-being?

Maimonides (1135-1204), Mishneh Torah, Laws Relating to Marriage 13:14

If a man says to his wife, "I do not wish to have your father, your mother, your brothers, or your sisters come to my house," his wish is to be honored, and she should visit them instead when anything happens to them. She should also visit her father's house once a month, and on each pilgrimage festival. They, however, should not visit her, unless something has happened to her, such as illness or a childbirth, for no one may be compelled to let others enter his or her premises.

Thus, also, if she says, "I do not wish to have your mother or your sisters visit me, nor do I wish to reside in the same courtyard with them, because they cause me harm and annoyance," her wish is to be honored, for no one may be compelled to let other people reside with him or her on one's premises.

Questions for Thought and Discussion

1. Under what circumstances must a daughter or son care for an elderly parent? Under what circumstances is the child exempt?

2. How does one care for parents who have Alzheimer's disease or another illness that makes them dependent? Would you agree with Maimonides or with Rabad?

3. Does a wife have the right to refuse to care for her husband's parents? Even if she has the right, could an American Jewish wife in the twentieth century actually refuse? And how do the modern wife's responsibilities to her in-laws compare to the modern husband's responsibilities to his in-laws?

Additional At-Home Activities

❖ If you are young, invite elderly relatives or friends to your home, perhaps for Shabbat dinner or on Shabbat afternoon. If they are willing, discuss their childhood and young adulthood. What generational differences and similarities do you perceive? If you are elderly, invite a young relative or friend to your home.

❖ Capture your family's or friends' life stories on tape. If you've heard the stories before but have forgotten the details, or if you wish to preserve a record for your own children, or if you want to reinforce shared values and increase closeness, use a camcorder or a tape recorder to chronicle the history of an aging relative or friend. Or, have your children interview and record the life histories of their grandparents or other relatives. Consult *Mishpahah: Hadassah's Hands-On Family History Project* kit. It provides straightforward instructions and carefully selected questions, a guide to recording individual family histories, and a videotape for preserving your recorded interviews. (This program can also be used to record the history of your Hadassah chapter or any other kind of extended family.) Call the National Programming Department, 212-303-8027, for more information or to order the kit.

INTEREST/STUDY GROUPS

Hold a discussion based on the following questions:

1. The *bubbe*—warm, loving, controlling, interfering, irritating, making gefilte fish—is an almost mythical figure. What accounts for the persistence of the myth? How does this affect women's lives today?

2. Re-read the biblical stories of Rebecca and Naomi. Have the low points in your life given you insight into people and situations? Were you able to use that insight in responding to challenges, as Rebecca and Naomi did? How else might you interpret their stories?

3. Is the wisdom of Rebecca and of Naomi uniquely feminine? If so, how?

4. Women's use of deception to achieve their ends is an emotionally-charged topic. In the Bible, however, both men and women use trickery to further God's work—Jacob, Rebecca's son, is a prime example (Genesis 27:1-38). How do we justify using deception in our own lives? Are we more likely to be deceptive when we are older, or are "woman's wiles" the province of the young?

MEETINGS

❖ Invite a gynecologist or endocrinologist to speak on menopause as experienced in different cultures. For instance, very few women in China suffer from hot flashes. In contrast, many women in America experience them. Your speaker might address how current research explains such cross-cultural differences. Is diet a factor? What other cultural factors have been implicated?

❖ Invite someone who is currently disabled, or someone who had been temporarily disabled, to speak on physical barriers for the handicapped. Are wheelchair ramps and elevators available for the handicapped in your local synagogues, Jewish community centers, and Jewish community organizations? If not, work toward eliminating obstacles to Jewish communal life.

❖ Invite a rabbi or Judaic scholar to discuss aging in the Jewish tradition. Discuss biblical and rabbinic models of older women. What can we learn from these models? How have older women been depicted in Jewish history? How has the model of aging changed in our own time?

❖ More than half of all women over age 65 are affected by osteoporosis. Discuss osteoporosis at a chapter or group meeting, and provide all members with the Hadassah issue card "Prevent Osteoporosis" and the pamphlet "Bare Bones Facts." Call Hadassah's National Order Department, 1-800-880-9455. "Prevent Osteoporosis" order number #R654f. Minimum order: 500 cards. Cost: $5.00 for 500. "Bare Bones Facts" order number #R662. Cost: free.

❖ Show the video *Gefilte Fish* (color, 15 minutes), which depicts three generations of Jewish women—grandmother, mother, and grown daughter—preparing to serve gefilte fish. Order the video for $34.95 (includes shipping and handling) from Ergo Media in Teaneck, NJ, 1-800-695-3746. Order #370. Follow up with a discussion of Jewish women and aging, perhaps focusing on some of today's positive role models, Betty Friedan and Ruth Bader Ginsburg, for example.

ANNUAL EVENTS

❖ Refer to the "Annual Events" section of "The Beauty Myth" to organize an Education Day on "Biblical Images of Women," pages 11-12.

❖ Conduct an Education Day or Evening on the Fifth Commandment: honoring our mother and father. Invite a rabbi or scholar to discuss the biblical injunction and later Jewish texts. Open up a discussion on the difficulties of obeying this commandment ourselves, and discuss as well the difficulties our children face in obeying the commandment. Issues to be addressed might include: the difference between "honor" and "reverence"; the adult child's needs versus the parent's needs—competing obligations; and the abusive parent—how far does honor go? Devote at least one session to the "woman-in-the-middle" or the sandwich generation—women who must care both for children and for parents. How do the Bible and rabbinic literature guide the woman in the middle? Discuss ways in which Jewish women today cope with the responsibilities to children, parents, and self. For background, read *The Jewish Woman in the Middle*, a Hadassah study guide. Call 212-303-8167 to order a copy.

HANDS-ON

❖ Visit a Jewish old age home, perhaps on Shabbat or a holiday. Most institutions welcome volunteers. Inquire in your community. If possible, arrange to visit with another Hadassah member. Working together will usually help you both to feel at ease. (Also inquire in local synagogues about *Bikkur Holim* societies to visit the sick. These groups offer volunteers the opportunity to work together in visiting nursing home and hospitalized patients.)

❖ Form a group to sit with or escort those going to the hospital for physical therapy, dialysis, chemotherapy, radiation, or other treatments. Create a schedule so that members of the group can rotate shifts.

❖ As a Hadassah unit, work in coalition with a "Meals on Wheels" program, delivering meals to aging and ill shut-ins.

---

1. Tikva S. Frymer-Kensky, *In The Wake of the Goddess: Women, Culture and the Biblical Transformation of Pagan Myth* (New York: Free Press; Toronto: Maxwell Macmillan Canada, 1992), page 13.

2. Irene Fine, *Midlife—A Rite of Passage* and *The Wise Woman: A Celebration* (San Diego: Women's Institute for Continuing Education, 1988).

3. Claudia V. Camp, *Wisdom and the Feminine in the Book of Proverbs* (Decatur, GA: Almond Press, 1985), page 81.

A Time to Mourn, A Time to Dance: An Unfinished Work in Progress

Gail Katz Meller

In 1989, Gail Katz Meller wrote in prose and poetry about her experiences as a widow of ten years. In 1997, she wrote the postscript that follows this article.

Young Widow in the Orthodox World

Pushing my way through an unpacked moving box, I smiled. The hubbub of moving, painting, starting kids off at yeshivah and bus stops had quieted down; the *yom tov* marathon of cooking and hosting had subsided; the children, one through eleven years old, were finally all sleeping through the night. On my birthday that week I would be thirty-one. We were at peace in our new house, and I thought of Stan and smiled. Now there would be time for us.

What does it mean? What do we learn from this when one week later this life of peace and love is finished?

It is five days after my thirty-first birthday. Stan is dying in an emergency room of myocardial infarction. But he was so healthy—a biker, nonsmoker—he had no heart problems, no blood pressure history, no familial health problems.

A young Israeli resident with a pained face is trying to explain to me, but he keeps shrugging his shoulders and few of his words make sense.

"We're going to keep trying, though, but it's really bad."

A heavyset nurse with bushy knit eyebrows shakes her head silently as she waddles toward my open hands with a heavy paper bag. Deadweight, it pulls at me. Through a fog of sirens deep inside my skull, I open it to find Stan's pants, shoes, cut open *tzitzit*, and shirt. Dry mouthed, I look up as the sad resident slowly moves toward me. My ears are ringing, but I can hear what he is telling me almost before he says it.

"I'm sorry. We.... He...." He is dead. My whole life, as I knew it, is dead.

"I need a phone."

"What?"

"I need a phone."

And in five minutes I call my rabbi, the rabbi who will deal with the medical examiner, the funeral chapel, the baby sitter, his parents, my two friends.

And yet....

But who will take care of me? Who? What about me? Who will hold me?

At dawn I wait for my children to awaken.

"*Ima?*"

"Leezie, there is a story...."

"*Ima*, what's wrong?"

"There is a story of a man who came home to see his wife and two sons, and his wife said, 'If a king lent you two jewels to enjoy, and then, after a time, he took them back.'" ...

"Oh, *Ima*, oh ... but I know that story," she wept, her head trembling in my lap.

"My son, *Abba* has died."

"But people go to the hospital to get better."

"He has died. The doctors couldn't make him better this time."

"But that doesn't happen, does it?"

"I'll hold you."

"No! No ... oh."

"My father's dead," the 4-year old announced at *shiva*. Then, "Listen, we're going to be big when we sit *shiva* for you, *Ima*, right? Right?"

For how can a boy so small survive without the father of his life—

Trying hats and zipping flies ...
Flying kites and dreams ...
And, ah, the littlest one, there is no milk left to nurse you.

Late into the night the *shiva* candle dances shadows around my cold walls. Sleep? As if I might ever sleep again as I once did. As if life would ever be safe as it once was. I creep upstairs in the dark, still house as a scream swells in my throat. My mouth is completely closed, yet my lungs scream raw anguish into the emptiness.

> *How can I raise*
> *four children alone?*
> *I am 31 years old*
> *And a widow with*
> *four children*
> *Who will take care*
> *of me?*
> *Who will hold me?*

It's like falling with your eyes open
Into a bottomless
Endless
blackness
only to fall still more.
My hands numb
I pull at the icy blankets
And edge stiffly between them
Biting my cheek to keep back
The
Scream.

I clutch my shoulders
And nod and rock
Aye ...

It's all a mistake
They meant to come get me ...
They got the wrong guy—
He'll be back—
It's a dream
What if—
I should have—

I should have
But
but
How can I raise four children alone?
I am 31 years old
And a widow with four children
Who will take care of me?
Who will hold me?

Father and Mother and More

The nightmare has only just begun.
There is business to be taken care of.
The banks close the accounts and the vault is sealed.
Social Security needs me for an interview.
His employer requests I come over to finish signing paperwork
    and clear out his office
The life-insurance policy—
Is there one? Is there? If there is, where is it? Where?
And how did he pay the bills? Master and VISA from every bank
    downtown?

Why didn't we practice my paying bills and managing
the bookkeeping? Because. That's why.

Because we never thought this would happen.

Not to us.

So I never handled billing. Not once. And as I sit down to
pay mortgage, utility, insurance, yeshivah tuition, car loan
and funeral bills that second week, I vomit all over the
desk.

Hey, Stan!! Hey!

And as I try to load the car to take the children away for
Shabbat, I can't get the clothing, pampers, and portacrib
in the way they had always fit; the trunk will not close!

Hey, Stan!

And the furnace needs water, and the bricks need pointing;
and the garage door doesn't close; and we have squirrels,
and I get weird phone calls, Stan! Stan!
And your health insurance dropped us
—and Ethan needs hernia surgery! And I need you! I need
you! Oh! Stan!

And Shana has begun to walk

And Dovie takes his guns to school

And Ethan is so very quiet

And Leezie tries to smile. Sometimes.

And I drive Ethan to *maariv* every night to say *kaddish*.
An 8-year old *kaddish*, Stan.

And I move with the screaming

Inside my head

Stan!

Stan!

The Early Years

Think of the Children

"You must be strong for your children,
You must—"
"There are the children to think of;
Remember the children,
Remember—"
"Think of the children."

They half wince when they see me
"You should only have *naches* from the children."
Only? Only? I should only have?
May God not punish me, is that all

There is to hope for? Is that to be my only blessing?
What will restore the well of strength
That I may give to their need
What about me?
Hey Stan!
Hey God!
What about me?

Widowspeak

Yes, dear world, I am married
I am married to a man who died,
I am married to a life that died
Our life
My life as I knew me
Who I was—

Life ahead—
        Dead.
All.
Each.
We—
I—
me—
Dead.

My ring—
His ring—
Our ring is in the bank vault,
Cool steel keeps it in its place below ground.

But I was his. I have his name to prove it.
And now that he is not
I am not.

Don't you see? You shake your head no,
but can't you see?
I was his
And now that he no longer lives
I am—
Nobody's.
I belong to a memory.
I belong with a memory.
I am a memory.

Then who is this person
who leaves for work daily
shielding the kids from the world?
Who is this woman who stretches and reaches
to make time and life go on?
Through nights—
and homemade soups—
Granola/dried flowers/sightseeing day trips—
taxes—
children frightened of the dark—
carburetors—
gravestones
not-quite broken arms/appendicitis
field mice/water bugs—
gland lumps—
insurances that won't renew—
twenty-one undone homeworks—
camp trunks/name tapes—
fever—
school bus accidents

And they say I should only have *simhahs*.

I remember I opened his closet
Three months after he was gone
And placed my hand on the shoulder
of his herringbone brown tweed suit
and slowly embraced the jacket
where his back once used to be—
Fingers moving slowly—
My head pressed to the lapel—
And a moan escaped
From somewhere
Locked deep beneath the pose
of
sanity.
And I stood inhaling his scent
A light warm softness that was him.
Solid.
There with me.
There for me.
Of me.
And my hand stroked the empty shoulder
slowly as I wept
until I sank

to the floor
Drained
Lost.

And later
when the wave of sorrow
passed
once again into silence,
I thought of at least three
things I should be doing.
Right away. Right away,
Up, up and away

Still at midnight
I look through the *Times*
How often I have fallen asleep
in this chair
Awake
so tired—
but sitting downstairs
still
unable
to get myself
to
go
up
to my room.
Sleeping alone is impossible
After the years of peace
as one.

He is dead.
Very.
I have stopped
touching
the spot where my ring once was
You know, with my thumb?
Only sometimes
I reach for
what was.

What was
Is not.
Yet I am quite married.
I am married to a life that died.

The Middle Years

Best Foot Forward: The Widow Dates

What shall I wear
That will help him decide
   to call back?
How can I capture his eye
That he will skim the list of one hundred names
   given him
Till he spots mine.
    Me!
Oh, me!
I'm over here!
   Yoo hoo!
I'm different from the others
Choose me
Oh, me
Choose
Oh choose
   me.

And don't wear those awful shoes
so frumpy, ich—
Buy a boot, for heaven's sake.
And no skirt and blouse
That's date dress for kids
Not
Adults
And his wife was
An adult,
dear,
So it's an adult he's looking for.
A dress or a suit. That's it. A dress
   or a suit.

But—he may come in a sweater, you know.
   It's happened that way before.
No.
You don't know, do you? How could
   you know?
No.
Sooo
A skirt, blouse and blazer
will juggle me through.

And it should be a blouse
that drapes beautifully.
And I guess I'd better
have my nails done.
Simply.
Colorless
but shining
would be best, yes?
And the right bag.
I'll need a new coat—mine is dead.
It's from another life
that no longer is who I am.
A new coat, yes.
Young—
with the times ...
Pretend.

Pretend this first date
Is simply to have
A lovely evening
Yes.
That this best behavior careful smiling
neat, supportive, quiet, genteel woman
Is really
me.

Putting my best foot forward
Trying not to let it end up in my mouth.

And Last Year

Phoenix

Moving
Shaking her feet slowly
    in disbelief
The phoenix stretched
Her long legs.
First one
Then the other
Shaking off the ashes of yesterday.
Strange, she thought,
Hm—

I would have sworn
    life was over—
I remember
I wanted to jump into the flames
    of yesterday's end
That I
    would
    be
    no
    more. That I would ache
    no more.
That I might die
if not instead of
    then
At least
    with
yesterday.

But—
but
I am
here.

Changed
yes, surely changed
But
yes,
yes
I am here.

She leaned back
and reached out
her neck
Her face
up
beyond the
    ruin.
the sun shone
    above her.
the soft wind
stroked her cheek
    calling her soul,
"Arise!"
Lifting her wings so slowly
she inhaled,

Then sighed—
Then breathed in again
Reaching higher
and higher
To embrace the day.

Oh, dear God—
    there *is* day!
There is *still*
    beautiful new day
beyond here—
Oh, look at the day!

A small movement in the
    clouds above
Held her a moment.
Drawn, she watched an arrow pierce
    the open space.

The geese followed the leader.

    Did you know that geese
    Mate for life?
    For life.
    But ...
    Well, but he can lead.
    And take care of
    And do things well—

    But is that enough for a goose?
    Silly goose.
    It needn't be so—
    Silly goose. If you let it be so
        It will be so.

And the Phoenix
stood
And looked at the ashes
    of yesterday.
And kissed them sadly
    with her soul.

And,
    turning her face to
        the sun

Arose
　　took flight,
　　　　to join
　　　　　　tomorrow.

POSTSCRIPT, MARCH 1997

Dear God
　　I know I'm in your hands
and if this—
　　this raising the kids
　　and living my life through
　　alone—
is my portion in life
　　my only portion
　　the portion left to me
then
　　then
　　I'd better
　　accept.
Except ...
maybe, just maybe
　　maybe—
and then
　　Milt.
　　I met him.
　　I found him.
　　God gave me him.
　　He found me
　　God gave him me.
So this is the next chapter.
　　This was supposed to happen
　　now.
　　Like this.
And each day enfolds
　　as it
　　needs to.

When my fairy godmother friend Chaya Fredel invited me to a singles party last January, I shuddered. A widow for over 17 years, I hated singles "meet-me-choose-me" events. "You come," she said firmly. "Milt will be there." Friends had tried to introduce us since the July before, but he wasn't interested. A widower for just over a year, he had said he thought he'd never be interested in meeting anyone. Period. So now Milt would be there. I didn't want to go. I stalled. It was late.

And then we met—and the air sparkled. The first crystals of snow began to fall as we talked and giggled and talked and sang and talked, and that was the beginning of the snow of 1996; we are sorry we inconvenienced the whole Eastern Seaboard, but Milt and I needed time to meet and talk. Monday's dinner date became a ten-hour snowed-in talktime. Then Tuesday was another ten hours (wonder of wonders those two school-closed days!). And then we had dinner and whispered and talked every day (with midnight phone calls and whispertalk again). And seven days after we met, we knew (but we knew all week, really, I guess) so seven days after we met ... we were engaged.

We married on March 12, a month and a half later (needing to delay until my son returned from Israel) and we've been moving in, selling a house, embracing both families and celebrating life and love. The seventeen-year winter of my life is past, the rains have come and gone, the voice of the turtledove is heard in the land. (Arise my love! Arise and come away!)

> For lo, the winter is past.
> The rains have come and gone
> the flowers appear on the earth
> and the voice of the turtledove is heard.
> Arise my love!
> Arise and come away!
> And after a long time
> of cold and silence
> it began to snow—
> and Menachem found Gitel
> and they talked
> and they talked
> and they reached out—
> and then a piece of the universe
> (a peace of the universe)
> was
>   whole
>   again.

"A Time to Mourn, A Time to Dance: An Unfinished Work in Progress" from Jewish Marital Status: A Hadassah Study, *Carol Diament, ed. (Northvale, NJ: Jason Aronson, 1989), pages 147-159. "Postscript, March 1997" written for* Jewish Women Living the Challenge.

GAIL KATZ MELLER teaches writing and literature at Edward R. Murrow High School in Brooklyn, New York, a communications arts school. She has also taught folk dance in Temple sisterhoods and to senior citizens in East Flatbush. She looks forward to finishing this unfinished work in progress.

P R O G R A M M I N G   I D E A S

AT HOME

Torah Table Talk   A discussion of Jewish thought and values with your family and/or friends. The Bible repeatedly enjoins us to care for the widow, the orphan, and the stranger, as the following passages indicate.

Exodus 22:21-23

You shall not ill-treat any widow or orphan. If you do mistreat them, I will heed their outcry as soon as they cry out to Me, and My anger shall blaze forth and I will put you to the sword, and your own wives shall become widows and your children orphans.

Rashi (1040-1105), Commentary on Exodus 22:21

The same law applies to every person, but Scripture speaks of the usual term [that is, the widow and the orphan], because they are weak in power and it is a frequent thing to afflict them.

Deuteronomy 16:10-15

Then you shall observe the Feast of Weeks for the Lord your God, offering your freewill contribution according as the Lord your God has blessed you. You shall rejoice before the Lord your God with your son and daughter, your male and female slave, the Levite in your communities, and the stranger, the fatherless, and the widow in your midst, at the place where the Lord your God will choose to establish His name. Bear in mind that you were slaves in Egypt, and take care to obey these laws.

After the ingathering from your threshing floor and your vat, you shall hold the Feast of Booths for seven days. You shall rejoice in your festival, with your son and daughter, your male and female slave, the Levite, the stranger, the fatherless, and the widow in your communities. You shall hold the festival for the Lord your God seven days, in the place that the Lord will choose; for the Lord your God will bless all your crops and all your undertakings, and you shall have nothing but joy.

Deuteronomy 27:16-19

Cursed be he who insults his father or mother.—And all the people shall say, Amen.

Cursed be he who moves his fellow countryman's landmark.—And all the people shall say, Amen.

Cursed be he who misdirects a blind person on his way.—And all the people shall say, Amen.

Cursed be he who subverts the rights of the stranger, the fatherless, and the widow.—And all the people shall say, Amen.

Questions for Thought and Discussion

1. Why does the Bible refer to widows in the singular?

2. How does Rashi explain the commandment not to ill-treat the widow or orphan?

3. What do the stranger, fatherless, and widow share in common?

4. Why does the Bible use the term "fatherless" rather than "orphan"? Is this language significant?

5. In Deuteronomy 16, what does the Bible command? To whom are these commandments directed? Who is included in the rejoicing? Is anyone excluded? (Note: Levites are included because they have no land of their own.)

6. In Deuteronomy 27, who is cursed and why? What do the cursed share in common?

Additional At-Home Activities

❖ Writing provides a catharsis for the complexity of emotion that accompanies extremely sorrowful experiences. Think about the most difficult period of your life, and write down words and phrases that come to mind. Also write down the words or sentences that are the most consoling. (Refer to the Programming Ideas of "On Sorrow and Silence" as well, pages 261-265.)

INTEREST/STUDY GROUPS

Hold a discussion based on the following questions:

1. Which of the following were (or would have been) helpful to Gail Katz Meller, and at what stages in her life after her husband's death?

   (a) reminding her to keep going for the sake of the children

   (b) giving advice on managing her finances

   (c) inviting her and her children for a meal on Shabbat

   (d) inviting her to lunch any day of the week

   (e) "fixing her up" on dates

   (f) having a male friend or relative act as a role model for her children

2. Judaism demands that the community attend to the needs of the widow and the orphan. In this day of governmental social services, are we still obligated as a Jewish community to provide for the widow and orphan? If yes, what form should this action take?

3. What are some of the differences between the needs of a young widow and an older widow? How well are we in the Jewish community meeting these different needs?

4. Is it possible to prepare ourselves for widowhood in advance? What can an ill spouse or a healthy spouse do in anticipation of this life change?

5. Some widows worry that they are not properly "acting like a widow." All of the following traits describe widows—but not all widows and not at all times. Discuss the traits below that best describe widows. Feel free to add.

   (a) being lonely and withdrawn

(b) putting on a good face for others even when she feels miserable

(c) participating actively in volunteer work

(d) traveling easily

(e) staying at home, not going out a lot

(f) "consulting" her dead spouse on decisions

(g) being independent

(h) being in need of attention and affection

(i) being angry and resentful

(j) socializing with other widows

(k) dating

6. Read aloud the poetry in Gail Katz Meller's article and share your responses.

MEETINGS

❖ Invite a rabbi and/or Jewish social worker to discuss working with widows and widowers. Follow up by reading aloud selections from Gail Katz Meller's poems, and discuss.

❖ Invite one or two widows, or a widow and a widower, to discuss their experiences with your members. Hold a question-and-answer session or small group discussions.

❖ Hold a panel discussion on the needs of widows and the Jewish community's responsibility to widows. Invite a rabbi, social worker, and two or three widows of different circumstances to sit on the panel. Explore how the needs of widows differ from those of other single women.

❖ View and discuss the 1970 film *Siege*, about an Israeli woman, Tamar, who loses her husband during the Six-Day War. Her husband's friends do not want his memory to be forgotten, and this forces Tamar into the role of the ever-mourning widow. Tamar, living with her young son, attempts to break away from the past, form new relationships, and lead a new life. Order *Siege* (black and white, 95 minutes, Hebrew with English subtitles) for $39.95 from Ergo Media in Teaneck, NJ, 1-800-695-3746. Order #544.

ANNUAL EVENTS

Refer to the "Annual Events" section of "On Sorrow and Solace" by Nessa Rapoport, page 265.

HANDS-ON

Refer to the "Hands-On" section of "On Sorrow and Solace" by Nessa Rapoport, page 265.

RECOMMENDED READING

Women's Health

Boston Women's Health Book Collective. *The New Our Bodies, Ourselves.* New York: Simon & Schuster, 1996.

Cobb, Janine O'Leary. *Understanding Menopause.* Toronto, Canada: Key Porter Books, 1989.

Cutler, Winnifred B., and Garcia, Celso-Ramon. *Menopause: A Guide for Women and Those Who Love Them.* New York: Norton, 1992.

Hoffman, Eileen. *Our Health, Our Lives: A Revolutionary Approach to Total Health Care for Women.* New York: Pocket, 1995.

Jacobowitz, Ruth S. *150 Most-Asked Questions About Osteoporosis: What Women Really Want To Know.* New York: Hearst, 1993.

Lark, Susan M. *The Menopause Self-Help Book.* Berkeley, CA: Celestial Arts, 1990.

Love, Susan M. *Dr. Susan Love's Breast Book.* Reading, MA: Addison-Wesley, 1991.

Love, Susan M. *Dr. Susan Love's Hormone Book: Making Informed Choices About Menopause.* New York: Random House, 1997.

National Osteoporosis Foundation. *Boning Up on Osteoporosis* (1991). Copies are $2.00. To obtain, write to: The National Osteoporosis Foundation, 1150 17th Street NW, Suite 500, Washington, DC 20036-4603. Other noteworthy publications by the Foundation are *Facts About Osteoporosis, Arthritis, and Osteoarthritis* (1991), *The Older Person's Guide to Osteoporosis* (1991) and *Stand Up To Osteoporosis* (1992).

The PDR Family Guide to Women's Health and Prescription Drugs. Montvale, NJ: Medical Economics, 1994.

Rinzler, Carol Ann. *Estrogen and Breast Cancer: A Warning to Women.* New York: Macmillan, 1993.

Utian, Wulf, and Jacobowitz, Ruth S. *Managing Your Menopause.* New York: Prentice Hall, 1990.

Body Image and Identity

Brumberg, Joan Jacobs. *Fasting Girls: The Emergence of Anorexia Nervosa as a Modern Disease.* Cambridge, MA: Harvard University Press, 1988.

Foster, Patricia, ed. *Minding the Body: Women Writers on Body and Soul.* New York: Doubleday, 1994.

Halprin, Sara. *"Look At My Ugly Face!" Myths and Musings on Beauty and Other Perilous Obsessions with Women's Appearance.* New York: Viking, 1995.

Marks, Marlene Adler. "Nice Jewish Girls," *Hadassah Magazine*, vol. 77, no. 10, June/July 1996.

Nesse-Biber, Sharlene Janice. *Am I Thin Enough Yet? The Cult of Thinness and the Commercialization of Identity.* New York: Oxford University Press, 1996.

Orbach, Susie. *Fat is a Feminist Issue: The Anti-Diet Guide to Permanent Weight Loss.* New York: Berkley Books, 1994.

Rosen, Jonathan. *Eve's Apple.* New York: Random House, 1997. (The female protagonist of this novel is anorexic.)

Waterhouse, Debra. *Like Mother, Like Daughter: How Women Are Influenced by Their Mothers' Relationship with Food—and How to Break the Pattern.* New York: Hyperion, 1997.

Wolf, Naomi. *The Beauty Myth: How Images of Beauty Are Used Against Women.* New York: Anchor, 1992.

Aging

Blank, Barbara Trainin. "Family Matter: Late Mitzvas," *Hadassah Magazine*, vol. 77, no. 10, June/July 1996.

Cole, Thomas. *The Journey of Life: A Cultural History of Aging in America.* New York: Cambridge University Press, 1992.

Doress, Paula Brown, Siegel, Diana Laskin, and the Boston Women's Health Book Collective. *Ourselves, Growing Older.* New York: Simon & Schuster, 1987.

Friedan, Betty. *The Fountain of Age.* New York: Simon & Schuster, 1993.

Greer, Germaine. *The Change: Women, Aging and the Menopause.* New York: Alfred A. Knopf, 1992.

Grumbach, Doris. *Extra Innings: A Memoir.* New York: Norton, 1993.

Grumbach, Doris. *Fifty Days of Solitude.* Boston: Beacon, 1994.

Kuhn, Maggie. *No Stone Unturned: The Life and Times of Maggie Kuhn.* New York: Ballantine, 1991. (Maggie Kuhn founded the Gray Panthers.)

Pogrebin, Letty Cottin. *Getting Over Getting Older: An Intimate Journey.* Boston: Little, Brown, 1996.

Sheehy, Gail. *New Passages: Mapping Your Life Across Time.* New York: Random House, 1995.

Shulman, Alix Kates. *Drinking the Rain*. New York: Farrar Straus Giroux, 1995.

Widows and Grieving

Broner, E. M. *Mornings and Mourning: A Kaddish Journal*. San Francisco: HarperSanFrancisco, 1994.

DiGiulio, Robert C. *Beyond Widowhood: From Bereavement to Emergence and Hope*. New York: Free Press, 1989.

Feinberg, Linda Sones. *I'm Grieving As Fast As I Can: How Young Widows and Widowers Can Cope and Heal*. Far Hills, NJ: New Horizon, 1994.

Graham, Laurie. *Rebuilding the House*. New York: Viking, 1990.

Graham, Virginia. *Life After Harry: My Adventures in Widowhood*. New York: Simon & Schuster, 1988.

Liss, Bonnie. *Cruising At 30,000 Feet: A Young Widow's Personal Account of a Year of Adjustment, Recovery, and Renewal*. New York: Macmillan, 1983.

Lopata, Helena Znaniecka, ed. *Widows*. Durham: Duke University Press, 1987.

Moffat, Mary Jane, ed. *In the Midst of Winter: Selections from the Literature of Mourning*. New York: Vintage, Random House, 1982.

Nudel, Adele Rice. *Starting Over: Help for Young Widows and Widowers*. New York: Dodd, Mead, 1986.

Rapoport, Nessa. *A Woman's Book of Grieving*. New York: William Morrow, 1994.

Reimer, Jack, ed. *Jewish Insights on Death and Mourning*. New York: Schocken, 1995.

Rice, Rebecca. *A Time to Mourn*. New York: NAL Books, 1990.

Yates, Martha. *Coping: A Survival Manual for Women Alone*. Englewood Cliffs, NJ: Prentice-Hall, 1976.

FAMILY AND HOME

In this unit, we present both positives and negatives of Jewish women's home and family lives.

The first issue concerns modern sexual norms. The pseudonymous writer Yeroham Tsuriel contends that in Judaism the concept of kedushah *(holiness) is tied to the concepts of self-restraint and discipline, applied both to the mind and to the body. The author adheres* to Orthodox Judaism, and he contends that single men and women are bound to the Jewish legal code of sexual purity. For him, premarital chastity is just as important as marital fidelity. In response, self-described "liberal Jew" Ellen Umansky argues that, for her, Jewish tradition has a voice but not a veto in the formation of ethical behavior. In stressing the *relationship* between individuals rather than their sexual purity, she contends that we hallow life when we regard other individuals as full human beings, and that any sexual standard that aims at moral excellence can be defended as being Jewish. For her, responsible decision-making, coupled with an emphasis on the sexual *relationship* between two human beings, should be the Jewish model for ethics. In the end, the debate between Yeroham Tsuriel and Ellen Umansky may say more about the split between the Orthodox and Reform approaches than about sexual relations.

The following three articles explore family relationships. In "Happy Marriages," Francine Klagsbrun analyzes the factors that enable marriages to endure. Although she writes for a wide audience of both Jews and non-Jews, marriage itself is a deeply-held Jewish value. And Klagsbrun writes: "It should be pointed out that the commitment to marriage by long-married couples is usually a commitment not only to a relationship, but also to marriage as an institution." Barbara Goldstein, in "*Mikvah* Blessings," writes about accompanying her soon-to-be-married daughter to a *mikvah* (ritual bath). As readers learn of a Jewish woman's way to prepare for marriage, Goldstein also reveals her closeness and love for her two daughters. The third piece on relationships is a short story, originally written in Hebrew by Savyon Liebrecht. "Apples in the Desert" presents the reconciliation of an Orthodox, religious mother with her secular, *kibbutz*-dwelling daughter.

Two articles explore two of the most distressing problems of today's Jewish community. Susan Alter writes of Jewish divorce law in "The Anchored Woman—A Cry for Help." According to *halakhah* (Jewish law), a wife is unable to divorce her husband. He must divorce her. The husband does so by handing his wife a *get* (writ of divorce). Many husbands, who have already separated from their wives or divorced them in civil court, refuse to give a *get*. Or, they use the opportunity to extort money from the women. These ex-wives who are still legally married are called *agunot*—chained ones. Susan Alter shows how the Conservative and Reform denominations have addressed the issue. The Orthodox community, however, has so far failed to free the *agunot*.

We also explore wife abuse in "A *Mezuzah* Does Not Ward Off Domestic Violence" by Rabbi Julie Ringold Spitzer. Despite persistent beliefs to the contrary, statistics indicate that domestic violence is as prevalent in the Jewish community as in the general population. Rabbi Spitzer also reports on the chilling statistic that abused Jewish women are likely to remain with their abuser twice as long as abused women in the general American population.

Finally, three essays analyze one of the most controversial issues of our day—interfaith marriage. Interfaith marriage particularly affects women, because in our society women, more than men, transmit values and customs to the next generation. In "The Jewish Community in Crisis—Two Views on Intermarriage," Egon Mayer argues that interfaith marriage is changing the character of Judaism, while Deborah Lipstadt provides an overview of recent demographic research and recommends that the Jewish community bid good-bye to those children of interfaith marriages who are being raised in another religion. Dr. Lipstadt asserts that the American Jewish community must spend its resources instead on enriching the lives of those families who actively seek a Jewish connection. Rabbi Harold Schulweis, for his part, questions the very idea of a Judeo-Christian synthesis, since the differences between Jewish and Christian theology and philosophy are deep and wide. He asserts that "Judeo-Christian" is a euphemism for spiritual emptiness. And, for those interfaith families raising their children as Jews, Paul and Rachel Cowan provide concrete advice.

THE *KEDUSHAH* OF MONOGAMY: A PERSONAL PERSPECTIVE

Yeroham Tsuriel

Yeroham Tsuriel, the pseudonym used by a young Orthodox Jewish man, wrote "The Kedushah of Monogamy*" in 1976, as the sexual revolution that had begun in the sixties spread throughout all sections of American society. In 1988, he wrote a postscript, condemning the self-righteous tone that had informed his earlier piece, yet sticking to his original conclusions.*

The seemingly irreconcilable conflict between the sexual norms of the Jewish tradition and contemporary sexual behavior is a problem with which an entire generation is wrestling. Perhaps more than any other, this problem causes the halakhic system to appear unlivable and irrelevant.

First, I wish to explain the stance from which I write. I am an Orthodox Jew, and as such I am totally committed to the authority of the traditional *halakhah* (Jewish law). My obedience to the Jewish norms of personal modesty and chastity derive from that source. At the same time, I have wrestled with this problem and understand the dilemma of this generation from within. While it is not customary among Jews to engage in public confession of sin, I must state that I have acted out a deep split within my own life: For nearly five years, I lived a pious Jewish life in all respects but the sexual. As one who has knowingly and willfully sinned, and has subsequently returned to the full demands of the Torah, I hope it will not seem presumptuous for me to say that I possess a certain understanding of both poles of this question and of how the gap between the modern and traditional positions may be spanned.

A few more words of background. During my college years, I lived an urbane and open lifestyle, which included many friendships with young women of greatly varied backgrounds. I remember at that time that my adherence to the *halakhah* helped to create an atmosphere of dignity and respect in my relationships with the opposite sex. Subsequently, I moved to another city, one of the centers of the emergent youth culture, and there, under the combined pressures of a personal religious crisis and the values prevalent in my environment, my sexual morality began to crumble....

In retrospect, it is no longer clear to me that single adulthood is responsible for the relaxed sexual morality of our generation. The reverse is true as well. Free sex encourages a casual attitude toward relationships which, in turn, discourages early marriages. The prevailing cultural prejudice that marriage is not necessary, and that a young couple ought to live together for a considerable time before marriage, discouraged me, for example, from cultivating relationships with women who adhered to the outmoded norm of premarital chastity. Furthermore, this prejudice against marriage encouraged predatory and exploitative approaches toward sexual partners, particularly on the part of men.

What can be done to civilize this jungle? I would contend that it is in the nature of this jungle to be a jungle. The chaotic irresponsible elements within sexuality are so close to the surface even among sensitive, gentle, cultured individuals that any such enterprise seems doomed to failure.

A letter from a friend of mine—a young woman who grew up in the atmosphere of the youth culture of the late sixties and, by a long and tortuous path, found her way to Judaism—portrays some of the issues involved in striking and eloquent terms.

> ... *Zenut* [promiscuity] ... is [one way] to make *Hashem*'s [God's] name have a foreign sound in His own world. A relationship whose commitment does not allow full expression of both people without fear of overstepping the boundaries ... can only be a fragmentation, creating a contradiction between one's soul and one's actions. Any lack of commitment in sexuality, which plumbs the depths of each, can make a habit of taking those discoveries lightly, releasing their energy into the air instead of embodying it in work that honors God's name.... Just as saying *Hashem* is He who has power to rule over all of "these" does not exclude any of the creation, so great is His oneness, so too *kedushah* [holiness] in sexuality does not limit one's ability to love or to give, but includes every possible relationship in its higher focus. It includes it and contains it in manageable, usable form. Only then can one avoid killing the Godly spark in oneself or another.

Kedushah, restraint, monogamy, seen not as puritanical restrictions or hatred of the human life force, but as a focusing of that energy. Perhaps here lies the beginning of an answer to the problem. There is a paradox in sexuality. It touches that which is most human in us, in binding us intimately to another person, and in bringing us close to the mysteries of our mortality; and at one and the same time it appears as a blind, chaotic drive, crying for release in any form. The modern view, based on a bowdlerized version of Freud, teaches that repression or sublimation of sexual energy is unhealthy and that orgasm is a value in itself. In contrast, the traditional Jewish view is based on the premise that this energy must be channeled and harnessed, in creating the bonds of the couple and the family, and through them, the larger community. To leave this energy at the level of mere pleasure-seeking is to fail in our task as human beings....

The teachings about sexuality touch chords that are close to the essence of the Jewish world view. Traditionally, the notion of *kedushah*, which is the highest rung of spiritual development that a human being can reach, is tied to the idea of self-restraint and discipline. In Judaism, this discipline is applied not only to the mind and higher human faculties but to basic biological drives. Moreover, "*kedoshim tihyu*," "you shall be holy" (Leviticus 19:2) is addressed not only to spiritual giants, but to every single Jew. These demands are not easy, and they cannot be explained simply in rational terms. One central idea in Judaism is that of the *hukkah*—that law that we obey even though we do not understand the reason for it—through which we surrender our reason and will to that of the Almighty. Underlying this is a profound awareness of the limits of the human intellect and of the ease with which the thinking processes of even the most sophisticated may be bent. This is the essential point of departure of Judaism from Western culture. For us, man is not the measure of all things.

Milton Himmelfarb, in an essay entitled "Paganism," observes that Judaism is defined by the sages as denial of paganism, and that two of the outstanding elements in paganism are its orgiastic approach to sex and its fascination with bloodshed. These three elements—idolatry, licentiousness, and murder—are linked together as the three acts for which a Jew is commanded to die in *kiddush Hashem*,[1] and they are also linked together in the passage from Leviticus 18 read on Yom Kippur afternoon.[2] Himmelfarb speculates on whether the current sexual

> Traditionally, the notion of *kedushah*, which is the highest rung of spiritual development that a human being can reach, is tied to the idea of self-restraint and discipline. In Judaism, this discipline is applied not only to the mind and higher human faculties but to basic biological drives.

libertarianism, which goes under the banner of gentleness and kindness ("Make Love, Not War"), won't, in the end, carry in its wake a new wave of paganism and irrationality that will involve not only unchastity, but cruelty and contempt for human life.

At one time, I believed that the *halakhah* ought to respond to current sexual morality through a liberalization of norms—opening the *mikva'ot* (ritual baths) to unmarried women, and exploring the possibility of a limited *heter* (permission from a rabbinic authority) for premarital relations. In fact, the prohibition on premarital intercourse is rather ambiguous.... Rabbi Yaakov Emden, in a responsum published in the mid-eighteenth century, concludes that, under carefully delineated circumstances, sexual relations without marriage are permissible. Among the preconditions are: (1) that the woman observe all the laws of *niddah*;[3] (2) that, for the duration of the relationship, known as *pilagshut* (concubinage, or half-marriage), both lovers be faithful to one another; (3) that the relationship be a public one, in which the man and his mistress live together; (4) that a rabbi be consulted in each individual case....

While Emden's view must be respected as the considered opinion of a major halakhic figure, I can no longer see this as the solution for our generation. The entire Jewish people rejected this view. Rav Hayyim of Brisk, when asked about this responsum, described Emden as a "knave within the bounds of Torah." At best, Emden's solution was intended to be used after the fact and not as an expression of what God's will as expressed in the Torah wants and demands of Jews.

How does one live according to God's will in the real world? There is no easy answer. The forces against it are many: the person's own sexual urge; the sexual stimuli that are ubiquitous in our culture; the need for human warmth and closeness that is expressed in the physical embrace; the social pressures urging one not to be "uptight" or "hung up," which, repeated often enough, lead one to doubt one's own position. Basically, the only way to preserve sexual purity is to build a strong, clear awareness that this is the true Jewish path and that only through it may one achieve *kedushah* and *toharah* (purification).

Maimonides sums up the seriousness of the laws of *arayot* (forbidden sexual relations) and the difficulty they pose. Perhaps we may gain strength from his words.

> There are no laws in the entire Torah which are as difficult for the majority of the people as those concerning *arayot*. The sages said that when Israel was commanded about *arayot* they wept and accepted the *mitzvah* grudgingly ... and they further said that one cannot find any community, at any time, in which there were not those who were guilty of illicit relations. Therefore, a man ought to bend his impulse in this matter and accustom himself to extra

holiness, purity of thought, and proper views in order to be saved from sin.... And he should avoid frivolity and drunkenness and sexual talk, for those are great factors leading to *arayot*. And he oughtn't to live without a wife, for by marriage he will attain greater purity. But greater than all of these, he should turn himself and his thoughts to words of Torah and broaden his mind in its wisdom, for sexual thoughts only grow strong in a mind which is empty of wisdom.

POSTSCRIPT 1988

Rereading "The *Kedushah* of Monogamy" after more than a dozen years is a strange experience. The author of the article was a young, earnest, unmarried man in his late twenties, who could devote most of his waking hours to study of Torah and reflection upon matters of Jewish philosophy and spirituality. The author of these lines is a man in his early forties, his everyday life filled with the responsibilities of family and profession. The former was rather naive, innocent, and optimistic about life, while the latter has both experienced and seen in others some of the pain and suffering that can be felt in intimate relationships.

While I still agree, in substance, with both the theoretical principles and the halakhic conclusions outlined in that article, I feel that there is more than a bit of self-righteousness in the tone. I find a certain lack of compassion or understanding for a person who cannot live up to the high standards of sexual morality I championed there. To put matters quite simply: the dream in which one marries as a young adult and settles down to live "happily ever after" with one's life partner is one that, for many people, does not seem to work. The social context in which there are more and more unmarried adults—whether due to divorce, homosexuality, or the simple inability to find a suitable partner—is one that cannot simply be ignored in a serious discussion of "sex and the tradition in the contemporary world." The needs, both for intimacy and love, and for sexual expression on whatever level, are among the most fundamental human needs. The two are of course interrelated. Sex is ideally expressed in a loving, caring, committed relationship, while feelings of love, which are in essence spiritual, are quite properly expressed in the realm of the physical (it is significant that our Rabbis always accepted this point and never developed concepts of "platonic" or "chaste" love such as are found in the medieval courtly or romantic traditions). Given this, can one realistically condemn those who are unable, for whatever reasons, to live "normal" family lives, to a life of extended celibacy? ...

As a Jew committed to the *halakhah*, I can perhaps advocate a liberal *pesak* (legal determination) permitting sexual relations between unmarried people under certain clearly defined conditions (that is, sexual faithfulness for the duration of the relationship and observance of immersion in the *mikvah*).[4] ...

Those of us living [today] may have a stronger sense than our forebears of the fragility and transient nature of human relationships, the pain and loneliness of life without love and intimacy, and the peculiar difficulties of finding one's way as a moral being in the world. Loyalty to the integrity of the *halakhah* and sympathy for one's fellow human being must constitute "two verses that come as one."[5] Together with the lofty ideals and calls for personal holiness, there must be compassion, love, and understanding for another human being in this confusing and value-shattering age.

"The Kedushah *of Monogamy" reprinted in* Jewish Marital Status: A Hadassah Study, *Carol Diament, ed. (Northvale, NJ: Jason Aronson, 1989), pages 63-69; originally published in* Response, Winter 1976-1977. *"Postscript 1988" originally published in* Jewish Marital Status.

"YEROHAM TSURIEL" is the pseudonym used at the time this article was written by Jonathan Chipman, a rabbi who has lived in Israel since 1974. Rabbi Chipman has translated into English many books and articles on the Bible and on Jewish mysticism, history, and thought. He is currently compiling a collection of his essays on contemporary Jewish issues.

Programming Ideas for "The *Kedushah* of Monogamy" are combined with Programming Ideas for the companion piece to this article, "The Liberal Jew and Sex" by Ellen Umansky. Refer to pages 71-74.

---

1. Jews are commanded to seek life. If forced to sin in order to stay alive, a Jew must commit the sin and preserve his or her life. However, if the sin involves idolatry, licentiousness, or murder, a Jew must choose to die in *kiddush Hashem* (sanctification of God's name) rather than commit the sin.

2. Milton Himmelfarb interprets a portion of the biblical passage as follows: "Unchastity is the piety of paganism. The things that are 'abominations' for Israel are the 'statutes' for the people of Egypt and Canaan.... Bloodshed is likewise the piety of paganism."

3. The laws of *niddah*—a woman's untouchability during menstruation and for seven days after menstruation ceases—are also referred to as the laws of family purity. Following the period of *niddah* (untouchability), a woman immerses herself in a *mikvah*. She and her husband are then able to touch each other and to have sexual relations.

4. This legal opinion is based on Rabbi Moses Isserles' interpretation of the *Shulhan Arukh, Even ha-Ezer* 26:1. (The *Shulhan Arukh*, written by Joseph Caro and with extensive glosses by Moses Isserles, is the definitive Jewish legal code. It is divided into four major sections; *Even ha-Ezer* is the section on marriage, divorce, and related topics.)

5. "Two verses that come as one" refers to reconciling two divergent interpretations of the Torah. The phrase is found in the Orthodox prayer service for weekday mornings before the *Kaddish De-rabbanan.*

THE LIBERAL JEW AND SEX

Ellen M. Umansky

D*r. Umansky's article was written in response to "The* Kedushah *of* Monogamy*" by Yeroham Tsuriel.*

In his article, Yeroham Tsuriel maintains that the halakhic Jew can best respond to the crumbling sexual morality of modern society by following these traditional Jewish sources that have understood "*kedushah* (holiness), restraint, and monogamy" to represent the Will of God. Although he states that his intent is to span "the gap between the modern and traditional positions," Tsuriel's rejection of what he considers to be "contemporary sexual behavior," and similarly, his rejection of any liberalization of halakhic norms, leads him to a reaffirmation of the traditional position as the only "true Jewish path." Tsuriel may feel that his conclusions are not mere restatements of the Orthodox position, because they emerge out of a long period of personal struggle, self-questioning, and doubt. However, the desired solution he claims to have discovered for "an entire generation" is, in fact, the position of the *Shulhan Arukh,* first presented by Maimonides in the *Mishneh Torah.* Tsuriel does not really offer us a way of spanning the gap between modern and traditional outlooks. Instead, he admonishes us to turn our backs on contemporary sexual mores and, as he has done, return "to the full demands of the Torah."

As a nonhalakhic Jew, it is difficult for me to accept Tsuriel's solution as my own. My source of ethics derives neither from the Talmud, commentators such as Maimonides, nor the *Shulhan Arukh*. Although I believe that there are ethical imperatives that each Jew must follow, I see these demands as rooted in the ethical autonomy of the individual and not in any external code of law. Careful thought, responsible decision making, and the conviction that what I have decided is "right"—and would also be "right" for others in a similar situation—are all important components in setting up an ethical standard of behavior. While Jewish tradition does influence my concept of morality, like Mordecai Kaplan, I recognize this tradition as having a voice but not a veto. Thus, ultimately, I must take the reasoned judgment of individuals as seriously as I do the demands of *halakhah*.

Orthodox Jews frequently remark that it is easier to be a liberal Jew than it is to be "fully observant." This kind of observation betrays a failure to take the demands of liberal Judaism seriously. For the liberal Jew who, like myself, is committed both to the rational capacity and ethical autonomy of individual persons as well as the preservation of Jewish religion and culture, making one's ethical standard both personal *and* Jewish, is often a difficult and painful process. Moreover, the inner struggle and lack of conviction that one's behavior is unquestionably right continue even after decisions have been made. While Tsuriel maintains that he too has struggled to reach the ethical (identified with God's Will), his admission that as an Orthodox Jew he feels "totally committed to the authority of traditional *halakhah*" makes his decision to follow the precepts of the *Shulhan Arukh* a foregone conclusion.

Essentially, I see Tsuriel's self-proclaimed struggle not as an attempt to discover the ethical, but as a growing recognition that one cannot be a pious Jew "in all respects but the sexual." If one is genuinely committed to Orthodoxy and sees this commitment as presupposing an adherence to the authority of traditional *halakhah*, then one cannot accept halakhic decisions only when it is convenient or desirable to do so. The fact that, as Tsuriel admits, "the [halakhic] prohibition on premarital intercourse is rather ambiguous" somewhat weakens but does not negate Tsuriel's conclusions. He rejects the liberalization of halakhic norms because he feels that such a measure would only be a compromising, convenient solution. He therefore states that "the solution for our generation" is an affirmation of premarital chastity, faithfulness within marriage, and adherence to the laws of family purity. Believing that God expects us to live up to these sexual standards, Tsuriel asserts that only those Jews who do so can attain a life that is both holy and pure.

As a liberal Jew, I can react to Tsuriel's article, but I cannot fully respond to it. Neither do I think that Tsuriel can fully respond to my own stance on sexual ethics. While both of us are Jews, our sense of what is Jewish vastly differs. Therefore, any attempt at real communication would have little chance of success. For Tsuriel, a position on sexuality that claims to be Jewish must follow "traditional *halakhah*." For me, any sexual standard that aims at achieving moral excellence can also be defended as Jewish. While, obviously, Jews are not the only people capable of positioning a morally excellent sexual standard, God's command to be holy gives us a special obligation to strive toward the highest level of ethical behavior. In formulating my own sexual ethic, then, I too have taken seriously God's command to be holy. However, I cannot believe that only by adhering to the norms of *halakhah* does one begin to make life sacred.

My standard of ethical sexual behavior stresses not the sexual purity of the individual, but rather the sexual *relationship* between two human beings. Its moral criterion rests with Martin Buber's concept of personhood and what it means to be fully human. While recognizing that "self-restraint and discipline" are important means of hallowing life, the sexual standard to which I adhere rejects the notion that premarital intercourse and the decision not to observe the family purity laws label one undisciplined and without self-restraint. Instead, it maintains that by treating someone as a whole person and not as a sex object, in Buber's language, as a "Thou" and not an "It," one transforms physical and potentially animalistic and exploitative behavior into expressions of warmth, caring, feeling, and love. This kind of physical intimacy is qualitatively different from acts of rape, sex performed only to satisfy one's sexual urges, and intercourse based not on mutual desire but on feelings of obligation. The extent to which it is transforming depends both on the depth of emotion involved and the degree to which the other's individuality and self-worth are considered.

Because my criterion of ethical sexual behavior is based on personhood, a relationship that most fully recognizes the humanity of the persons involved is necessarily on a higher ethical level than the sexual relationship based only on mutual consent. Premarital sex becomes unethical when an individual treats another solely as a sex partner, an "It" instead of a "Thou." Intercourse between two people who love each other is more ethical than intercourse based on mutual

> *My standard of ethical sexual behavior stresses not the sexual purity of the individual, but rather the sexual relationship between two human beings. . . . The sexual standard to which I adhere rejects the notion that premarital intercourse and the decision not to observe the family purity laws label one undisciplined and without self-restraint.*

agreement, and intercourse within marriage (if entering into a marital relationship is the deepest expression of love that two people can offer) represents the highest level of human sexual intimacy. To strive toward moral excellence, however, this relationship should be monogamous. Extramarital affairs jeopardize feelings of trust, honesty, and closeness, and indicate a weakening of one's marital (or what Eugene Borowitz calls a "love for life") commitment. Therefore, moral excellence is incompatible with marital infidelity, because such affairs reduce the strength, and significance, of the marital bond. This is as true of premarital relations as of intercourse within marriage.

While, as human beings, we have an obligation to strive toward that which is morally excellent, even if one formulates an ideal standard of sexual behavior, it may not be possible to attain that ideal at every stage of one's life. An I-Thou relationship based on mutual love and a desire to spend one's life together necessitates that the individual first find a Thou to whom this kind of commitment can be made. Moreover, even if one has found such a person, he or she may not be ready to enter into a marital relationship. Instead, that individual may choose to spend some time discovering his or her own set of values, self-identity, and personal sense of direction. Undoubtedly, it is possible to achieve these ends within marriage. However, the independence and greater flexibility that singleness affords make single adulthood a stage in one's life that should neither be minimized nor, I think, missed.

The liberal Jew knows of no pre-established path to holiness. Thus, in order to seriously consider God's command to be holy, he or she must first recognize that which can make life sacred. To me, one hallows life when one regards others as persons. As Buber states, we must often perceive the world and those people within it as objects of our experience. Yet when we encounter another human being as a Thou, "we are touched by a breath of eternal life," for all of us have been created in God's image.

Reprinted in Jewish Marital Status: A Hadassah Study, *Carol Diament, ed. (Northvale, NJ: Jason Aronson, 1989), pages 70-73. Originally published in* Response, *Winter 1976-1977.*

ELLEN M. UMANSKY, Ph.D., is the Carl and Dorothy Bennett Professor of Judaic Studies at Fairfield University in Fairfield, Connecticut, and a teaching associate of CLAL, the National Jewish Center for Learning and Leadership. Her most recent work is Four Centuries of Jewish Women's Spirituality: A Sourcebook, *co-edited with Dianne Ashton. She is also author of* Lily Montagu and the Advancement of Liberal Judaism: From Vision to Vocation.

PROGRAMMING IDEAS

AT HOME

Torah Table Talk   A discussion of Jewish thought and values with your family and/or friends. Nahmanides' *Iggeret HaKodesh (The Holy Letter)* is a candid essay on marital sexuality. Rabbi Moses ben Nahman (1194-1270) is known as Nahmanides or the Ramban. He was a leading biblical and talmudic commentator, and he was also a philosopher, poet, and physician. The passage below is taken from Morris J. Sugarman's translation of *Iggeret HaKodesh* (in *Ethical Literature, Teacher's Edition* [West Orange, NJ: Behrman House, 1987], pages 31-32). The study questions that follow were written by Nina Dubler Katz (page 34). This table talk would be particularly appropriate for families with older children or teens.

Nahmanides, Iggeret HaKodesh

Know that the sexual intercourse of a man with his wife is holy and pure.... No one should think that sexual intercourse is ugly and loathsome....

We the possessors of the Holy Torah believe that God ... created all ... and did not create anything ugly and shameful....

The mystery of humankind includes the mystery of wisdom, understanding and knowledge. Know that the male is the mystery of wisdom, and the female is the mystery of understanding. And the pure sex act is the mystery of knowledge. If so, it follows that proper sexual union can be a means of spiritual elevation when it is properly practiced, and the mystery greater than this is the secret of the heavenly bodies when they unite in the manner of man and woman.

A husband should speak with his wife with the appropriate words, some of erotic passion, some words of fear of the Lord....

A man should never force himself upon his wife and never overpower her, for the divine spirit never rests upon one whose conjugal relations occur in the absence of desire, love, and free will....

One should never argue with his wife, and certainly never strike her on account of sexual matters. The Talmud ... tells us that just as a lion tears at his prey and eats it shamelessly, so does an ignorant man shamelessly strike and sleep with his wife....

A man should not have intercourse with his wife while she is asleep, for then they cannot both agree to the act. It is far better to arouse her with words that will placate her and inspire desire in her.

To conclude, when you are ready for sexual union, see that your wife's intentions combine with yours. Do not hurry to arouse her until she is receptive. Be calm, as you enter the path of love and will.

Questions for Thought and Discussion

1. Which arguments does Nahmanides present to support his position that sexual intercourse is not "ugly and loathsome"?

2. Nahmanides seems to be reacting to sexual abuses which existed in his society. What were those abuses?

3. What do you consider the main sexual problem in our society? Can you point to the causes of this problem?

4. Most people agree that Western society has undergone a sexual revolution in recent years. What are the key changes?

5. In what sense does Nahmanides use the term "mystery"? How, specifically, would you explain the mystery of wisdom and the mystery of understanding? Do you agree with the distinction he draws between the respective natures of men and women? What does he mean by the mystery of knowledge, and what does this term reveal about the Jewish view of sexual intercourse?

6. How would you explain the concept of "love and will" as it is set forth by Nahmanides?

7. What specific values pertaining to sexual relations can be drawn from Nahmanides' essay? Can they pertain to a sexual relationship in which the parties are not married?

Additional At-Home Activities

❖ Discuss sexual matters regularly with your children, so that you can be a guide and a resource for them as their own sexuality develops. When watching television shows, videotapes, or movies together, note how sexual relations are portrayed, and offer your own comments and critique based upon your Jewish values and goals.

INTEREST/STUDY GROUPS

Hold a discussion based on the following questions:

1. Do you believe that the sexual freedom of the past thirty years has contributed to the postponement of marriage until the late twenties, thirties, and even forties? In what ways? What else has contributed to later marriages today than forty years ago?

2. Has the AIDS epidemic changed attitudes toward sexual freedom?

3. How might it be possible for a non-religious Jew to accept the ideas presented in "The *Kedushah* of Monogamy"? How could the non-religious Jew work toward making sexual intercourse a matter of *kedushah*, holiness?

4. How does the stance of "The *Kedushah* of Monogamy" diverge from or adhere to socially-accepted notions of sexuality? (Consider that Christian religious teachings are the source of much current thinking on the topic—for instance, Paul taught that it "is better to marry than to burn.")

5. In choosing a pseudonym in 1976, Jonathan Chipman chose "Yeroham

Tsuriel." The first name *Yeroham* is derived from the Hebrew word meaning "mercy" or "compassion," and *Tsuriel* means "God is my rock." What might the author's choice of name mean?

6. In your opinion, which of the following must be adhered to? Why or why not? (a) premarital chastity
(b) fidelity within marriage
(c) the laws of family purity, which include abstention from sex for approximately two weeks every month and the wife's monthly visits to the *mikvah*

7. Do you agree with Ellen Umansky that the ideal "standard of ethical behavior stresses not the sexual purity of the individual, but rather the sexual *relationship* between two human beings ... and [that] intercourse within marriage represents the highest level of human sexual intimacy"?

8. Discuss Ellen Umansky's contention that monogamous, loving marriage is the highest "moral excellence" possible for a couple. Should all couples aim for this goal?

9. Discuss why Ellen Umansky has a dispute with the concept of sexual purity and with adherence to *halakhah*.

10. Ellen Umansky states that she can react to "The *Kedushah* of Monogamy," but cannot fully respond to it. Because she and its author strongly disagree on what it means to be Jewish, she suggests that any attempt at communication would have little chance of success. What are the implications of this statement? Would you agree that Jews of different denominations have little chance for communication on controversial topics?

11. Writer and therapist Lisa Aiken observes that Jewish single men and women may or may not have sex together on their first date, but they would never, ever discuss their respective salaries until well after they had established a relationship. She asks, why may sex be shared when finances must remain private? Current attitudes toward sex and money differ greatly from earlier centuries, when Jewish marriages were arranged only after the parties had a full understanding of each other's economic status. Discuss. Should sex be more private today? Should discussions of money be more open?

MEETINGS

❖ Invite a local rabbi or Judaic scholar to lead a discussion on change within the Jewish tradition, as exemplified by the edict of Rabbeinu Gershom that outlawed polygamy among Ashkenazi Jews. Prior to 1040, Jewish men had been legally permitted to have two or more wives and even to keep concubines. Thus, the idea of male sexual restraint is relatively recent in Jewish history. The prohibition against polygamy is certainly not found in the Bible or the Talmud (although the Rabbis of the Talmud write under the assumption that, in general, each man will have only one wife). If external moral standards dictated to Rabbeinu Gershom in the eleventh century, why should they not also influence us today as well? Or, do you agree with the author of "The *Kedushah* of

Monogamy" that the Jewish sexual laws should remain unaltered today regardless of external moral criteria?

❖   Invite a local rabbi or Judaic scholar to discuss Jewish views of sexuality, as discussed in the Bible, Talmud, and the writings of medieval Jewish scholars. For follow up discussion: What are the implications of these views for women and men today?

ANNUAL EVENTS

❖   As part of an Education Day or Evening, organize a panel of Jewish rabbis and scholars of different perspectives—for example, an Orthodox halakhic scholar, a non-Orthodox rabbi, a psychologist, a historian, a feminist theologian—to discuss Jewish views on sexuality. Suggested topics include: the laws of *taharat hamishpahah* ("family purity"); premarital sexuality; sexuality as depicted in Bible and Talmud; opinions on concubines; the divine presence in the sexual relationship.

HANDS-ON

❖   Organize a pot-luck Friday night Shabbat dinner for singles, and discuss Jewish views of sexuality—before marriage and in marriage. Use the excerpt from the Ramban's *Iggeret HaKodesh*, "The *Kedushah* of Monogamy," and "The Liberal Jew and Sex" as the starting points for discussion. You might work in partnership with a synagogue or community organization, and invite a well-known guest speaker. Publicize the dinner, and hold it in a large space. Or your Hadassah chapter or group might host a more intimate dinner for ten to twenty singles in a private home.

Happy Marriages

Francine Klagsbrun

What are the characteristics of long, satisfying, happy marriages? There is no formula, no single recipe that will produce the perfect marriage, or even a working one. Rather, there are certain abilities and outlooks that couples in strong marriages have, not all of them at all times, but a large proportion a good part of the time. They fall, it seems to me, into eight categories.

An Ability to Change and Tolerate Change

Change is inevitable in marriages as in life. Partners become involved in work and pull back from work; children are born, go to school, leave home; spouses age, get sick, drop old interests, take on new ones, make new friends, live through the sorrows of old ones; parents get old and die; couples move from apartments to houses and back to apartments, from one town to another. Changes bring anxieties and disequilibrium. Yet in the strongest marriages, each partner is able to make "midcourse corrections, almost like astronauts," as one psychiatrist put it. That is, they are able both to adapt to the change that is happening in the marriage or in the other partner and, when called for, to change themselves.

Couples [who married before the seventies] have lived through some of the most rapid and overwhelming social change in modern history.

These people married at a time when marriage had a set form, when husbands knew that their work was to provide for the family, and wives knew that theirs was to care for the home and children. During the course of these marriages, the world turned upside down. Marriage was ridiculed as a dying institution. Husbands who played out the traditional roles they had been taught as children were now seen as "insensitive patriarchs," while wives were "oppressed." Along with the rhetoric came real change, a new emphasis on a woman's right to seek her own work outside her home and on a man's responsibility to his home and to his family. The changes brought chaos to many marriages.

> *In the strongest marriages, each partner is able to make "mid-course corrections, almost like astronauts," as one psychiatrist put it. That is, they are able both to adapt to the change that is happening in the marriage or in the other partner and, when called for, to change themselves.*

In the marriages that have remained strong and viable, partners have had the flexibility to change their marriages to incorporate new ideals.

Great changes have taken place in couples who have shifted their life patterns as social values have shifted. The women who have gone to work or back to school years into their marriage have come to see themselves as different beings than they were in their earlier days. Their husbands have accommodated to those changes and have changed themselves. They have taken on household tasks they would not have dreamed of when they first married. More important, they have changed inwardly, many of them acknowledging their wives' ambitions and accomplishments. One tiny manifestation of these changes in long marriages are the numbers of no-longer-young men I see at dinner parties automatically getting up to clear the table or serve a course, while their wives sit and chat with guests. Such acts are not merely gestures; they represent an inner change.

But there is an attitude toward change in long marriages that goes far beyond the social issues. People who stay happily married see themselves not as victims of fate, but as free agents who make choices in life. Because they choose to be married to each other, a choice they make again and again, they are open to changing themselves, pulling away from what *was* in order to make what *is* alive and vital. In other words, as much as they are able to, they try to control their lives, rather than drifting along.

In the best of marriages, change takes place in a context. It is contained within the boundaries of the marriage. Within those boundaries each partner acts and reacts, bending to the changes in the other and in the world outside. And even while they change, couples recognize that some things cannot change and should not change—and that leads to the second characteristic of long-term marriages, and its major paradox.

An Ability to Live With The Unchangeable

This means to live with unresolved conflict when necessary. The simultaneous acceptance of change and lack of change in long marriages is summed up by the words of a shopkeeper, married thirty-eight years: "You have to know when to holler and you have to know when to look away."

A statement made by many couples when asked about the "secrets" of their happy marriage was, "We don't expect perfection." They would go on to explain that their marriage had areas that were far from perfect, qualities in one another that they wish could have changed but they have come to recognize as qualities that will never change. Still, they live with those unchangeable, and sometimes disturbing, qualities, because, as one woman said, "The payoff is so great in other areas."

Long-married couples accept that there are some deep-seated conflicts—about personality, habits, styles of dealing with things—that will never be solved. In the best of situations, they stop fighting and they go about their lives instead of wasting their energies on a fruitless struggle to settle differences "once and for all."

The point is not that we must all sit back and let life wash over us without trying to shape and control what happens to us. The point is that we can best control our lives—and our marriages—by acknowledging that some things cannot be turned around, and apply our strengths where they *can* make a difference.

An Assumption of Permanence

Most marriages, first, second, or later, begin with the hope and expectation that they will last forever. In marriages that do last, "forever" is not only a hope but an ongoing philosophy. The mates do not seriously think about divorce as a viable option. Certainly there are "divorce periods," times of distancing and anger, but even if divorce itself crosses the minds of the couple, it is not held out as an escape from difficulties. This attitude that a marriage will last, *must* last (not because some religious authority or family member says so, but because the marriage is that important to the couple), tempers a husband's and a wife's approach to conflicts and imperfections. They see the marriage as an entity in itself that must be protected. In today's terminology, they are committed to the marriage as well as to each other.

The commitment, however, is *not necessarily equal* at all times. In marriage after marriage, I had the impression that one partner more than the other was the "keeper of the commitment." One usually seemed more willing to give in after a fight or more prone to compromise to avoid the fight altogether and hold the marriage on a steady keel. That partner may have been the more dependent one, but was just as likely to be the stronger and more mature one, the one more able to swallow pride, break stalemates, and see the other's point of view. Caring and dedication to the marriage, however, must be strong enough on the part of both partners so that when the "commitment keeper" pulled back, or refused to be the conciliator on some issue, the other moved in and took over that role. The commitment to marriage is not always top priority in both partners' lives at the same time, but it is usually top priority for one or the other at different times.

It should be pointed out that the commitment to marriage by long-married couples is usually a commitment not only to a relationship, but also to marriage as an institution. Mae West remarked that "marriage is an institution, and who wants to live in an institution?" But to couples who value marriage, the institution adds stability and order to life, transmits ideals from one generation to the next, and provides a structure within which a woman and a man can entrust their souls to each other, knowing that they will be sheltered and protected by its permanence.

Trust

This is a word used again and again by couples, and it means many things. It means love, although people tend to use the word "trust" more often than they use "love." In part this is because "love" is an overused word, and one whose romantic meanings have overshadowed the deeper, more profound meaning of the love that binds married people. In larger part it is because feelings of love may wax and wane in the course of a marriage—in times of anger, for example, few people can keep in touch with those feelings—but trust is a constant; without it there is no true marriage. Trust also implies intimacy, or, rather, it forms the base for the closeness that couples in good marriages have established.

Once that trust exists, there is no set form intimacy must assume. Not every couple in a strong marriage communicates as openly as the much-publicized communication ideals of our society would have them. Some do. Some are open and loose with each other, ventilating feelings and sensations freely. In other families, one partner, or both, may be more closed off, less able or willing to pour out heartsounds. But these marriages have their own ways of being intimate, which grow from the trust between partners. It may be that one partner is expansive while the second is silent, relying on the first for emotional expressiveness. Or it may be that both are somewhat restrained in revealing sensitivities, yet they understand each other and feel comfortable with the more limited interchanges they have. There are many styles of relating among long-married couples, and no one seems better than another as long as each couple is satisfied with its own style.

The trust that lies at the heart of happy marriages is also the foundation for sexual enjoyment among partners. When mates speak about sexual loving, they almost always speak about trusting feelings that had expanded over the years. "Sex is richer and deeper for us," said one woman. "We trust each other and we're not ashamed to get pleasure." Trust is also the reason invariably given for a commitment to monogamy, as in "I may be tempted, but I wouldn't want to violate our trust." When a partner has had a fling or brief affair, trust is the reason most often offered for having ended it or for avoiding further extramarital involvements. In short, trust is regarded by many couples as the linchpin of their marriage.

A Balance of Dependencies

This is another way of saying a balance of power. "Dependency" is preferable, even though "power" is a sexier word; it better conveys the way couples see and regard one another. They speak of needing each other and depending on each other, and in doing so, they are not speaking about the weaknesses of marriage, but about its strengths. In the best of marriages, partners are mutually dependent; interdependent is another way of saying that. They are aware of their dependencies and not ashamed to cater to them, acknowledging openly their debt to one another.

Rarely are husband and wife equally dependent on each other at any particular point. Rather, the dependencies tip back and forth during the course of a marriage, each spouse nurturing the other as needed, so that over time, a balance is established, and that balance keeps the marriage strong and stable.

Dependency, it needs to be added quickly, does not mean an obliteration of self. No matter how close or how interdependent a couple, each spouse must retain an individuality, a sense of self. If one or the other loses that individuality and becomes completely submerged or exploited by the other, one or both partners usually become deeply unhappy in the marriage. Even in the most traditional marriages, where a woman's social identity may be tied to her husband's occupation or profession, the women who speak most convincingly about the satisfactions of their marriages are women who view themselves as individuals and who do not rely on their husbands to make them feel worthy.

An Enjoyment of Each Other

Wives and husbands in satisfying long marriages like each other, enjoy being together, and enjoy talking to each other. Although they may spend evenings quietly together in a room, the silence that surrounds them is the comfortable silence of two people who know they do not *have* to talk to feel close. But mostly they do talk. For many couples conversations go on continually, whether the gossip of everyday living or discussions of broader events. And they listen to each other. I watch the faces of people I interview and watch each listening while the other speaks. They might argue, become irritated, or jump in to correct each other, but they are engaged and are rarely bored.

They enjoy each other physically also, and sexual pleasures infuse many marriages for years and years. Sexual electricity can be sensed between some partners. A different kind of warmth emanates from others, a feeling of closeness and affection. They hold hands, they touch, they smile, and they speak of sex as "warm and loving," as one woman said, "maybe not the wildness of our early marriage, but very pleasing."

They laugh at each other's jokes. Humor is the universal salve and salvation, easing tensions and marriage fatigue. "If you can laugh about it," many say, "you know it will be all right." And for them it is.

They find each other interesting, but they do not necessarily have the same interests. And that is a surprise. Far fewer couples than would be expected speak about sharing interests or hobbies.

Some make fewer concessions than others to their spouse's interests. They might take separate vacations, or go to the movies or lectures with friends rather than with each other. And for some married people, having separate interests makes each more interesting to the other. The only danger in this kind of separateness, especially for new marriages, is in its extreme. Spending a great deal of time apart is bound to cut into the closeness a husband and a wife build up. As in so many areas, couples in strong marriages try to find a balance between participating in each other's activities and going their own ways.

But if sharing interests is not a prerequisite for a rewarding marriage, sharing *values* is. Values refer to the things people believe in, the things they hold dear and worthy. The philosopher Bertrand Russell explained their importance in marriage well when he wrote, "It is fatal ... if one values only money and the other values only good works."

Mates who feel well-matched share a common base of values even when they disagree about other things. One couple describes having their biggest arguments about money. He loves to spend whatever they have on clothes, records, and the theater; she watches every cent, wearing the same dress again and again. Yet they had an instant meeting of minds when it came time to buy a cello for their musically gifted daughter. They bought the best they could afford, even using a good part of their savings, because they both value their child's music education above anything else money can buy.

For some couples, religion is the value that informs everything else in life. These couples are a minority in our secular society. But those who do value religion consider it the strongest bond in their lives, and many attribute the happiness and stability of their marriage to that bond.

For all marriages, sharing values enhances the intimacy and mutual respect spouses feel, adding to their enjoyment of each other.

A Shared History that is Cherished

Every couple has a story, and couples in long marriages respect their own stories. They are connected to each other through these stories, and even the sadnesses they share are a valued part of their history. "Our life is like a patchwork," one woman said. "We pull in red threads from here and blue threads from there and make them into one piece. Sometimes the threads barely hold, but you pull hard at them and they come together, and the patchwork remains whole."

People in long marriages value their joint history. When their ties in the present get raggedy, they are able to look to the past to find the good they shared, rather than give in to the disillusionments of the moment. Their sense of history also gives them respect for time. They know, by looking backward, that changes take time and that angers vanish with time, and they know that there is time ahead for new understandings and new adventures.

Luck

It has to be said, because everyone said it. With it all, the history and the trust, the willingness to change and to live without change, people need a little bit of luck to keep a marriage going.

You need luck, first of all, in choosing a partner who has the capacity to change and trust and love. In their book *Marriage and Personal Development*, psychiatrists Rubin Blanck and Gertrude Blanck make the case that marriages work best when both partners have reached a level of maturity before marriage that makes them ready for marriage. They are quite right. The only difficulty is that few people are terribly mature when they marry, certainly not people in first marriages who marry young, and not even many people in second marriages. Yet many marriages work because partners mature together, over the years of matrimony. So, you need a little luck in choosing someone who will mature while you, too, mature.

And you need a little luck in the family you come from and the friends you have. A horrendous family background in which parents abuse their children or offer no love can set up almost insurmountable obstacles to the ability to sustain a marital relationship. Yet there are couples in long, happy marriages who did have devastating backgrounds. Often they were able to break the patterns they had known because of the encouragement of an aunt or an uncle, a grandparent, a teacher, a friend. They were lucky in finding the support they needed.

Then, you need a little luck with life. A marriage might move along happily and smoothly enough until a series of unexpected events rains down on it. A combination of illnesses or job losses, family feuds, or personal failures might push the marriage off-course, when without these blows, it could have succeeded. Every marriage needs some luck in holding back forces that could crush it.

These aspects of luck may be out of our power to control. But the good thing about luck is that it is not all out of control. Many people who consider themselves happy in a marriage speak about themselves as being lucky. Since they seem to have the same share of problems and difficulties as anyone else, sometimes even more than their share, luck in marriage, as in life, seems to be as much a matter of attitude as of chance. Couples who regard themselves as lucky are the ones who seize luck where they are able to. They are not blind to the soft spots of their marriages—nobody denies difficulties; they just consider the positives more important. So they say they are lucky. And they are. They have grabbed luck by the tail and have twisted it to their own purposes.

"Happy Marriages" is an abridged version of the article reprinted in Jewish Marital Status: A Hadassah Study, *Carol Diament, ed. (Northvale, NJ: Jason Aronson, 1989), pages 135-144, and originally published in* Married People: Staying Together in an Age of Divorce *(New York: Bantam Books, 1985).*

FRANCINE KLAGSBRUN has written and edited more than a dozen books. Her newest work is Jewish Days: A Book of Jewish Life and Culture Around the Year. *Other books include* Married People: Staying Together in the Age of Divorce *and* Voices of Wisdom: Jewish Ideals and Ethics for Everyday Living. *Her articles have appeared in* The New York Times, Newsweek, *and* Ms. *She is a regular columnist for* The Jewish Week *and* Moment *magazine, and she has lectured widely on family issues, feminism, and Judaism.*

PROGRAMMING IDEAS

AT HOME

Torah Table Talk   A discussion of Jewish thought and values with your family and/or friends. The *ketubah* is the marriage contract that is signed and read aloud at all Orthodox and Conservative and many Reform wedding ceremonies. *Ketubah* literally means "written," and the document is written in Aramaic, the language of the *Gemara*. It records the obligations that a husband undertakes upon marriage, as enumerated in the Talmud. The *ketubah*, designed as a legal protection for the wife in the event of divorce or the death of her husband, first came into widespread use in the first century before the common era. The *ketubah* translated below is used by modern Orthodox Jews today.

On the ... day of the week, the ... day of the month ... in the year five thousand seven hundred and ... since the creation of the world, the era according to which we reckon here in the city of (name of city, state, and country), that (name of bridegroom) son of (name of bridegroom's father) of the family (bridegroom's surname) said to this maiden (name of bride) daughter of (name of bride's father) of the family (bride's surname), "Be my wife according to the law of Moses and Israel, and I will cherish, honor, support, and maintain you in accordance with the custom of Jewish husbands, who cherish, honor, support, and maintain their wives faithfully. And I here present you with the marriage gift of virgins, two hundred silver *zuzim* (monetary units), which belongs to you, according to the law of Moses and Israel; and I will also give you your food, clothing, and necessities, and live with you as husband and wife according to the universal custom." And (name of bride), this maiden consented and became his wife. The trousseau that she brought to him from her father's house in silver, gold, valuables, clothing, furniture, and bedclothes, all this (name of bridegroom), the bridegroom accepted in the sum of one hundred silver pieces, and (name of bridegroom), the bridegroom consented to increase this amount from his own property with the sum of one hundred silver pieces, making in all two hundred silver pieces. And thus said (name of bridegroom) the bridegroom, "The responsibility of this marriage contract, of this trousseau, and of this additional sum, I take upon myself and my heirs after me, so that they shall be paid from the best part of my property and possessions that I have beneath the whole heaven, that which I now possess or may hereafter acquire. All my property, real and personal, even the shirt from my back, shall be mortgaged to secure the payment of this marriage contract, of the trousseau, and of the addition made to it, during my lifetime and after my death, from the present day and forever." (Name of bridegroom), the bridegroom, has taken upon himself the responsibility of this marriage contract, of the trousseau and the addition made to it, according to the restrictive usages of all marriage contracts and the additions to them made for the daughters of Israel, according to the institutions of our sages of blessed memory. It is not to be regarded as an indecisive contractual obligation or as a mere formula of a document. We have followed the legal formality of symbolic delivery (*kinyan*) between (name of bridegroom) son of (name of bridegroom's father), the bridegroom, and (name of bride) daughter of (name of bride's father), this maiden, and we have used a garment legally fit for the purpose, to strengthen all that is stated above,

AND EVERYTHING IS VALID AND CONFIRMED.

Attested to (signature of witness), Witness
Attested to (signature of witness), Witness

Questions for Thought and Discussion

1. The *ketubah*, based upon Jewish society in talmudic times, specifies the obligations of the husband to the wife. The wife may accept the *ketubah* or she may refuse to accept the *ketubah*, but there is no comparable document that she

must sign. Today, many Conservative and Reform *ketubot* specify the mutual obligations of both wife and husband. However, no Orthodox authority recognizes the legality of an innovative contract. Discuss.

2. The husband agrees to "cherish, honor, support, and maintain" his wife. Why is there no mention of love?

3. The husband promises: "I will also give you your food, clothing, and necessities, and live with you as husband and wife according to the universal custom." According to the Torah, a husband has three duties toward his wife: to provide her with food, clothing, and sexual intercourse. Why is sex a husband's duty? Why is sex considered a duty of the same importance as food and clothing?

4. The *ketubah*, a contract that must be signed prior to the wedding ceremony and delivered to the bride, is a type of prenuptial agreement. How does it differ from prenuptial agreements currently being written? How is it similar?

5. Jewish marriage is considered a spiritual, holy union. Yet the marriage contract is, in essence, a business agreement. Why?

6. Daniel I. Leifer writes: "The detailed economic arrangements spelled out in the extensive second section of the traditional *ketubah* are no longer observed even by many people who operate in an otherwise traditional context. References to the *mohar* (marriage gift) of two hundred silver *zuzim* and to the *nedunia* composed of the wedding outfit, are waived today in many traditional divorce proceedings" ("On Writing New *Ketubot*," in *The Jewish Woman: New Perspectives*, Elizabeth Koltun, ed. [New York: Schocken, 1976], page 51). Yet the *ketubah* itself warns us not to regard the document "as an indecisive contractual obligation or as a mere formula." How can we reconcile these statements?

Additional At-Home Activities

❖ If you are married, discuss with your husband Francine Klagsbrun's eight characteristics of happy marriages. How are these characteristics different from/similar to those of good friendships?

❖ Invite one or more single people to your home for a Shabbat or holiday dinner.

INTEREST/STUDY GROUPS

Hold a discussion based on the following questions:

1. Francine Klagsbrun writes of eight characteristics that underlie happy marriages. Rank these characteristics in order of importance. Is there consensus among group members, or is each member's ranking unique? Should any characteristics be added to the list below? If so, rank them as well.

    (a) ability to change and tolerate change
    (b) ability to live with the unchangeable

(c) assumption of permanence

(d) trust

(e) balance of dependencies/balance of power

(f) enjoyment of each other

(g) shared history that is cherished

(h) luck

2. Is there anything characteristically Jewish in Francine Klagsbrun's eight characteristics for a happy marriage? If yes, describe.

3. Respond to the statement: "People who stay happily married see themselves not as victims of fate, but as free agents who make choices in life."

4. Francine Klagsbrun writes that happily married couples are "committed to the marriage as well as to one another." Do you agree? Do you think divorce is prevalent today because couples lack commitment to the institution of marriage?

5. Think of the best marriages you know. How do they exemplify Francine Klagsbrun's eight characteristics? In what ways do the couples enjoy each other? How have the wife and husband changed together over the years? What unchangeable things do they live with?

6. Francine Klagsbrun emphasizes shared values. In your opinion, what is the most important value a couple can share?

7. Daniel B. Syme, in "The Jewish Wedding Then and Now" (adapted from *The Jewish Home* [New York: UAHC 1989]), lists the advice given by the rabbis of the Talmud on choosing a future wife:

(a) Marry the daughter of a learned man.

(b) Marry a woman of the same age, or about the same age.

(c) Marry a woman of the same or lower social class.

(d) Marry a woman of a different complexion, lest children be too pale or too dark.

(e) Marry a woman of a different height, lest children be too tall or too short.

(f) If possible, avoid marriage to a widow or a divorcee.

(g) Don't marry for money.

Which of these rules translate into sound advice for modern men choosing wives and modern women choosing husbands? Which are inappropriate? Consider happy marriages that you know. How many of these rules did the wife and the husband follow?

MEETINGS

❖ View and discuss the 1978 film *A Seal Upon Thy Heart* (color, 30 minutes). A young couple embraces a Jewish lifestyle, showing why "Jewish marriage means more than just owning a *ketubah* and silver candlesticks." A videotape is available for $39.95 from Ergo Media in Teaneck, NJ, 1-800-695-3746. Order #854.

❖ Invite a rabbi or Jewish historian to discuss marriage, its history in Torah and Talmud, changes in sex-role-based divisions of labor over time (note especially changes from Jewish marriages in nineteenth century Eastern Europe to marriages in the United States, and changes from the early part of the twentieth century to today), and current challenges.

❖ Invite a Jewishly-knowledgeable marriage counselor to discuss her or his work. Does your speaker agree with Francine Klagsbrun on the characteristics of happy marriages? How does therapy enable couples to resolve differences? How does Judaism inform your speaker's work?

❖ Invite a Jewish family services staff member, Jewish community center staff member, or synagogue director to discuss how your local Jewish community addresses the needs of single women who wish to marry or to remarry. How are the needs of single parents met? Discuss as well the activities of your Hadassah chapter or group in reaching out to singles.

❖ Visit a museum to view illuminated *ketubot*. These reveal some of the most beautiful artistry created by the Jewish people from the middle ages to the present day.

❖ Invite a guest speaker (or several speakers) to discuss the *ketubot* used by the different streams of Judaism. Read selections from *ketubot* used by Orthodox, Conservative, Reconstructionist, and Reform Jews.

ANNUAL EVENTS

❖ Organize an event where Jewish singles can meet and get to know each other. Consider these options:
  (a) *Kallah* (Shabbat retreat) at a Young Judaea camp or other rural setting.
  (b) Israeli film series with follow-up discussion sessions.
  (c) Trip with accompanying scholar to points of Jewish interest. (Call the Travel Department, 212-303-8031, for assistance. Or call the Membership Division, 212-303-8061, for information on Vanguard outings.)

❖ Organize an Education Day or Evening on love, sex, and marriage in the Jewish tradition. Invite scholars to speak on three different topics. For example: marriages in the Bible—functional and dysfunctional; marriage in the Talmud; the ban on polygamy; the laws of family purity; Jewish views on sexuality; sociology of Jewish marriage from the middle ages to modernity; the Song of Songs and the spirituality of marital imagery (God and Israel as husband and wife, Shabbat as bride); Jewish courtship—from matchmakers to singles bars; the Jewish wedding; marital therapy.

HANDS-ON

❖ Visit a *sofer* (scribe) to see how different *ketubot* are written.

❖ To honor a member on a milestone wedding anniversary, create a quilt incorporating Jewish themes and themes from her marriage. (A theme quilt of a bride and groom would also be a lovely wedding gift.) The Women's League for Conservative Judaism prints instructions on designing a quilt. For information on ordering, write to: 48 East 74th Street, New York, NY 10021.

❖ Establish (or encourage Jewish singles to establish) a Vanguard steering committee to plan and hold events for singles. Vanguard lectures, dances, trips, and other events give Jewish singles an opportunity to meet, have fun, and get to know each other—and ultimately become partners in happy marriages! For details on Vanguard, call Hadassah's National Membership Division at 212-303-8061.

❖ Invite Jewish singles in your community to participate in a day of group volunteer service. Coordinate the day with the local Vanguard steering committee. One option is to sponsor a clothing drive with a charitable organization. Then, as a group, spend one day sorting the clothes. Another option is to work together at a soup kitchen, particularly on Christmas or Easter, holidays when Christian volunteers are likely to be unavailable. A third option would be a project sponsored together with an environmental organization— clearing a park of trash, reintroducing native species of plants in a wildlife refuge, etc. The object is to provide women and men with opportunities to meet while doing worthwhile work.

MIKVAH BLESSINGS

Barbara Goldstein

"Blessed are You O Lord who has kept me in life, has sustained me and enabled me to reach this moment."

Many times, in the course of my life, I have had the pleasure and the privilege of reciting *sheheheyanu*. I never take this blessing for granted— even when I light *yom tov* candles. I feel its meaning in the power of a particular moment. But this day, the 12th of Elul 5748, the *sheheheyanu* was different, even if only for a brief glimmer of time.

My second daughter was about to be married. It was Thursday and Devra's wedding was Sunday. The wedding and the *mikvah* visit were timed to her menstrual cycle. "Going to the *mikvah*?" her friends and many of mine queried. The bemused expressions on their faces spoke more than volumes.

I too once had, and still have, many negative feelings about the entire concept of *mikvah*. The idea that, as women, we are physically impure and require purification is abhorrent to me. From the time of marriage through all of our childbearing years, we are "defiled" for half of our lives. Leviticus 18:19 prohibits conjugal relations for seven days during a woman's period of uncleanness. The Torah restriction of seven days was then extended by the rabbis for another seven days—*niddah*. Why *mikvah* at all? Since the destruction of the Temple, none of the other ritual purifications are necessary. Why single out women? Is it because we can't find any more red heifers?[1] Nevertheless, despite my ambivalence, I advocate *mikvah* because I know from my own experience that it can be spiritually transcending. Furthermore, it is exclusively a woman's *mitzvah*, one of only three, and is, therefore, mine. It ties me to generations of Jewish women who went to *mikvah* before me. Nor do I, a Conservative Jew, choose to allow it to become solely the property of Orthodox women.

*D*espite my ambivalence, I advocate *mikvah* because I know from my own experience that it can be spiritually transcending.

The first thing I had to do, then, was to find out where the *mikvah* was located. I knew there was one in Highland Park, a town five minutes from me. Whom should I ask? The thought occurred to me to call the kosher pizza place. I did, and they gave me the telephone number and address. I telephoned and made an appointment for Thursday morning. I told Devra that going during the day is a privilege granted only to brides. We entered a Word War II suburban house and were escorted by two children into the waiting room of the "ritualarium." I had forgotten the English word for *mikvah*. That is why I couldn't find the number in the phone book.

We sat for a few moments when Sara, the "*mikvah* lady," appeared and greeted us. Radiant, a young *ba'alat teshuvah*, she told us of her encounter with the Chabad *Hasidim* at the University of Buffalo while she and her husband were shelling shrimp in a nearby restaurant. She showed us around the building and then asked if Devra had prepared herself at home. We said "no," and Devra went into the washroom with Shira, her older sister, who accompanied us. Shira had been married several months earlier in Jerusalem, where she, too, had gone to the *mikvah*. In Israel, the spirituality we so eagerly sought was totally destroyed, because a bride must present proof of her immersion to the *Rabbanut* before a *ketubah* can be issued. In our people's history, an act of faith was never meant to be legislated.

Now Shira was here for the wedding and was anxious to assist her sister, Devra, with her first *mikvah* visit. My own mind raced back twenty-seven years to my first *mikvah* experience. I was then the bride and my mother thought I was "crazy" to want to go to "that place," as she filled me with bizarre stories of her own unpleasant *mikvah* reception before her wedding.

In considering our grandmothers' and mothers' generations, the *mikvah* of that time, in a poor immigrant neighborhood, was indeed likely to be dingy and dark. My mother feared going to the *mikvah*. In ominous tones she warned me that they would cut my hair and nails to the quick. How sad, I thought, that my mother had refused to share this special moment with me, as I was about to do with my own daughter.

I walked into the washroom and saw my two "little girls" playing. Shira was washing Devra's hair, using a cup, as I used to. "Put your head back so that the soap doesn't run into your eyes." It would be the last time the two sisters would have this moment together, as one was already married and the other was on the threshold of *huppah*. "Okay," they said, "we're ready." Having gone through the checklist, removing nail polish, toenail polish, etc., we called for Sara.

From the washroom a door led into the actual *mikvah*. Devra descended the stairs and was ready for the immersion. "All the way under," Sara said softly. Devra immersed herself, and as she did, I heard the sounds of *tekiah teru'ah*. I realized that Sara's husband was upstairs reciting his morning prayers which were followed by his blowing of the *shofar*, as is customary in the month of Elul. The piercing sound of the *shofar* heralded the occasion appropriately. "Kosher," Sara exclaimed as Devra recited the blessing. Shira and I answered, "amen"; our eyes filled with tears of joy. Shira's younger sister, my daughter, Devra, was now indeed a *kallah*. She emerged, nymph-like, from the water and ascended the stairs glistening from the softness of the rain water. Sara wrapped her in a sheet and wished her *mazal tov*! Devra radiated beauty and sanctity, the kind of glow that comes from within as the *Shekhinah* shines through.

She got dressed. I inquired what the fee was. Sara waved her hand, "Brides are free," she said. I thanked her and gave her *hai*. She asked Devra where she was going to live. When she heard Puerto Rico, she said, "Shh—just go right into the ocean!"

Sara's last words to us were, "Remember, a child born of *mikvah* carries a special blessing." And so I thought: My blessings were not all luck, for my three children were conceived after *mikvah*.

As we drove away, the conversation turned to Masada. Devra reminisced about our trips to Masada and explanations of the ancient *mikvah* there. Suddenly she felt connected to 2,000 years of her people's history. She was at one with the past—even as she was about to create a new link to the future.

It was hard to explain to everyone what had happened. One rabbi asked if *mikvah* wasn't superfluous, considering that most brides aren't virgins. I answered, "All the more reason, a bride and groom enter the *huppah* with their sins washed away." The *huppah* and *kiddushin* create a new beginning. What better way for the bride than through *mikvah*—"*mayim hayim*" (living waters)—to prepare herself for the groom and for the life they are about to begin.

I spent the rest of the day suffused with joy. The unique action bonded the three of us. I prayed that each of my daughters would one day have the same privilege with their daughters. A new Jewish home was about to be consecrated. My husband and I had given our all to make this happen. We are grateful to God that we have reached this season.

From Jewish Marital Status: A Hadassah Study, *Carol Diament, ed. (Northvale, NJ: Jason Aronson, 1989), pages 122-125.*

BARBARA GOLDSTEIN is a member of the Hadassah National Board, and currently serves on the Executive Committee. From 1980 to 1984, she served as National Jewish Education chair.

PROGRAMMING IDEAS

AT HOME

Torah Table Talk   A discussion of Jewish thought and values with your family and/or friends. This selection is from Chapter 15 of the Book of Leviticus, the third book of the Torah.

Leviticus 15:1-33

The Lord spoke to Moses and Aaron, saying: Speak to the Israelite people and say to them:

When any man has a discharge issuing from his member [literally, his flesh], he is unclean. The uncleanness from his discharge shall mean the following—whether his member runs with the discharge or is stopped up so that there is no discharge, his uncleanness means this: Any bedding on which the one with the discharge lies shall be unclean, and every object on which he sits shall be unclean. Anyone who touches his bedding shall wash his clothes, bathe in water, and remain unclean until evening. Whoever sits on an object on which the one with the discharge has sat shall wash his clothes, bathe in water, and remain unclean until evening. Whoever touches the body of the one with the discharge shall wash his clothes, bathe in water, and remain unclean until evening. If one with a discharge spits on one who is clean, the latter shall wash his clothes, bathe in water, and remain unclean until evening. Any means for riding that one with a discharge has mounted shall be unclean; whoever touches anything that was under him shall be unclean until evening; and whoever carries such things shall wash his clothes, bathe in water, and remain unclean until evening. If one with a discharge, without having rinsed his hands in water, touches another person, that person shall wash his clothes, bathe in water, and remain unclean until evening. An earthen vessel that one with a discharge touches shall be broken; and any wooden implement shall be rinsed with water.

When one with a discharge becomes clean of his discharge, he shall count off seven days for his cleansing, wash his clothes, and bathe his body in fresh water; then he shall be clean. On the eighth day he shall take two turtledoves or two pigeons and come before the Lord at the entrance of the Tent of Meeting and give them to the priest. The priest shall offer them, the one as a sin offering and the other as a burnt offering. Thus the priest shall make expiation on his behalf, for his discharge, before the Lord.

When a man has an emission of semen, he shall bathe his whole body in water and remain unclean until evening. All cloth or leather on which semen falls shall be washed in water and remain unclean until evening. And if a man has carnal relations with a woman, they shall bathe in water and remain unclean until evening.

When a woman has a discharge, her discharge being blood from her body, she shall remain in her impurity seven days; whoever touches her shall be unclean until evening. Anything that she lies on during her impurity shall be unclean; and anything that she sits on shall be unclean. Anyone who touches her bedding shall wash his clothes, bathe in water, and remain unclean until evening; and anyone who touches any object on which she sat shall wash his clothes, bathe in water, and remain unclean until evening. Be it the bedding or be it the object on which she has sat, on touching it he shall be unclean until evening. And if a man lies with her, her impurity is communicated to him; he shall be unclean seven days, and any bedding on which he lies shall become unclean.

When a woman has a discharge of blood for many days, not at the time of her impurity, or when she has a discharge beyond her period of impurity, she shall be unclean, as though at the time of her impurity, as long as her discharge lasts. Any bedding on which she lies while her discharge lasts shall be for her like bedding during her impurity; and any object on which she sits shall become unclean, as it does during her impurity: whoever touches them shall be unclean; he shall wash his clothes, bathe in water, and remain unclean until evening.

When she becomes clean of her discharge, she shall count off seven days, and after that she shall be clean. On the eighth day she shall take two turtledoves or two pigeons, and bring them to the priest at the entrance of the Tent of Meeting. The priest shall offer the one as a sin offering and the other as a burnt offering; and the priest shall make expiation on her behalf, for her unclean discharge, before the Lord.

You shall put the Israelites on guard against their uncleanness, lest they die through their uncleanness by defiling My Tabernacle which is among them.

Such is the ritual concerning him who has a discharge: concerning him who has an emission of semen and becomes unclean thereby, and concerning her who is in menstrual infirmity, and concerning anyone, male or female, who has a discharge, and concerning a man who lies with an unclean woman.

Questions for Thought and Discussion

1. Both emissions caused by disease and emissions resulting from healthy functioning result in ritual impurity, which prevents the person from entering the Tabernacle. In order to become ritually pure, a man or woman must (a) bathe in water and (b) launder his or her clothing. However, emissions caused by disease—either discharge from the penis or abnormal vaginal bleeding—require the bringing of a sacrifice in addition to the bathing and laundering. What might this symbolize?

2. How is ritual impurity transmitted from one person to another? What can we conclude?

3. Though procreation is a biblical commandment, and though Jewish commentators write of the holiness of marital sexuality, sexual intercourse renders both the man and the woman ritually impure, so that they are unable to enter the Tabernacle. Why? Consider that many ancient Near Eastern religions included sexual activity as part of their temple rites.

4. The Bible enjoins both men and women to "bathe in water," women after menstruation and men after emission of semen. Over the course of time, however, Jewish authorities ruled that men need not go to the *mikvah* following loss of semen, but could remain in their state of ritual impurity. Women, however, were required to immerse in the *mikvah* after menstruating, and rather than waiting seven days as specified in the Bible, they were now required to wait fourteen. What can we conclude?

INTEREST/STUDY GROUPS

Hold a discussion based on the following questions:

1. What are your personal feelings about *mikvah*? Are these feelings based on actual experience? (Encourage members who have been to a *mikvah*—including those who became Jews through the Orthodox or Conservative conversion process—to share their experiences with the study group.) Did your mother or grandmother go to a *mikvah*? Did she ever accompany you or your sisters to one? In what ways were your family's *mikvah* experiences similar to or different from Barbara, Shira, and Devra Goldstein's?

2. Barbara Goldstein relishes the ritual of the *mikvah*. While she acknowledges that many women have negative feelings, she also reasons that Jewish women should preserve (and reinvigorate) the immersion ritual because it is one of the few rituals in Jewish women's unique possession. Do you agree that we should retain the institution of *mikvah*? Why or why not?

3. What Jewish rituals, besides *mikvah* immersion, are solely female experiences? Can universal rituals be further enhanced to emphasize their applicability to women? Would Jewish women in the past have been able to give clearer answers to these questions? Do Orthodox women today have more experiences that are solely for women? If so, how might that affect marriage and family life?

4. Do you think that single women should be allowed to use the *mikvah*, either as a form of spiritual cleansing or as a prelude to resuming sexual activity after menstruation? Is there room for redefining *mikvah* to fit the present day, when many Jews are sexually active for nearly a decade prior to marriage?

5. By going to the *mikvah* together, the mother and her two daughters share a strong sense of spiritual enhancement. Imagine going to a *mikvah* with your mother, your sister, or your daughter. Would she agree to accompany you? Why or why not? Could you ask her? Why or why not? What spiritual experiences

have you shared with your mother? With your daughter? With your sister? How can you build upon these experiences?

6. What rituals did your mother share with you prior to your wedding? What rituals did you (or will you) share with your daughter? Did these rituals help you to adjust to your new married status? Did these rituals have a Jewish, spiritual component? What other pre-wedding rituals helped you (or your husband) adjust to marriage?

7. What other Jewish rituals, in addition to *mikvah* immersion, have both valid feminist interpretations and valid patriarchal interpretations?

MEETINGS

❖ Invite a guest speaker to discuss the Jewish laws of family purity, including *mikvah* immersion. How do these laws affect relations between husband and wife? The family purity laws involve a two-week period of celibacy, beginning when the wife menstruates, followed by a *mikvah* immersion, followed then by a two-week period of sexual activity. When the woman again menstruates, sexual activity between wife and husband is again prohibited. If possible, arrange for a female Judaic scholar who herself adheres to these laws to address your chapter or group, and also invite a woman who went to the *mikvah* only prior to her marriage.

ANNUAL EVENTS

❖ Include a session on *mikvah* use today as part of a Women's Symposium or Education Day or Evening on Jewish women's spirituality. See the "Annual Events" section of "The Future for Jewish Women" by Vanessa L. Ochs for additional topics, page 238.

HANDS-ON

❖ Arrange a visit to a *mikvah*. Have a knowledgeable Hadassah member, one of the women associated with the *mikvah*, or an Orthodox guest speaker explain the steps in the ritual of *mikvah* immersion.

❖ Create a *huppah* for a family member about to be married. Write to the Women's League for Conservative Judaism to order instructions on putting together a "Family Memento *Huppah*" (ch# 162), 48 East 74th Street, New York, NY 10021.

---

1. The red heifer was sacrificed and its ashes were used in the ritual purification of persons and objects defiled by a corpse (Numbers 19).

Apples from the Desert

Savyon Liebrecht

All the way from the Orthodox quarter of Sha'arei Hesed in Jerusalem to the great stretch of sand where the driver called out "Neve Midbar" and looked for her in his rear-view mirror, Victoria Abravanel—her heart pounding and her fists clenched—had only one thing on her mind. She took some bread in brown paper and an apple with a rotten core out of her string bag and joined the blessing on the fruit to the prayer for travel, as prescribed. Her eyes were fixed on the yellowing landscape spread out in front of her—and her heart was fixed on her rebellious daughter Rivka who left the Orthodox neighborhood six months ago and went to live on a kibbutz of secular Jews. Now, Victoria had found out from her sister Sara that Rivka was sharing a room with a boy, sleeping in his bed and living as his wife.

All through the eight-hour trip, she pondered how she would act when she was face to face with her daughter: maybe she would cajole her as if she weren't angry with her, teach her about a girl's honor in a man's eyes, explain sensitive issues, one woman to another. Or maybe she would start out with cries of despair, shout out the grief, the disgrace that Rivka had brought down on their noble family, shriek like a funeral mourner until the neighbors heard. Or maybe she would perform her mission stealthily, draw her daughter away from there with false news and then put her in her room under lock and key and obliterate all trace of her. Or maybe she would terrify her, tell her about Flora, Yosef Elalouf's daughter, who fell in love with some boy, gave up her virginity for him and he deserted her; so she lost her mind and wandered around the streets, pulling little children by the ear.

On the road from Beersheva, she came up with something new: she would attack the boy with her nails, rip off his skin and poke out his eyes for what he did to this change-of-life daughter of hers. Her daughter would come back to Jerusalem with her. Which was what she promised her sister: "I'll bring her back by the hair."

From her sister Sara, Victoria already knew that her daughter was sixteen when she met him. He was an army officer and was brought in to tell them about military service for Orthodox girls. Later on, there was a fuss about letting people from the army come and poison the girls but the venom had already worked on Rivka. Cunningly, he'd sent her letters, through a friend, even after he went back to his kibbutz. And she, the fool, who was known for neither grace nor beauty—even when she was a baby, people would mistake her for a boy—she fell for it, and when she was eighteen, she picked up and went to him in the desert.

The further Victoria got from Beersheva, the more her heroic spirit deserted her and the pictures in her imagination made her sigh: What if Rivka turned her back on her and threw her out? What if the boy raised his hand to hit her? How would she spend the night if they locked her out, and the bus doesn't leave till tomorrow morning? What if they didn't get her message? She didn't know anything about traveling, hadn't been out of the neighborhood since the barren Shifra Ben-Sasson of Tiberias gave birth four years ago.

But when the driver called out "Neve Midbar" again and found her in his mirror, she got off the bus, pulling her basket behind her. She stood there in the sand, the dry wind struck her throat. How could you leave the pure air and beautiful mountains of Jerusalem—and come here?

By the time she came to a path and found a woman to ask about Rivka, drops of sweat were streaming from her kerchief. Coming toward them, on the opposite path, was a girl also wearing pants whose hair was cut short. "Here's Rivka," said the woman. Just as Victoria was about to say: "That's not the one I meant"—she recognized her daughter and burst into a shout which rang like weeping. The girl put down the laundry basket she was carrying and ran to her, her head thrust forward and her eyes weeping.

"What's this ... what's this...?" Victoria scratched her nose. "Where are your braids? And those pants ... that's how you dress ... *oy vey!*" Rivka laughed: "I knew that's what you'd say. I wanted to get dressed but I didn't have time. I thought you'd come on the four o'clock bus. When did you leave home? Six? Come on. Enough crying. Here's our room. And here's Dubi."

Stunned by the short hair, the frayed trousers with patches on the back and the shoes spotted with chicken droppings, Victoria found herself squeezed in two big arms, a fair face was close to hers, and a male voice said: "Hello, Mother." Her basket was already in his hand and she—not understanding herself, her hands suddenly light—was drawn after her daughter into a shaded room and seated on a chair. There was a glass of juice in her hand at once; her eyes looked but didn't know what they saw and, later on, she'd remember only the double bed covered with a patchwork quilt and the voice of the giant with golden hair saying "Welcome, Mother." And, as soon as she heard him say "mother" again, very clearly, she swallowed some juice which went down the wrong way and started choking and coughing; the two of them rushed to her and started pounding her on the back like a child.

"Leave me alone," she said weakly and pushed them away. "Let me look at you," she said after a moment. Once again she scolded Rivka: "What is this, those pants? Those are your Sabbath shoes?" Rivka laughed: "I'm working in the chicken coop this week. They brought in new hens. I usually work in the vegetable garden. Just this week in the chicken coop."

Weary from the journey, confused by what she was seeing, shaken by the vicissitudes of the day and straining to repress her rage which was getting away from her in spite of herself, and always remembering her mission, Victoria sat down with her daughter Rivka and talked with her as she had never talked with her children before in her life. She didn't remember what she talked about and she didn't remember when the boy who called her mother left, only her eyes saw and knew: her daughter's face looked good. Not since Rivka was a little girl had she seen her eyes sparkle like that. Even her short hair, Victoria admitted to herself, made her look pretty. Not like when she wore a skirt and stockings, with her broad shoulders, like a man dressed up in women's clothes.

"You don't miss the neighborhood?"

"Sometimes. On holidays. I miss the Shabbat table and the songs and Aunt Sara's laugh. But I like it here. I love working outside with the animals.... You too, I miss you a lot."

"And Papa?" Victoria asked in a whisper into the evening light filtering in.

"Papa doesn't care about anybody. Especially not me. All day long in the store and with his books and prayers. Like I'm not his daughter."

"God forbid! Don't say such a thing," Victoria was scared. Of the truth.

"He wanted to marry me off to Yekutiel's son. Like I was a widow or a cripple."

"They talked. You heard. We don't make forced matches. And anyway, Yekutiel's son is a genius."

"A pale, sick genius, like he sits in a pit all day long. And anyway, I don't love him."

"What do you think? You think love is everything?"

"What do you know about love?"

"What does that mean?" Victoria was offended and sat up straight. "This is how you talk to your mother around here?"

"You didn't love Papa and he didn't love you." Rivka ignored her and went on in the silence that descended: "I, at home ... I wasn't worth much."

"And here?" Victoria asked in a whisper.

"More."

A question began to take shape in Victoria's mind about Dubi, the fair-haired giant but the door opened, a light suddenly came on, and he himself said: "Great that you're saving electricity. I brought something to eat. Yogurt and vegetables on a new plastic plate, that's OK, isn't it? Then, Rivka, you should take Mother to Osnat's room. It's empty. She must be tired."

In the room that went out to the darkening fields, Victoria tried to get things straight in her heart. But years of dreariness had dulled her edge and yet she already knew: she wouldn't bring her daughter back to Jerusalem by the hair.

"Why did it take you half a year to come here?" Rivka asked.

"Your Papa didn't want me to come."

"And you, you don't have a will of your own?" And Victoria didn't have an answer.

When Dubi came to take her to the dining hall, she poured all her rage on him and yet she was drawn to him and that only increased her wrath.

"What's this Dubi, what kind of name is that?" Anger pulled words out of her mouth.

"It's Dov, after my mother's father. The Germans killed him in the war."

"That's a good name for a baby, Dov?" She hardened her heart against him.

"I don't mind." He shrugged, and then stopped and said with comic seriousness: "But if you do—I'll change it tomorrow." She strained to keep from laughing.

In the evening, the two of them sat at the table with their eyes on Rivka as if she were all alone in the big hall, walking around with a serving cart, asking people what they wanted.

"You want something else to drink, Mother?" she heard him ask and returned the question angrily:

"You call me mother. What kind of mother am I to you?"

"I'm dying for you to be my mother."

"Really? So, who's stopping you?" she asked and her sister Sara's mischievousness crept into her voice.

"Your daughter."

"How is she stopping you?"

"She doesn't want to be my wife."

"My daughter doesn't want to get married. That's what you're telling me?"

"Exactly."

As she was struggling with what he said, he started telling her about the apple orchard he was growing. An American scientist who grew apples in the Nevada desert sent him special seeds. You plant them in tin cans full of organic fertilizer and they grow into trees as high as a baby with little roots and sometimes they produce fruit in the summer like a tree in the Garden of Eden. Apples love the cold, he explained as their eyes wandered after Rivka, and at night, you have to open the plastic sheets and let the desert cold in. At dawn, you have to close the sheets to preserve the cold air and keep the heat out.

"Really," she muttered, hearing these words now and thinking about what he said before. Meanwhile, somebody came to her and said: "You're Rivka's mother? Congratulations on such a daughter." And suddenly her heart swelled in her.

Then she remembered something that came back to her from long ago and far away. She was fifteen years old. On Saturdays in the synagogue, she used to exchange glances with Moshe Elkayam, the goldsmith's son, and then she would lower her eyes to the floor. In the women's section, she would push up to the wooden lattice to see his hands that worked silver and gold and precious stones. Something arose between them without any words and his sister used to smile at her in the street. But when the matchmaker came to talk to her about Shaul Abravanel, she didn't dare hurt her father who wanted a scholar for a son-in-law.

At night, when Rivka took her back to her room, she said: "You came to take me back to Jerusalem, right?"

Her mother chose not to answer. After a pause, she said apropos of nothing: "Don't do anything dumb."

"I know what I want. Don't worry about me."

Victoria plucked up her courage: "Is it true what he told me, that you don't want to marry him?"

"That's what he told you?"

"Yes or no?"

"Yes."

"Why?"

"I'm not sure yet."

"Where did you learn that?"

"From you."

"How?" Victoria was amazed.

"I don't want to live like you and Papa."

"How?"

"Without love."

"Again love!" She beat her thighs until they trembled. A gesture of rage without rage. They reached the door. Victoria thought a moment about the bed with the patchwork quilt and heard herself asking: "And the *Shema* at bedtime, do you say that?

"No."

"You don't say the *Shema*?"

"Only sometimes, silently. So even I don't hear it myself," said Rivka, laughed and kissed her mother on the cheek. Then she said: "Don't get scared if you hear jackals. Goodnight." Like a mother soothing her child.

Facing the bare sand dunes stretching soft lines into the frame of her window as into the frame of a picture, Victoria said a fervent prayer, for both of them, her and Rivka. Her heart both heavy and light: "... Let not my thoughts trouble me, nor evil dreams, nor evil fancies, but let my rest be perfect before Thee...."

And at night she dreamed.

In the dream a man approaches white curtains and she sees him from behind. The man moves the curtain aside and the trees of the Garden of Eden are in front of him: the tree of life and the tree of knowledge and beautiful trees in cans of organic fertilizer. The man goes to the apple tree, there is a lot of fruit on it, and the fruit drops off and rolls into his hands and, suddenly, the fruit is small and turns into stones. Victoria sees: handfuls of precious stones and gold and silver in his white fingers. Suddenly, the man turns his face, and it's Moshe Elkayam, the goldsmith's son and his hair is flaming.

How could she describe to her sister, who had never known a man, or to her husband, who had never touched her with love—how could she describe the boy's eyes on her daughter's face?

All the way back to Sha'arei Hesed she sat, her eyes still holding onto their rage but her heart soothed, her basket at her feet and, on her lap, a sack of apples hard as stones that Dubi gave her. She remembered her daughter asking: "You see that everything's fine, right?"—her fingers on her mother's cheek; and Dubi's voice saying: "It'll be fine, Mother."

All the way, she pondered what she would tell her husband and her sister. Maybe she would sit them down and tell exactly what happened to her. When the bus passed the junction, she considered it. How could she describe to her sister, who had never known a man, or to her husband, who had never touched her with love—how could she describe the boy's eyes on her daughter's face? When the mountains of Jerusalem appeared in the distance, she knew what she would do.

From her sister, who could read her mind, she wouldn't keep a secret. She'd pull her kerchief aside, put her mouth up to her ear, like when they were children, and whisper, "Sarike, we've spent our lives alone, you without a husband and me with one. My little daughter taught me something. And us, remember how we thought she was a bit backward, God forbid? How I used to cry over her? No beauty, no grace, no intelligence or talent, and as tall as Og, King of Bashan. We wanted to marry her off to Yekutiel and they were doing us a favor, like Abravanel's daughter wasn't good enough for them. Just look at her now." Here she would turn her face to the side and spit spiritedly against the evil eye. "Milk and honey. Smart too. And laughing all the time. Maybe, with God's help, we'll get pleasure from her."

And to her husband, who never read her heart, she would give apples in honey, put both hands on her hips, and say: "We don't have to worry about Rivka. It's good for her there, thank God. We'll hear good things from her soon. Now, taste that and tell me: apples that ripen in summer and they put them in organic fertilizer and their roots are small—did you ever hear of such a thing in your life?"

Translated by Barbara Harshav

From Ribcage: Israeli Women's Fiction, *Carol Diament and Lily Rattok, eds. (New York, Hadassah, 1994), pages 71-80.*

SAVYON LIEBRECHT *was born in Munich, Germany in 1948, the child of Holocaust survivors, and came to Israel as an infant. She has published three collections of short stories, and has also written scripts for television. She lives in Tel Aviv with her husband and two children. "Apples in the Desert" was written in 1986.*

PROGRAMMING IDEAS

AT HOME

Torah Table Talk #1 A discussion of Jewish thought and values with your family and/or friends. The Fifth Commandment is stated twice in the Torah, with one significant difference, which the Rabbis of the Talmud analyze. The passages from the Talmud and from Maimonides have been altered to achieve gender neutrality.

Exodus 20:12
Honor your father and your mother, that you may long endure on the land that the Lord your God is assigning to you.

Leviticus 19:3
You shall each revere your mother and your father, and keep My Sabbaths: I am the Lord your God.

Babylonian Talmud (compiled between 200 and 500), Kiddushin 31b
Our Rabbis taught: What is "reverence" and what is "honor"? "Reverence"

means that children must not stand nor sit in their father's place, contradict his words, nor tip the scales against him. "Honor" means that children must give their parents food and drink, clothe and shelter them, and lead them in and out.

Babylonian Talmud (compiled between 200 and 500), Kiddushin 30b-31a

It is revealed and known to God Who decreed and the world came into existence that a child honors the mother more than the father because she sways the child by words. Therefore, the blessed Holy One placed the honor of the father before that of the mother. It is revealed and known to God Who decreed and the world came into existence that a child reveres the father more than the mother because he teaches the child Torah, and therefore the blessed Holy One put reverence of the mother before that of the father.

Maimonides (1135-1204), Mishneh Torah, Laws Relating to Rebels 6:9

One who strikes his or her child has transgressed the commandment not to place a stumbling block before the blind.

Questions for Thought and Discussion

1. Jewish sages have categorized the Ten Commandments into two groups of five commandments each. The first five are said to involve obligations between a person and God, and the next five are said to involve obligations between one person and another. The commandment to honor parents is the fifth—thus classified as one of our obligations to God. Why do the rabbis consider honoring parents to be a way in which we fulfill our obligation to God?

2. How do the Rabbis of the Talmud define "honor" and how do they define "reverence"? Note that Leviticus 19:3 is sometimes translated into English as "You shall each fear your mother and father." Do you agree with the Rabbis that a child is more inclined to honor the mother and to revere (or fear) the father? Why then must each parent be both honored and revered?

3. What connections—literal and metaphoric—are there between honoring parents and "enduring on the land"? What connections are there between revering parents and keeping the Sabbath?

4. Why is striking one's child similar to putting a stumbling block before a blind person?

5. Considering the commandment to honor and revere parents, how might an abused child be allowed, according to the Rabbis, to protect herself or himself? What types of self protection might the Rabbis prohibit?

Torah Table Talk #2   Lea Goldberg (1911-1970) was one of Israel's best known poets. Here a secular granddaughter speaks of her religious grandmother. The translation below, by Ezra Spicehandler, is reprinted from *The Modern Hebrew Poem Itself*, edited by Stanley Burnshaw, T. Carmi, and Ezra Spicehandler (Cambridge, MA: Harvard University Press, 1989), pages 128-129.

Lea Goldberg, "From My Mother's Home"

My mother's mother died
In the spring of her days. And her daughter
Did not remember her face. Her portrait, engraved
Upon my grandfather's heart,
Was erased from the world of images
After his death.

Only her mirror remained in the home,
Sunken with age into the silver frame.
And I, her pale granddaughter, who does not resemble her,
Look into it today as into
A pool which conceals its treasures
Beneath the waters.

Very deep down, behind my face,
I see a young woman
Pink-cheeked, smiling.
And a wig on her head.
She puts
An elongated earring on her ear-lobe, threading it
Through a tiny hole in the dainty flesh
Of her ear.

Very deep down, behind my face,
The bright goldness of her eyes sends out rays,
And the mirror carries on the tradition of
The family:
That she was very beautiful.

Questions for Thought and Discussion

1. In what ways does the speaker "not resemble" her grandmother?
2. What treasure does the speaker seek in the depths of the mirror?
3. What does the speaker of this poem feel toward her mother or her grandmother? Can we tell? Can we guess?
4. How does the speaker of the poem judge herself?
5. What, if anything, can we conclude about relationships in this family?

Additional At-Home Activities

❖ Share stories of yourself and your mother with your children. You might want to record the stories for posterity. Call the National Programming Department, 212-303-8027, for information on *Mishpahah: Hadassah's Hands-On Family History Project* kit.

❖ Explore your eating habits and philosophies with your mother or your daughter. Prepare food together, and collect healthful recipes for a family cookbook. If your daughter is a pre-teen or young teenager, encourage her to take an active role in planning and preparing meals. Have her plan the menu for one multi-course meal. As you prepare the meal together, discuss the kosher laws as well as the importance of nutrition and good eating.

❖ Together with your mother or daughter, decide on a *tzedakah* project to which you will both contribute financially. If possible, also donate your time, and work together for a cause you both believe in.

INTEREST/STUDY GROUPS

Hold a discussion based on the following questions:

1. In "Apples from the Desert" a mother learns from her daughter. What have you learned from your daughter(s)? What have you taught your mother?

2. Victoria Abravanel realizes that a secular life suits her youngest child better than a religious life. In American Jewry today, we occasionally read or hear of the opposite: parents whose children find that a more observant way of life brings them satisfaction. Discuss how your own choices about religion have affected your parents, and how your children's choices have affected you. (For thought: Is the very idea of a religion's suitability or lack of suitability for a given individual a secular idea? How might this story have differed if Savyon Liebrecht had been a member of Victoria Abravanel's world? Also for thought: Both Victoria and Rivka are influenced by their male partners in their choice between religious and secular. What is your own experience of men's influence on women's choice?)

3. Rivka chooses rural, agricultural labor in contrast to her mother's urban existence. This is a choice made by very few American Jews. What is your own attitude toward agricultural labor? Would you feel differently about your daughter working on the land of Israel or on the land of, say, California?

4. Consider the typically female occupations in which we observe Rivka, carrying laundry and serving food (while Dubi learnedly discusses agricultural techniques). Nonetheless, Rivka is sexually liberated, and she demands the right to think for herself and make her own choices—at least as far as her emotional/sexual/romantic future is concerned. Do these facts represent a contradiction? If so, what can we conclude?

MEETINGS

❖ Ask a knowledgeable member to discuss mother-daughter relationships in recent Jewish fiction, or invite a guest speaker. Compare the mother-daughter relationship in "Apples from the Desert" to the relationships in contemporary American Jewish women's fiction. Sylvia Barack Fishman's anthology, *Follow My Footprints: Changing Images of Women in American Jewish Fiction* (Hanover, NH: University Press of New England, 1992), offers selections from Vivian Gornick's *Fierce Attachments*, Anne Roiphe's *Lovingkindness*, Gloria Goldreich's

Four Days, and Gloria Kirchheimer's "Food of Love"—all exploring the bonds between mothers and daughters.

❖ Organize a meeting for mothers and daughters on weight and body image. Ask a member to speak on *Like Mother, Like Daughter: How Women Are Influenced by Their Mothers' Relationship with Food—and How to Break the Pattern* by Debra Waterhouse (New York: Hyperion, 1997). The author documents a destructive cycle of dieting and overeating, untangling a complicated web of mother-daughter food connections. Follow the book report with a discussion session.

ANNUAL EVENTS

❖ Organize an Education Day or Evening on Jewish mothers and daughters. Consider the following three sessions: a presentation by a family therapist who works with daughters and mothers; a talk by a scholar of literature on mothers and daughters in contemporary American Jewish fiction (refer to "Meetings" section above); and a panel discussion by several articulate Hadassah women— mothers and daughters. Questions for the panel to address: How is the Jewish mother/daughter relationship unique? What strengthens this relationship? What hobbles it?

HANDS-ON

❖ Organize a kosher cooking class for mothers and daughters. If there is a kosher cooking class already offered in your community (through the Jewish community center, a synagogue, etc.), work with the sponsoring organization to enroll mothers and daughters. If no class is available, ask a local kosher caterer if he or she would be willing to teach one. As the class proceeds, encourage the mothers and daughters to share cooking tips and favorite recipes.

❖ Host a mother/daughter outing to a place of Jewish interest, such as an exhibition of the work of a Jewish woman artist, or a performance of a Jewish theater or musical piece.

❖ Co-sponsor a mother/daughter volunteer event in coalition with a local organization or institution. For example, mothers and daughters might clean up a playground, paint a day care center or nursery school, deliver food to shut-ins, or co-sponsor a blood drive.

❖ Organize a book club for pre-teen and young teenage daughters and their mothers. The girls choose the books, although the mothers have veto power. Choose books with Jewish themes once every three or four books. (Refer to Teresa Barker's *The Mother-Daughter Book Club* [New York: HarperPerennial, 1997].)

THE ANCHORED WOMAN—
A CRY FOR HELP

Susan D. Alter

Susan Alter has been advocating for "anchored women" for many years. Since addressing the 1987 Hadassah National Convention (her speech is the basis of this article), she has continued to work on their behalf.

The agunah—*chained woman*—*is a woman who remains married according to Jewish law, but in actuality she has no marriage. Robert Gordis, in* Jewish Marital Status, *lists four main categories of* agunah:

1. A husband divorces his wife in civil court but refuses to give her a get, *either because of vindictiveness or greed. He may try to extort money in exchange for the* get. *Or a husband separates from his wife but refuses to agree to either a civil or a Jewish divorce, again because of vindictiveness or greed.*

2. A husband abandons his wife or disappears without a trace, and he has not given his wife a get. *(Abandonment was a common problem in the early years of this century. The Yiddish newspapers regularly published photos of husbands who had left their wives, asking readers to locate the missing men.)*

3. A husband is lost in military action or dies in an explosion, and there is no physical evidence that he is dead.

4. A childless widow, according to halakhah, *requires* halitzah *(release) from her husband's brother before she may remarry. The woman's brother-in-law refuses to release her.*

In all of these cases, the woman is still legally married. Consequently, she is unable to remarry and unable to have children with another man.

As explained in the article below, the Reform and Conservative denominations have solved the problem of the agunah *for their members, but these solutions are unacceptable to Orthodox Jews. In recent years, Orthodox Jewish women have adopted several approaches. One approach has been to use the civil courts or legislatures for redress. A number of women have sued rabbinical courts in the American civil courts, protesting against the rabbis' unjust decisions. And in 1992 the New York State Legislature, responding to requests by several Orthodox groups, enacted the Amendment to the Equitable Distribution Act, which permits civil court judges to take into account refusal to grant a* get *when deciding distribution of marital assets.*

Yet even after a decade of activism, Susan Alter's statement of 1987 remains true: "It is the responsibility of the Orthodox rabbis to exercise their rabbinic duty to find an halakhic way to free women from unwanted marriages." Today, the numbers of anchored women continue to increase, and Orthodox women continue to urge rabbinic authorities to find a halakhic way to free each and every agunah.

Harei at mekudeshet li betaba'at zo kedat Moshe veYisrael!
Behold, thou art betrothed unto me according to the laws of Moses and Israel!

Under the bridal canopy, the bride extends her right forefinger and the bridegroom places a circlet upon her finger and declares for her, the witnesses, and all to hear the words stated above. These words establish the strong personal bond and the religious, legal framework for the Jewish marriage, which for centuries was the key to the survival of the Jewish people.

Sadly today, the soaring divorce rate compels a review of the marital status of the Jewish woman because of her inability, in too many cases, to obtain a valid Jewish divorce from her husband. The instability of marriage and egregious behavior of many Jewish husbands toward their wives has created a crisis. Recalcitrant husbands who have refused initially to give their wives a *get* are agreeing to do so, in many cases, only after having extorted a huge amount of money from their wives and/or family. Sums upwards of $100,000 are not uncommon. Having no choice but to remain an *agunah*, women are forced to pay an unconscionable sum in exchange for a *get*. In other cases, assets such as stocks, jewelry or a house are demanded. In a rising number of instances, husbands are requiring not only visitation rights, which is customary, but total custody of their children in exchange for their wives' freedom.

Also, more and more frequently, women are willing to remarry without a *get*. Under the spoken or unspoken credo, "I have but one life to live, " Jewish women who have waited a number of years to obtain a *get* and discover that they will never be able to do so are marrying without having been properly divorced according to Jewish law. This is, indeed, a major tragedy for the Jewish community. For under Jewish law, such women are considered adulteresses since they are legally—from a Jewish perspective—still married to their former spouses. If children should result from such a second marriage, they are considered "*mamzerim,*" bastards, according to *halakhah*, Jewish law, and a separate set of discriminatory rules applies to them.

Obviously, if women could initiate a Jewish divorce, just as their husbands are entitled to do under Jewish law, this problem would not exist. However, only the husband can initiate a divorce. The consequences, as we have seen, are sad and painful. It would be useful in our discussion to review the history of Jewish divorce and to see whether any steps have been taken in the past to alleviate this condition.

The rules governing Jewish divorce are based upon only one short phrase in the Book of Deuteronomy 24:1. It is written: "*Vekhatav lah sefer kritut venatan beyadah.*" And he shall write her a bill of divorcement and give it to her.

According to the talmudic interpretation of this verse, it is only the husband who can present his wife with a bill of divorce. It must be initiated voluntarily by the husband and must not be given under duress or coercion. How then did the Jewish leaders respond to a situation in which the husband refused to give his wife a *get*? When circumstances arose where the Rabbis felt that a divorce should be given, despite the husband's unwillingness to do so, they allowed the woman to initiate an action whereby her husband was compelled to issue her a divorce even when he absolutely resisted. This *takkanah*, or legislative amendment, was introduced as early as 650 CE. Maimonides, centuries later, justified this rabbinic initiative by explaining that even though a coerced divorce according to Jewish law is invalid, the Rabbis could nevertheless compel the husband to initiate the divorce. This was done on the assumption that only the husband's evil inclination prevented him from acting properly, "according to the will of the Rabbis," and coercing him, therefore, was not unacceptable because it simply subdued his evil disposition and allowed his good intentions to come out. This legal fiction demonstrates how far the Rabbis extended themselves in an attempt to free a woman from an unwanted marriage and how sympathetic they were to her plight.

What is fascinating for us to note today is that the *takkanah* was enacted because of the "lively action" of the Jewish women of the time. Having been refused divorces by their husbands, they fraternized with the gentiles and made themselves unseemly in the eyes of their husbands, thereby forcing their husbands to divorce them. The Rabbis of the time were gravely concerned that the husbands were giving their wives a *get* under duress (which was not legal), and therefore "dreadful consequences would ensue." In order to avoid these "dreadful consequences," and in order to insure a proper Jewish divorce, the Rabbis decided to allow wives to petition the court for a divorce.

Unfortunately, this *takkanah* was abruptly rejected and its effectiveness terminated by Rabbeinu Tam, a leading halakhic figure, and others in France, in the twelfth century. They said that the *takkanah* was valid and applicable for only a specific period of time because of circumstances that were then prevalent.

Interestingly, however, early in the eleventh century, Rabbeinu Gershom, the greatest scholar of his time in Germany, reacted to the social situation of his generation by enacting two very important *takkanot* dealing with marriage and divorce that are honored to this day. Finding that husbands were abusive to their wives and were divorcing them against their will, he enacted a *takkanah* that a woman could no longer be divorced without her consent. The second *takkanah* of Rabbeinu Gershom (known as the *herem* of Rabbeinu Gershom) outlawed polygamy.

In the year 1573, in Scotland, an apocalyptic event occurred whose reverberations are still being felt to this day. For the first time, secular courts were given jurisdiction over divorce actions. This also occurred in France in 1792 and was followed in other European countries. Until the introduction of secular divorces, the religious courts of Europe—Christian or Jewish—had total control over the institutions of marriage and divorce.

This situation raised the specter that a Jewish couple could be deemed divorced by the laws of the state or country in which they lived, and yet remain married in the eyes of Jewish law, unless a *get* was given and accepted.

The introduction then of civil divorce and the inability of the Jewish court to compel a husband to give a *get* created the irreconcilable tension between the two systems of law that exists today. This tension produced the anomaly that a woman might be divorced under the law of the land without being free to remarry under Jewish law because of the refusal of her husband to give a *get*. The Reform movement addressed this issue early in its history by renouncing the need for a Jewish divorce and by accepting a secular divorce as a valid termination of a Jewish marriage.

The Conservative movement in 1954 tried to address this issue in a different fashion. Conservative rabbis inserted into the *ketubah*, a document presented by the groom to the bride, which embodies the obligations undertaken by the husband, a modification designed to solve the problem. This modification declares that the bride and bridegroom agree, in the event of the civil dissolution of their marriage, to recognize the *beit din* of the Rabbinical Assembly and the Jewish Theological Seminary as having the authority to counsel them and to summon either party at the request of the other for the purpose of effecting a valid Jewish divorce. In a test case of this new Conservative *ketubah*—Avitzur vs. Avitzur—the Court of Appeals, the highest court in the State of New York, held that it was not a violation of the separation of church and state clause of the Constitution, if it were to enforce that portion of the *ketubah*, which merely compelled the husband to submit to the decision of an agreed-upon panel of arbitrators—in this case, a rabbinical court.

The Avitzur case raised the problem of whether an action by a secular court to compel a husband to give a *get* constituted an unacceptable coercion of the husband, since under Jewish law a husband must give a *get* voluntarily. The Conservative position, however, was that the court was, in effect, enforcing the decision of the *beit din* (rabbinical court) and that in reality the rabbis had initiated and decreed the action.

In summary, the issue of solving the Jewish divorce question has been dealt with differently by the different branches of Judaism. Reform Judaism relies on a civil divorce, eliminating the need for a *get* altogether. Conservative Judaism has introduced a prenuptial agreement as part of the *ketubah*, which will benefit all marriages from the date of its inception. Orthodoxy remains divided over the acceptance of any prenuptial agreement, even one written in a document separate from the *ketubah*. Therefore, the major problem of the *agunah* is in the Orthodox community in which women are still totally dependent upon the good will of their husbands in obtaining a *get*.

The truth is that for the Orthodox community, the issue is one of *halakhah*, Jewish law. Because too many of today's divorcing husbands are hostile toward their wives, it is estimated (because we do not have the wherewithal to determine any definite statistics) that thousands of women are *agunot*—women who are anchored to unwanted marriages—or who, out of desperation, are toying with possible adulterous relationships. It is the responsibility of the Orthodox rabbis to exercise their rabbinic duty to find an halakhic way to free women from unwanted marriages as their predecessors did in the *takkanah* of the early seventh century.

We understand that perhaps feelings of true modesty and even inadequacy may be preventing the rabbis from initiating creative halakhic approaches to this critical situation. Especially as they compare themselves to the *gedolim* (halakhic giants of old), they may genuinely fear to enact new amendments. This is a totally unjustified position to assume, how-

> *Because too many of today's divorcing husbands are hostile toward their wives, it is estimated . . . that thousands of women are agunot—women who are anchored to unwanted marriages—or who, out of desperation, are toying with possible adulterous relationships.*

ever, since the leadership of every generation is obligated to confront and resolve the problems of its day.

We, the victimized underclass, can no longer permit dalliance in seeking a solution to redress the egregious wrongs suffered by many Jewish women. As indicated earlier, the number of *agunot* is staggering and growing every day. We, Jewish women and Jewish daughters, must encourage, nay, compel our rabbinic leaders to act, using whatever means necessary to correct this tragic situation.

From Bat Kol: Hadassah Jewish Education Guide, *Fall 1987, pages 30-34.*

SUSAN D. ALTER is a founder of Agunah, Inc. as well as a founding member of the International Committee for Women of the Wall (ICWOW). She served on the New York City Council from 1978-1991, and is currently a member of the Board of Directors of the Economic Development Corporation of the City of New York.

PROGRAMMING IDEAS

AT HOME

Torah Table Talk   A discussion of Jewish thought and values with your family and/or friends. Deuteronomy 24:1-4 describes the divorce procedure of the Israelite tribes, and also bans remarriage to a former wife. The selections from the Mishnah, compiled and written by about 200, are only a few of the details specified in the Jewish laws relating to marriage and divorce.

Deuteronomy 24:1-4

A man takes a wife and possesses her. She fails to please him because he finds something obnoxious about her, and he writes her a bill of divorcement, hands it to her, and sends her away from his house; she leaves his household and becomes the wife of another man; then this latter man rejects her, writes her a bill of divorcement, hands it to her, and sends her away from his house; or the man who married her last dies. Then the first husband who divorced her shall not take her to wife again, since she has been defiled—for that would be abhorrent to the Lord.

Mishnah, Kiddushin 1:1

By three means is the woman acquired and by two means she acquires her freedom. She is acquired by money or by writ or by intercourse. "By money"—the School of Shammai say: By a *dinar* or a *dinar's* worth. And the School of Hillel say: By a *perutah* or a *perutah*'s worth. And how much is a *perutah*? The eighth part of an Italian *issar*. And she acquires her freedom by a bill of divorce or by the death of her husband. A deceased brother's wife is acquired by intercourse and she acquires her freedom by *halitzah* or by the death of her deceased husband's brother.

Mishnah, Kiddushin *1:2*

A Hebrew bondman is acquired by money or by writ; and he acquires his freedom by [service lasting six] years or by [the entering in of] the year of Jubilee or by [redeeming himself at] his outstanding value. The Hebrew bondmaid has the advantage of him in that she acquires her freedom also through [manifesting] the tokens [of puberty]. The bondman that has his ear bored through is acquired by the act of boring, and he acquires his freedom by [the entering in of] the year of Jubilee or by the death of his master.

Mishnah, Ketubot *7:8*

If defects were found in [a wife] while she was yet in her father's house, the father must bring proof that these defects arose in her after she was betrothed, and that his field was laid waste. If she had entered into the control of the husband, the husband must bring proof that these defects were in her before she was betrothed, and that his bargain was a bargain made in error. So says Rabbi Meir. But the Sages say: This applies only to secret defects; but he may not make complaint of manifest defects. And if there was a bathhouse in that town he may not make complaint even of secret defects, since he can inquire about her from her women kinsfolk.

Questions for Thought and Discussion

1. List the ways in which a wife is likened to property.
2. Why might Jewish law forbid remarriage to a former wife?
3. How does a bondman (an indentured servant) become free? How does a married woman who wants a divorce become free?
4. What do you think is meant by the wife's "defects" in the excerpt from *Ketubot*?

Additional At-Home Activities

❖ If you know a woman undergoing a separation or divorce, or one who is currently divorced and alone, invite her to join you for a Shabbat or a holiday dinner. Be her friend.

INTEREST/STUDY GROUPS

Hold a discussion based on the following questions:

1. Susan Alter notes the tension felt by an *agunah* living according to *halakhah* even though the *halakhah* binds her in a marriage from which she seeks

to be free. Discuss how this dilemma is similar to or different from other dilemmas in which individuals must wrestle with Jewish law. Do you know of any areas of Jewish practice that have been altered (or for which loopholes have been created) in modern times? Why have some elements of *halakhah* been altered by rabbis through the ages, while the laws of Jewish divorce have not?

2. In modern times Jewish communal authority is so diminished that rabbis are unable to compel a husband to present his wife with a *get*. However, the authority still exists to require that a woman have a *get* before remarrying. Why has the authority to compel the wife to follow the law remained while the authority to compel the husband been diminished?

3. With which of the following do you agree and why?

(a) The approach of the Conservative movement in dealing with Jewish divorce law—encouraging a prenuptial agreement that states that, in the event of the civil dissolution of their marriage, the bride and groom agree to recognize the *beit din* (court) of the Rabbinical Assembly to compel either party to effect a valid Jewish divorce—is a legitimate means of staying within the authority of *halakhah* and at the same time of working to relieve the suffering of many *agunot*.

(b) The approach of the Conservative movement in dealing with Jewish divorce law is a manipulation of *halakhah*. The emphasis of this approach is more on avoiding church/state complications than on working within the confines of Jewish law to solve this problem.

MEETINGS

❖ Discuss Chaim Grade's *The Agunah* (New York: Menorah, 1978; translated from the Yiddish by Curt Leviant). This 1961 novel focuses on a young woman of Vilna whose husband has not returned from World War I, and the city's involvement in her struggle to remarry. Questions to ponder: Who has the authority to interpret *halakhah*? Are interpretations done in the name of God? Discuss the statement by Curt Leviant: "The tragedy of the *agunah*, a hapless woman caught in a current too powerful for her, is the tragedy of all situations revolving around the strictures of law." If there are *agunot* in your community, invite them to join your discussion.

ANNUAL EVENTS

❖ Include a guest speaker from Agunah, Inc. or from ICAR (International Coalition for Agunah Rights) as one part of an Education Day or Evening on Jewish women's issues. Provide Hadassah's "Free the *Agunah*" issue cards to participants. (Call the National Order Department 1-800-880-9455. Order number: #R654g. Minimum order: 500 cards. Cost: $5.00 for 500.)

HANDS-ON

❖ As a group, write to Agunah, Inc. at 463 East 19th Street, Brooklyn, NY 11226. This organization deals with individual cases of recalcitrant husbands.

Express your support and request a copy of its materials, which explain in detail the dimensions of the problem and how to address it.

❖ If you are a member of an Orthodox congregation, encourage your rabbi to act on behalf of *agunot*. Make him familiar with Agunah, Inc. materials. Also inform him of ICAR (International Coalition for Agunah Rights), an umbrella organization which is composed of Jewish women's organizations, including Hadassah. ICAR's primary goal is to devise and implement strategies to motivate the Orthodox rabbinate to recognize the inequity of Jewish divorce and to find a way to free *agunot* from their chains.

A MEZUZAH DOES NOT WARD OFF DOMESTIC VIOLENCE

Rabbi Julie Ringold Spitzer

At a recent gathering in my hometown, a friend of the family overheard me say that I often spoke on the subject of domestic violence and abuse in Jewish families. "Oh really," he said, "I didn't know that there was much domestic violence in the Jewish community. I don't know of any." And then he stopped in mid-thought. At that very moment he remembered a horrific murder-suicide that had occurred in his own neighborhood some years earlier. People he knew well. A model family to the neighbors. A nice Jewish family. "I guess it does happen," he admitted, "but is it really happening in that many of our families?"

The latest FBI statistics are telling: about 30 percent of the women murdered in 1990 were killed by husbands or boyfriends. Every 15 seconds on average, a woman is beaten by her husband or boyfriend. An estimated 95 percent of assaults against spouses are committed by men against women. "In this country, domestic violence is just about as common as giving birth," according to Health and Human Services Secretary Donna Shalala.

But what about Jewish families?

Unfortunately, we have far more anecdotal information than actual statistics. But what information we do have paints a surprising picture:

❖   An early study of the Los Angeles Jewish community (Giller and Goldsmith, 1980) indicated that abuse was as common in Jewish homes as it was in the community at large, affecting about 20 percent of all Jewish families.

❖   Barbara Harris, who works with domestic violence in the New York Jewish community, reports that the problem impacts on 15 to 19 percent of Jewish homes.

❖   One recent publication on domestic violence in the Jewish community estimated that 5 percent of Israeli women experienced abuse at the hands of husbands or boyfriends. Others put the number much higher.

❖   Jewish Family Service agencies around the country have all documented cases of abused women (and children). Many now have special programs to address the issue and report a rise in reported cases of abuse once staff has been trained on the subject.

Abuse in Jewish homes need not be limited to a husband physically abusing his wife. Once defined by a repeated cycle of tension leading to a violent attack, followed by contrition on the part of the abuser, abuse in relationships, most experts now realize, is based on a pattern of power and control. The abuser seeks to control the victim by assertions, both great and small, of his power over her. This pattern often wears down the resistance and the self-esteem of the victim, who then appears to others as somehow being to blame for not leaving. The emotional entanglements of such relationships are complex. The victim often feels love for the abuser, reasoning that if only she were able to do what he wanted, the abuse would end. Such reasoning is false. More often than not, what the woman does has little to do with the abusive behavior of the man. And, when left unchecked, this pattern of power and control leads to increasingly violent episodes. The only way to end the abuse is to break the cycle, to leave, or to have the abuser leave. Unfortunately, one of the most dangerous times for a woman is after she has left the relationship. Many women are therefore reluctant to leave such abuse, or they return home after having left for a brief period.

For Jewish women, there may be other factors in not wanting to leave an abusive home. Our tradition has accorded to the wife the responsibility for maintaining *shalom bayit*, or peace in the home. There are many sad stories of women who bravely share their plight of abuse with a rabbi. The rabbi, on more than one occasion, has then told the woman to go home and change her behavior, indicating that whatever is wrong at home must be her fault. Statistics indicate that Jewish women stay in abusive relationships twice as long as other women for this and other reasons. Such abuse need not be limited to married women and men. It can be found among dating couples, after a marriage has ended, and between couples of the same sex. Furthermore, the abuse need not be only violent and physical. Jewish women have also reported sexual abuse (forced sexual activity, including violation of an observant woman's time of physical separation from her husband) and emotional abuse (constant degrading comments, tormenting threats about children or pets, extreme restrictions upon her behavior, limiting of her social contacts, and so on).

Is abuse in Jewish homes something unique to the late twentieth century? Sadly, it is not. Actual instances of one spouse abusing the other in our Hebrew Scriptures are less obvious, but many read the words of Psalm 55 as if spoken in the voice of an abused woman: "For it was not an enemy that taunted me, then I could have borne it; Neither was it my adversary that did magnify himself against me, then I would have hid myself from him. But it was you, a man my equal, my companion, and my familiar friend ... He put forth his hands against them that were at peace with him; He profaned his covenant. Smoother than cream were the speeches of his mouth, but his heart was war; His words were softer than oil; Yet were they keen-edged swords."

Throughout rabbinic literature there are specific references to women who come with complaints of abuse to the authorities of their day. Some place the responsibility for a man's behavior on the woman, but many are understanding of her plight, and less tolerant of the abuser. One such figure is Rabbi Meir of Rothenberg, who lived in Germany in the thirteenth century. In his work of *responsa* (responses to Jewish legal questions), he writes: "One deserves greater punishment for striking his wife than for striking another person, for he is enjoined to respect her. Far be it from a Jew to do such a thing" (*Even haEzer* #298). Physical abuse was considered by many authorities as grounds for granting the woman a divorce.

> There are many sad stories of women who bravely share their plight of abuse with a rabbi. The rabbi, on more than one occasion, has then told the woman to go home and change her behavior, indicating that whatever is wrong at home must be her fault.

Today, violence and abuse continue to be a reality in far too many Jewish homes. It is one of the better kept secrets of our community. In the last ten years, the number of Jewish women's organizations and Jewish family service agencies breaking the silence has been heartening. In many large Jewish communities, and some smaller ones, abused Jewish women know that there is someone who will believe their stories. Kosher meals in shelters, Jewish safe homes, and Shabbat kits are some of the services that can be found in a growing number of locales. Still it is not enough. Writers like Blu Greenberg can make claims that the religious community is silent on the subject because there is much more yet to be done.

What can you do? Education is the key to prevention. Sponsor a speaker or a program in your synagogue or chapter meeting. Research the available resources in your community and provide a list that can be posted on bulletin boards and in more private places (like the inside of a women's restroom). Establish links with agencies that provide services to abused women, and let them know that there are special needs that Jewish women might have. Let them know that Jewish women are abused, too. (Many in the community buy into the myth that all Jewish families are places of peace and harmony.) Sponsor drives for toiletries or clothing in consultation with shelter programs. Work toward legislative reform in your community. (In many states, for instance, marital rape is not recognized as a crime.)

In *Pirkei Avot*, we learn that one who saves a single life indeed saves an entire world. Even if abuse and violence were happening in only one Jewish family, we would be compelled to act. Somewhere out there, be it a stranger or a friend, as many as one out of every five Jewish women is subject to abuse at the hands of a loved one. Each of us can help to save a life. Each of us can save an entire world.

From The American Scene, *Fall 1994, pages 1-4.*

RABBI JULIE RINGOLD SPITZER is Regional Director of the Union of American Hebrew Congregations Greater New York Council of Reform Synagogues.

PROGRAMMING IDEAS

AT HOME

Torah Table Talk   A discussion of Jewish thought and values with your family and/or friends. The three selections are from: the *Gemara* of the Babylonian Talmud, the legal writings of Maimonides; and from Joseph Caro, author of the *Shulhan Arukh*, the authoritative code of law for Orthodox Jews throughout the world. In this passage, he cites Rabbi Simhah ben Shmuel of Speyer (twelfth to thirteenth centuries), writing a response to a Jewish legal question.

Babylonian Talmud (compiled between 200 and 500), Gittin 6b
Rabbi Yehuda said in the name of Rav, if a man terrorizes his household, he will eventually commit three sins: unchastity, blood shedding, and desecration of the Sabbath.

Maimonides (1135-1204), Mishneh Torah, *Laws Relating to Marriage 21:10*

A wife who refuses to perform any kind of work that she is obligated to do [according to Jewish law] may be compelled to perform it, even by scourging her with a rod.

If the husband claims that she is not doing her work, while she claims that she has not refused to work, another woman or some neighbors should be asked to stay with them. This matter should be handled according to what the judge may consider feasible.

Rabad (Rabbi Abraham ben David of Posquires) (twelfth century)

(Commenting on Maimonides)

It is not possible. I have never heard of corporal punishment for women. Rather her [financial] allowance is diminished for her needs and her food until she complies.

Joseph Caro (1488-1575), Beit Yosef, Even Ha-Ezer *154:15*

In a responsum of Rabbeinu Simhah, it is written, "It is an accepted view that we have to treat a man who beats his wife more severely than we treat a man who beats another man, since he is not obligated to honor the other man, but is obligated to honor his wife—more, in fact, than himself. And a man who beats his wife should be put under a ban and excommunicated and flogged and punished with various forms of torment, one should even cut off his hand if he is accustomed to it [wife-beating]. And if he wants to divorce her, let him divorce her and give her the *ketubah* payment." He goes on to write: "You should impose peace between them, and if the husband does not fulfill his part in maintaining the peace but continues to beat her and denigrate her, let him be excommunicated, and let him be forced by gentile [authorities] to give her a writ of divorce."

Questions for Thought and Discussion

1. Does the excerpt from the Talmud state that terrorizing the household is sinful in and of itself? Why or why not?

2. For Rabbi Yehuda, the three sins that follow from abusive behavior are roughly equivalent in moral degradation. What do the three sins represent? Why will an abuser eventually become unchaste and why will he desecrate the Sabbath?

3. Jewish legal writings, from the middle ages to the twentieth century, includes both denunciation of all violence against a wife and qualified permission to beat a wife, as the brief excerpts here indicate. Why might different halakhic experts hold such different opinions?

4. Rabbi Simhah seems almost contemporary in his wholehearted condemnation of the abusive husband, even to the point of advising that, if the abuse continues, the wife must appeal to the gentile courts to enforce a *get*. (Certainly an unusual recommendation!) Maimonides, however, had permitted wife-beating when a wife refused "to perform any kind of work." Similarly, many later writers were reluctant to accept an abused wife's testimony, requiring

independent corroboration that her husband abuses her. How are these various attitudes toward domestic violence echoed in our own time?

5. Rabbi Simhah writes, "You should impose peace between them." Is a reconciliation between the abused and the abuser possible? How might "peace" between husband and wife be defined? How might it be monitored?

INTEREST/STUDY GROUPS

Hold a discussion based on the following questions:

1. How have your own attitudes toward domestic violence changed over the past two decades?

2. Rabbi Spitzer states: "Statistics indicate that Jewish women stay in abusive relationships twice as long as other women." One reason for the statistic, she states, is that rabbis in the past were likely to blame the abused woman for the lack of *shalom bayit* (peace in the home), and a rabbi would therefore encourage a woman to return to her abuser and treat him better. What other reasons could account for this troubling statistic?

3. Rabbi Meir of Rothenberg argues that because a man is legally bound to respect his wife, he deserves greater punishment for striking her than for striking another person. Until very recently, the opposite has held true in the United States: A man who beat his wife could expect lenient punishment while a man who beat a stranger could expect harsh punishment. Discuss the attitudes toward family and toward privacy that would have caused medieval European Jewish society and mid-twentieth century American society to hold these opposite viewpoints.

MEETINGS

❖ Rabbi Spitzer states: "Education is the key to prevention." Sponsor a speaker or a program on domestic violence in your synagogue, or in your Hadassah region, chapter, or group. Discuss Jewish communal attitudes, the myths and realities of domestic violence. Provide a list of resources to all participants—hotline number, battered women's shelter, and agencies that provide counseling to abused women.

ANNUAL EVENTS

❖ Sponsor a seminar on domestic violence together with the American Affairs/Domestic Policy chair and Israel, Zionist and International Affairs chair. The National Hadassah Education/Public Policy Division offered the following four-part seminar in February 1995. Use this seminar as a model, and adapt it for your community. Provide all participants with Hadassah's "Stop Domestic Violence" issue card to spark their interest in membership. (Call the National Order Department at 1-800-880-9455. Order number: #R654c. Minimum order: 500 cards. Cost: $5.00 for 500.)

Domestic Violence—In the United States, in Israel, and in Jewish Law

9:30-10:30	**A Victim's Perspective** *Lisa Haberman, social worker*
10:45-11:45	**An American Perspective** *Mindy Perlmutter, educator*
12:00-1:00	Lunch
1:15-2:15	**An Israeli Perspective** *Blu Greenberg, author and lecturer*
2:30-3:30	**A Jewish Legal and Ethical Perspective** *Aviva Comet-Murciano, social worker, therapist, educator*

HANDS-ON

❖ Research the available resources in your community that provide help to battered women, and provide a list that can be posted on bulletin boards and in more private places (like the inside of a women's restroom).

❖ Establish links with agencies that provide services to abused women, and let them know that there are special needs that Jewish women might have. Let them know that Jewish women are abused, too. (Many in the non-Jewish community buy into the myth that all Jewish homes are places of peace and harmony.)

❖ Sponsor drives for toiletries or clothing after consultation with local shelters to determine their needs.

❖ Work toward legislative reform. The National American Affairs/Domestic Policy Department (212-303-8136) can provide you with up-to-date information on the Violence Against Women Act. Work toward reform at the local and state level as well. In many states, for instance, marital rape is not recognized as a crime.

❖ Work together with US-Israel Women to Women (275 Seventh Avenue, 8th floor, New York, NY 10001; phone 212-206-8057; fax 212-206-7031) or with the New Israel Fund (165 East 56th Street, New York, NY 10022; phone 212-750-2333; fax 212-750-8043) to assist battered women's shelters in Israel.

❖ Encourage your rabbi to deliver a sermon on domestic violence. Refer her/him to the *Resource Guide for Rabbis on Domestic Violence*, edited by Maya Townsend, published in 1996 by Jewish Women International (formerly B'nai B'rith Women). For further information, write to: Jewish Women International, 1828 L Street, NW, Suite 250, Washington, DC 20036; phone 202-857-1300; fax 202-857-1380.

THE JEWISH COMMUNITY IN CRISIS—TWO VIEWS ON INTERMARRIAGE

Egon Mayer and Deborah E. Lipstadt

RE-DRAWING THE CIRCLE

by Egon Mayer

A demographic revolution is underway. Largely because of the success of the American-Jewish community, we are witnessing the transformation of our families through intermarriage. Today's Jews are intermarrying at five to seven times the rate that their parents did.

We American Jews have prided ourselves on being the people who went from Poland to polo in three generations, and we must be realistic about our priorities and our policy positions. Demanding Jewish outcomes to our children's marriages is not enough, we also have to opt for Jewish lifestyles. As American Jews, though, we have opted to live primarily as Americans in our professional, political, and economic lives, and as Jews in our leisure time. Jewishness may occupy a great deal of our mental and emotional lives, but when we look at how we commit our time—our day-to-day engagements, our social life—Judaism has no primacy. We can lament this, but we cannot deny it.

In America, a romantic marketplace determines mate selection, not the desires of parents, grandparents, or community leaders. Most Americans follow their personal inclinations in mate selection, and we Jews are Americans. It is improbable that many of us would sublimate or suppress our individual inclinations for the good of the larger community.

To insure Jewish marital outcomes, we must increase our involvement in the romantic marketplace where mate selection occurs. To date, the Jewish community has not had much impact. Most American Jews are marrying at age 26 to 28, and the organized Jewish community has—at best—only minimal contact with that age group. By all means, we should support Jewish education. We should send children to Israel when they are in high school or college, but we cannot expect those experiences to determine whom they will marry ten years later! We must project a Jewish image into the world view of the 26 to 28 year old. We have to create forums in which young men and young women meet, fall in love, and marry.

We American Jews have prided ourselves on being the people who went from Poland to polo in three generations, and we must be realistic about our priorities and our policy positions.

Besides assuring Jewish marital outcomes, we must stop berating intermarrieds for the success of the American-Jewish community. We American Jews have succeeded all too well, and we don't like what we see. We have become secularized. *Halakhah* (Jewish law) is too demanding, too authoritarian, and does not allow for enough initiative on the part of the individual. As devoutly individualistic Americans, we do not like constraint. However, when we then think about our traditions, we feel guilty, and our kids take the blame. Residual guilt can never assure the survival of a community.

We can only attract young adults if our community offers something exciting, passionate, and caring. This kind of Jewish community will attract men and women. A community of guilt and anxiety will not. A community that admonishes the 28 year old for having fallen in love (at long last!) and having chosen to marry will never be appealing. That is the dilemma we face today. We have to own up to our American way of life. We have to recognize, that in a voluntary community, individuals make life choices that suit their needs but not necessarily the needs of the Jewish community. Nevertheless these individuals want to be Jewish. That is the mystery.

When we look at the [National Jewish Population Survey] data and recite the alarming statistics, we must remember that the people who gave us those numbers were delighted that the Jewish community had reached out to ask them about their Jewishness. Even though every answer they gave to our questions sounded like a non-Jewish answer—they haven't been in a synagogue in years; they wouldn't know *tefillin* if they tripped over them—they did want to spend time talking to our researchers about their Jewish identity, and they did want to participate in Jewish family celebrations. As a community, we have to let them know that we do want them to remain part of us. I believe that when we do reach them, we will be astonished to find that their Jewishness looks different from ours, but they will in fact be the bearers of continuity.

I would like to conclude with the following lines from the poet Edwin Markham, as taught to me by the late Paul Cowan:

He drew a circle to shut me out.
A renegade, a heretic, a thing to flout.
But love and I had the wit to win.
We drew a circle to close him in.

REACH OUT TO KEEP SOMEONE

by Deborah E. Lipstadt

The statistics on intermarriage are staggering: according to the National Jewish Population Survey, 52 percent of all Jews who are marrying today are choosing to marry non-Jews. This figure seems even more shocking when we compare it to the 1960 figure of approximately 9 percent. The vast majority of non-Jewish mates of intermarried couples do not convert, and in homes where one parent is a non-Jew, only 28 percent of the children are raised as Jews. Clearly, 72 percent are *not* being raised as Jews. Furthermore, we now have adequate data to show that the intermarriage rate for children of mixed marriages is 90 percent. However, the intermarriage rate of children of conversionary Jews (that is, where one partner has converted to Judaism) is the same as the rate of born Jews. This important statistic shows that conversion strengthens the Jewish community.

Charles E. Silberman in his 1985 book, *A Certain People: American Jews and Their Lives Today*, very optimistically argued that intermarriage was not a danger, because it brought people into Judaism. Silberman now indicates that if he were to write that book today, knowing the results of the National Jewish Population Survey, he would come to a different conclusion. In his book, he overestimated the ability of mixed households to transmit the Jewish heritage to the next generation.

What are the policy implications of the findings on intermarriage? What, if anything, can we as a community, can Hadassah as an organization, do? And what can all of us, individually, do about it?

Responses to the findings of the survey have varied greatly. On one side, there are people who throw up their hands in defeat. "Intermarriage," they argue, "shows that the non-Jewish world is too much with us. Therefore, we should become quite insular and limit our interactions with the non-Jewish world. It is the quality of Jewish life—and not the quantity of Jews—that we must worry about. We can write off the intermarrieds and forget about them."

Unless you live in certain areas of Crown Heights, this response bears no relationship to reality. Very few Jewish men and women are willing to forget about the rest of the world.

At the other end of the spectrum, there are people who say: "It's time to stop saying that intermarriage is wrong, because that simply alienates those who are intermarried and pushes them further away from Judaism. Stop the *angst*, and instead let's devote ourselves to outreach so that we can bring the intermarrieds closer to the Jewish community."

This suggestion sounds appealing, because it resolves the problem by saying, "It's no longer a problem. We just have to live with it." Also, the suggestion lets us feel good by giving us something to do, that is, it presents the seeming panacea of outreach. The proposed solution, however, has serious failings, because the outreach lacks a target population. If we want a Jewish community that is more than a shadowy reflection of what it was, then undirected outreach is not the answer. The vast majority of intermarrieds have no interest in affiliation. Even though 62 percent of them attend a Seder and 59 percent kindle the *menorah*, they are far from making a commitment to a Jewish life. As my teacher Marshall Sklare, of blessed memory, taught, Passover and Hanukkah observance are the Jewish rituals that are closest to prevalent American customs. First, because of the proximity in time between Hanukkah and Christmas, far more people light Hanukkah candles than hear the *Megillah* of Esther. Second, the connection of both Pesah and Hanukkah to ideas of renewal and revolt reflects basic American ideals, and thus these celebrations mesh with American traditions more than, for example, putting on *tefillin*. We cannot, therefore, derive much comfort from Seder-going and *menorah*-lighting statistics. People can perform these rituals and raise their children as non-Jews, even take them to church on Sundays.

In an open society, we have to respect the decision of those people who have chosen not to marry Jews. On a personal level, they and their children are a part of our families, and they must continue to be the recipients of our love. But many of those who marry non-Jews have, in effect, decided not to be part of the Jewish community. On the levels of faith, belief, and identity, many of the intermarrieds—most notably those who are raising their children as non-Jews—have made the decision to distance themselves from us. As a community we must bid good-bye to many of the children of intermarrieds. We need to draw community boundaries, so that Jewish identity can be effectively transmitted. If people have no interest in affiliating with the Jewish community and with Judaism, should our limited resources be expended on enticing them back into the fold?

If however, they or their children want to be a part of the Jewish community, we must welcome them with open arms, ease their path, and do everything possible for them. Many intermarrieds are raising their children as Jews, and these families are likely to respond to outreach. They are the ones on whom we should spend community resources. We should especially target those who have expressed an interest in conversion. We must show these men and women that they are an integral part of our community and not peripheral to it. *All vestiges of negative or quizzical attitudes toward converts must be totally eradicated.* Not only are these attitudes counter-productive to the future of the Jewish community but, much more important, they are in opposition to Jewish law. *Halakhah* says that we must joyously welcome converts into our lives. We have been giving a mixed message for too long. We owe too many converts a sincere apology for how we have treated them.

We cannot only *hope* that our children marry Jews. Nor can we just give them an unambiguous message that we expect them to do so. We must also stack the deck to try to make sure that they do. Many parents drop the kids off at Sunday school, afternoon class, or even day school, and expect that the staff will be responsible for transmitting Jewish identity. Parents who practice car-pool Judaism must evaluate the message they are sending their children, and elevate the Jewish content of that message. They must show that being Jewish means something to them personally, that it is an integral part of their lives. They cannot wait until the child is an adult to transmit that message.

Organizational Judaism is also not sufficient. Those whose Jewish identity is expressed solely through the work they do for Jewish organizations or for the Jewish community must recognize the limits of the message *they* are sending. Living as organizational Jews without weaving consistent practice of Jewish tradition and Jewish learning into our lives is not enough.

Our love for Judaism and Jewish tradition must be woven into the very fabric of our lives. Synagogue attendance and celebration of the Shabbat on a consistent basis are two significant steps. Consistency and celebration are the keys. Judaism must be something that enhances and elevates our lives.

Many intermarrieds are raising their children as Jews, and these families are likely to respond to outreach. They are the ones on whom we should spend community resources. We should especially target those who have expressed an interest in conversion. We must show these men and women that they are an integral part of our community and not peripheral to it.

From Textures, Hadassah National Jewish Studies Bulletin, *May 1993, vol. 11, no. 2. The article is adapted from speeches presented at the "Jewish Community in Crisis" plenary sessions at the National Hadassah Convention in Washington, DC in July 1992.*

EGON MAYER, Ph.D., is Professor of Sociology at Brooklyn College and Director of the Center for Jewish Studies of the Graduate School of the City University of New York. He also directs the Jewish Outreach Institute, which helps interfaith families integrate within the Jewish community. Dr. Mayer is the author of Love & Tradition: Marriage Between Christians and Jews.

DEBORAH E. LIPSTADT, Ph.D., is Dorot Professor of Modern Jewish and Holocaust Studies at Emory University in Atlanta. Her latest book is Denying the Holocaust: The Growing Assault on Truth and Memory, *the first full-length study on those who attempt to deny the Holocaust. She is also the author of* Beyond Belief: The American Press and the Coming of the Holocaust.

PROGRAMMING IDEAS

AT HOME

Torah Table Talk A discussion of Jewish thought and values with your family and/or friends. The following two selections from the Bible speak very differently of interfaith marriages. In the Book of Ruth, we read of Ruth's faithfulness to Naomi. In the Book of Ezra, the people of Israel leave Babylon and return to Jerusalem. In the passage below, Ezra addresses the Israelite men who have married "foreign women."

Ruth 1:1-20, 4:13,16,17

In the days when the chieftains ruled, there was a famine in the land; and a man of Bethlehem in Judah, with his wife and two sons, went to reside in the country of Moab. The man's name was Elimelekh, his wife's name was Naomi, and his two sons were named Mahlon and Chilion—Ephrathites of Bethlehem in Judah. They came to the country of Moab and remained there.

Elimelekh, Naomi's husband, died; and she was left with her two sons. They married Moabite women, one named Orpah and the other Ruth, and they lived there about ten years. Then those two—Mahlon and Chilion—also died; so the woman was left without her two sons and without her husband.

She started out with her daughters-in-law to return from the country of Moab; for in the country of Moab she had heard that the Lord had taken note of His people and given them food. Accompanied by her two daughters-in-law, she left the place where she had been living; and they set out on the road back to the land of Judah.

But Naomi said to her two daughters-in-law, "Turn back, each of you to her mother's house. May the Lord deal kindly with you, as you have dealt with the dead and with me! May the Lord grant that each of you find security in the house of a husband!" And she kissed them farewell. They broke into weeping and said to her, "No, we will return with you to your people."

But Naomi replied, "Turn back, my daughters! Why should you go with me? Have I any more sons in my body who might be husbands for you? Turn back, my daughters, for I am too old to be married. Even if I thought there was hope for me, even if I were married tonight and I also bore sons, should you wait for them to grow up? Should you on their account debar yourselves from marriage? Oh no, my daughters! My lot is far more bitter than yours, for the hand of the Lord has struck out against me."

They broke into weeping again, and Orpah kissed her mother-in-law farewell. But Ruth clung to her. So she said, "See, your sister-in-law has returned to her people and her gods. Go follow your sister-in-law." But Ruth replied, "Do not urge me to leave you, to turn back and not follow you. For wherever you go, I will go; wherever you lodge, I will lodge; your people shall be my people, and your God my God. Where you die, I will die, and there I will be buried. Thus and more may the Lord do to me if anything but death parts me from you." When [Naomi] saw how determined she was to go with her, she ceased to argue with her; and the two went on until they reached Bethlehem.

When they arrived in Bethlehem, the whole city buzzed with excitement over them. The women said, "Can this be Naomi?" "Do not call me Naomi," she replied. "Call me Marah [Hebrew for *bitter*], for Shaddai has made my lot very bitter....

So Boaz married Ruth; she became his wife, and he cohabited with her. The Lord let her conceive, and she bore a son.... Naomi took the child and held it to her bosom. She became its foster mother, and the women neighbors gave him a name, saying, "A son is born to Naomi!" They named him Obed; he was the father of Jesse, father of David.

Ezra 1:2-3; 7:1,6; 10:1-4, 10-11

Thus said King Cyrus of Persia: The Lord God of Heaven has given me all the kingdoms of the earth and has charged me with building Him a house in Jerusalem, which is in Judah. Anyone of you of all His people—may his God be with him, and let him go up to Jerusalem that is in Judah and build the House of the Lord God of Israel....

After these events ... Ezra came up from Babylon, a scribe expert in the Teaching of Moses which the Lord God of Israel had given, whose request the king had granted in its entirety, thanks to the benevolence of the Lord toward him....

While Ezra was praying and making confession, weeping and prostrating himself before the House of God, a very great crowd of Israelites gathered about him, men, women, and children; the people were weeping bitterly. Then Shecaniah son of Jehiel of the family of Elam spoke up and said to Ezra, "We have trespassed against our God by bringing into our homes foreign women from the peoples of the land; but there is still hope for Israel despite this. Now then, let us make a covenant with our God to expel all these women and those who have been born to them, in accordance with the bidding of the Lord and of all who are concerned over the commandment of our God, and let the Teaching be obeyed. Take action, for the responsibility is yours and we are with you. Act with resolve!" ...

Then Ezra the priest got up and said to them, "You have trespassed by bringing home foreign women, thus aggravating the guilt of Israel. So now, make confession to the Lord, God of your fathers, and do His will, and separate yourselves from the peoples of the land and from the foreign women."

Questions for Thought and Discussion

1. The selection from the Book of Ruth shows Ruth's remarkable attachment to Naomi. What might account for such devotion? Is there anything or anyone in your life to which you have felt such a passionate attachment?

2. David, the King of Israel, is the great-grandson of Ruth, and Judaism teaches that the messiah will be of the line of David and of Ruth. Why?

3. Why were the Israelites who returned to Jerusalem after being exiled in Babylon concerned about their foreign wives and children? What decision did Ezra make? Why? If he had to make this decision today, what other edicts might he issue? List these alternative edicts.

4. What does the selection from the Book of Ezra imply about the relative importance of our relationship to God, to husband/wife, and to children? How can we reconcile our own feelings about these relationships?

Additional At-Home Activities

❖ Invite an interfaith family to join you for a Shabbat or holiday dinner. And, if your guests are interested in learning more about Jewish living, have them help you prepare for a future Shabbat or holiday meal. If you yourself are part of an interfaith family, discuss with your guests how your family came to celebrate Shabbat or Jewish holidays together. What problems have you encountered, and what resolutions have you achieved?

INTEREST/STUDY GROUPS

Hold a discussion based on the following questions:

1. How do you react emotionally to Egon Mayer? To Deborah Lipstadt?

2. Egon Mayer ends his article with a poem by Edwin Markham. Who is the "he" drawing the first circle? Why might this circle be drawn? Who is the "we" drawing the second circle?

3. Professor Mayer notes that many of the respondents to the 1990 population survey, although they don't know *tefillin* from tortillas, readily identify themselves as Jews and are pleased to discuss their Jewish identity. Why? (And what does this imply for those of us who do know about *tefillin*?)

4. How do you respond to the statement "reject intermarriage, not the

intermarried"? What are the implications? How can the two—the act of intermarrying and the people who commit the act—be separated?

5. Discuss Egon Mayer's assertion that interfaith marriage is changing Judaism as we know it. How has Judaism changed already? What changes are likely in the future?

6. The Torah states "You too must befriend the stranger, for you were strangers in the land of Egypt" (Deuteronomy 10:19). What does "befriend the stranger" mean to you? Deborah Lipstadt asserts that, in general, American Jews have NOT befriended converts to Judaism. Describe the ways in which your family, your synagogue, your Hadassah group, and other Jewish communal organizations befriend converts. If these ways are inadequate, what improvements are needed?

7. Genesis chapter 18 tells of Abraham and the strangers who approach his tent. Abraham greets them eagerly and offers food and drink, providing future generations with a model of hospitality. Later commentators say that Abraham kept all four flaps of his tent open, so that he could see strangers coming from all directions. What might influence us today *not* to befriend the stranger? What may cause us to close the flaps of our metaphorical tents?

8. Analyze "The Stranger in the Bible" by Elie Wiesel (in *The Kingdom of Memory: Reminiscences* [New York: Schocken, 1995]) in relation to interfaith families and converts to Judaism. Wiesel describes the three terms Scripture uses for "stranger"—*ger, nokhri,* and *zar.* How do these terms apply to both the non-Jews and their Jewish spouses in modern American Jewish communities?

MEETINGS

❖ Organize a meeting on Jewish communal responses to interfaith marriage—"inreach" versus "outreach." Inreach focuses on strengthening the Jewish commitment of those who consider themselves and their children a part of the Jewish community. Outreach focuses on drawing interfaith couples and their children into the Jewish community. Because of limited finances, Jewish organizations must decide which response to emphasize. How are funds allocated in your community? How much responsibility does the community have to provide a hook or incentive to interfaith families? What individual and communal actions and attitudes could turn the alienated Jew and the non-Jewish spouse into a committed Jewish family?

As an exercise, have members imagine that they sit on the board of a foundation that funds Jewish continuity projects, and they are now examining grant proposals. Some proposals focus on inreach and some on outreach. Have different members present arguments for inreach and for outreach proposals. How would your "board" allocate funds?

❖ Invite two or three converts to Judaism to discuss their experiences. Why did they choose to become Jews? In what ways did they "try on" Judaism before making a commitment? How did they react to the conversion process? How has the Jewish community welcomed them? Many converts have reported that both Jewish communal organizations and individual Jews have been unwelcoming. If your speakers' experiences are similar, what action would they recommend? If possible, also invite a Jewish professional who works with non-Jews planning to convert to Judaism. What can the Jewish community, and in particular your Hadassah group or chapter, do to make converts, and those considering conversion, welcome?

❖ Conduct a role-playing workshop. Present role play assignments to small groups. One member should serve as moderator of this activity. First, allow a few minutes for the groups to decide how to present their role play. Then have the groups present their interpretations of the situations below. A few clarifying questions can be asked at the end of each presentation. After all the presentations are completed, discuss the different interpretations.

(a) You and your husband are Holocaust survivors. Your adult daughter brings her non-Jewish boyfriend home to meet you. How do you react?

(b) After several years of living together, your son announces his plans to marry his non-Jewish girlfriend. Decide whether or not to attend the wedding. Tell your son your decision.

(c) You and your daughter have not spoken since she married a non-Jewish man. Now your first grandchild has been born. You and your husband must decide whether to visit your daughter, son-in-law, and their new baby. What do you do?

(d) You are a Jewish woman in your twenties. You meet a wonderful non-Jewish man at a party and soon become serious. You date for eight years, and are still deeply in love. But your religious differences stand as an obstacle to marriage. What do you and he decide to do?

(e) Your daughter has been involved with a non-Jewish boyfriend, who is liked by everyone in your family, including you. She announces to you that she wants to marry him, but will not do so if you object. What do you say?

(f) You are a non-Jewish woman married to a Jewish man. Your wedding was a civil ceremony, and your husband's parents did not attend. You have now reconciled with your in-laws, and you and your husband have agreed to attend synagogue services to celebrate his nephew's becoming a bar mitzvah. How do you feel upon entering the synagogue?

ANNUAL EVENTS

❖ Organize an Education Day or Evening on interfaith marriage. Invite one or two Jewish scholars to speak, and hold a panel discussion with four to six Jews and non-Jews involved in interfaith marriages. The schedule below is adapted from the Pascack Valley Chapter of the Northern New Jersey Region's Education Day, organized by Jewish Education chair Barbara Newman. The panel discussion which is included as the day's third seminar is based on a session organized and moderated by Ruth G. Cole, currently National IZAIA Chair, for the Shatil Group of New York Chapter. Use the following schedule as a model, and adapt it to the expertise of speakers available in your community.

Interfaith Marriage—Crisis or Congratulations?

8:30-9:00   Registration and continental breakfast

9:00-9:15   **Introductory remarks** (delivered by chapter president)

9:15-10:30   **History of Interfaith Marriage** (delivered by historian)
Jews have been marrying non-Jews since biblical times. Historically, the rate of interfaith marriages (and of conversions) increases or decreases in response to societal antisemitism. The first Jewish interfaith marriage in America took place in 1654, only six years after Jews first arrived here. In the early years of the twentieth century, only two percent of American Jews married non-Jews. Today, half of all American Jews choose non-Jewish spouses.

10:45-12:00 **Interfaith Marriage and the American Jewish Community** (delivered by sociologist or demographer)
What percent of non-Jewish spouses convert to Judaism? What percent of Jewish spouses convert to their partner's religion (almost always Christianity)? About 40 percent of interfaith couples practice both religions in their home. In a minority of interfaith families, neither spouse follows any religious rituals. Will interfaith marriage undermine Judaism in America? How have the split on patrilineal descent and the "Who is a Jew" controversy affected interdenominational and Israel-diaspora relations?

12:15-1:30   Lunch

1:30-3:00   **Panel on Interfaith Marriage** (moderated by a Hadassah member)
Four panelists were interviewed: an adult child of an interfaith marriage; a Jewish man married to a Catholic woman, together raising a Jewish child; a Jewish woman married to a Catholic man; a female rabbi who herself was raised as a Methodist.

3:00-3:30   **Closing Remarks: What Our Community Can Do**

❖ Together with other Jewish community organizations (synagogues, women's groups, community centers, federations) sponsor an Introduction to Judaism seminar for converting Jews. Contact the Outreach Department of the Union of American Hebrew Congregations, 838 Fifth Avenue, New York, NY 10016; 212-650-4230.

❖ At an Education Day or Evening or at a Women's Symposium, hold one or two sessions on conversion to Judaism. One session might be a panel interview and discussion with four or five Jews by choice (refer to the "Meetings" section, pages 135-136), and one session could explore the history of conversion and offer current perspectives. Jewish tradition for the past 1,600 years has discouraged potential converts. For instance, rabbis require potential converts to ask three times to study Judaism before they are accepted as students. However, prior to the fourth century, proselytization was prevalent in Jewish communities. Then, in 315 Emperor Constantine prohibited male conversions to Judaism, and in 337 his son Constantius prohibited female conversions as well. Constantius also prohibited intermarriage between Jews and Christians. Continuing anti-Jewish bias prevented Jews from seeking converts for the next millennium and a half. Now, in the twentieth century, should we reconsider proselytizing?

HANDS-ON

❖ Sponsor a model Seder and invite interfaith families as the guests of your chapter or group. Have all participants take turns reading selections from the Haggadah aloud in English, and at intervals have Hadassah members read aloud their own explanations and personal reflections. Encourage questions and discussion, and sing Passover songs. Provide resource information for participants to take home.

❖ At your chapter or group meetings, set up a holiday table with the ritual objects and traditional foods of the next upcoming Jewish holiday. This will introduce the intermarried non-Jews to Jewish customs and traditions, and will provide concrete, non-threatening education on Jewish life. Provide take-home information about the holiday, its meaning and traditions. For brief profiles of the holidays, as well as resource lists of Jewish holiday guide books, contact the Jewish Education Department at 212-303-8167.

❖ Establish, or work with, a local Vanguard steering committee to help Jewish singles meet (and eventually marry each other). The Vanguard steering committee, made up of single Jewish women and men, plans and holds events that appeal to young singles. Call 212-303-8061 for more information on Vanguard.

PEERING INTO THE LIMBO OF JUDEO-CHRISTIAN

Rabbi Harold M. Schulweis

In the wake of Pope John Paul II's visit to America, a revival of Christian-Jewish anecdotes took place. One such story told of Cohen's conversion to Catholicism, for reasons unknown. The Knights of Columbus hosted a banquet in Cohen's honor. Called upon to speak, Cohen looked at his audience, devoted lay Catholics, priests, bishops, monsignors, and began his address: "Fellow *Goyim*."

That genre of Jewish humor is meant to console. It insinuates that the conversion has not taken and that an ineradicable residual identity remains: a Jew remains a Jew, even after conversion.

The challenge to Jewish identity comes less from outright conversion than from surreptitious deconversion. The hyphen, not the cross, dissolves Jewish identity. The Judeo-Christian hyphen is turned into a sign of identity. While Judaism and Christianity may appear different, stripped of externals, they are the same. Blue and white lights or red and green fixtures, hot-cross buns or *latkes*, they all signal the same directions.

The Judeo-Christian hyphenation is a theological triumph for those who sought to break the hyphen and free Christianity from its Jewish origins. The defenders of the Judeo-Christian link warned the church that for Christianity to sever its Jewish bonds is to attach Christianity to pagan roots. To cut the grafted branches from the good olive tree would cut off Christianity from its authenticating Jewish root (Romans 11:17). Yet for all the benefits in the grafted hyphen for Jews and Christians alike, there are serious liabilities in the assumption that deep down Judaism and Christianity are twin faiths without significant difference.

Consider the case of two attractive, intelligent, young people, very much in love, who enter my study. He, a Jew named Sam. She, a Christian named Peggy. Their object is matrimony, and the subject is a rabbi liberal enough to officiate at the mixed union or alongside a liberal priest. Neither seeks conversion. They seek an Equal Opportunity Cleric.

The challenge to Jewish identity comes less from outright conversion than from surreptitious deconversion. The hyphen, not the cross, dissolves Jewish identity. The Judeo-Christian hyphen is turned into a sign of identity.

They each have vague sentimental attachments to the faith in which they were raised and genuine filial fidelities to their parents. They have thought out the dilemma of raising their children. They will offer them the dual advantages of two religious civilizations. "If it's a boy, we'll have him both circumcised and baptized," they agree. Far from seeing conflict in the arrangement, they are convinced that the wisdom of both Old and New Testaments will enrich their lives and confirm Malachi: "Has not one Father created us. Has not one God made us." They see vindication in the similarities of the mother-sister traditions. Toward their own and each other's religious belief and practice, they offer benign neutrality.

The discussion wandered. At one point, possibly out of frustration, I asked them what they thought of my officiating as both rabbi and priest. They were taken aback at this bold ecumenicism. "You're not serious?" they asked. "Well, let's play it out. I know the church sacrament, the nuptial blessings, and I certainly know the seven blessings of the Judaic tradition," I said. Peggy thought such synchronistic virtuosity a bit too much. She couldn't quite conjure up the union of surplice and *tallit*, swinging rosaries and *tzitzit* fringes. Still, if we have one Father, why not one rabbi-priest?

They were not slow to see the *reductio ad absurdum* of my argument.

The rabbi-priest idea dropped, Peggy went on to explain that she was not a practicing Christian. Why then, I asked her, was it so important to have her child baptized? She answered with a personal anecdote of a cousin whose infant had died. "If that happened to me, I couldn't face the thought that my child was unbaptized." Unbaptized, her child would be suspended between heaven and hell, consigned to *limbus infantum*. I asked about the status of her husband-to-be. Would an unbaptized Sam be subject to limbo or damnation? Would her beloved Sam be saved? There followed a long and deep silence.

In that silence, I pondered over the neglect of Jewish theology and philosophy in Sam's life. Sam's Jewishness—he had attended a Jewish day school and performed well at his bar mitzvah—amounted to casual observances of a pastiche of rituals, a vague sentimentality toward

Jewishness, and an attachment to his Jewish parents.

But Judaism offered him no way of mapping the world, no distinctive view of human nature, God's character, or the quest for meaning. Sam was liberal in the manner of polytheists for whom every god is good enough. For Sam, and for Peggy as well, religions are all the same. If they appeared indifferent, it was because for them there were no true differences between the traditions. It seemed such a shame to dissolve a love because of a few ethnic residual memories. Preference for a colored Easter egg or a Seder burnt egg, a swaying evergreen or a shaking *lulav*, are more matters of taste than of principle.

But in truth there are radical differences between Christianity and Judaism and for their sake, and that of their children, Peggy and Sam ought to understand them, for they entail world views and values that affect them more than they think.

Original Sin and Other Differences

To begin with, Christianity is rooted in the dogma of original sin. By "original" is not meant the invention of new sins, but inherited sin (*erbsuende*) traced back to Adam and Eve's initial disobedience of God's prohibition against eating of the Tree of Knowledge. That *culpa originales* is transmitted to every living human action "by generation, not by initiation." That sin is not a consequence of an individual's choice, but is a congenital curse from which there is no human cure. Only by faith (*sola fide*) in the incarnation of the man-God and his unmerited kindness in dying for God's children is the stain of inherited sin wiped out. The crucified Christ is the sinless sacrifice that alone can loosen Eve's children from the grip of Satan.

"Whoever eats my flesh and drinks my blood has eternal life and I will raise him in the last day" (John 6:53). That promise is ritualized in the eucharist, mass, or communion sacrament wherein the miracle of transubstantiation or consubstantiation takes place. The wine and wafer are transformed into the blood and flesh of Christ crucified. To what degree of literalism such transformation is understood remains a Christian debate that need not concern us here. But no matter the version of the sacrament, it is a far cry from the wine of *kiddush* that remains wine and the *hallah* of the *motzi* that remains bread.

Baptism is a sacrament critical for Christian salvation. The Roman Catholic rite of baptism includes exorcism of the Prince of darkness. The priest blows on the face of the infant ordering the spirit of Satan to depart, moistens his thumb to touch the ears and nostrils of the infant, and asks the *patrini*—the sponsors of the child—to renounce the power and pomp of Satan. Those who are baptized and who believe are saved; those who refuse are stigmatized by the inherited sin that remains indelibly inscribed in the unredeemed soul. We may better appreciate Peggy's serious concern over the infant's baptism and her silence over its absence in Sam's life.

When during the trial of Adolph Eichmann, a Canadian Christian minister flew to Jerusalem to offer Eichmann's soul the opportunity to confess his belief in Christ, reporters asked him whether Eichmann's confession would save his soul. The minister affirmed that it would. Asked whether the soul of Eichmann's victims would be saved without such confession, he answered "no." "No one comes to the Father but by me," said Jesus, according to John 14:6.

For many of the Church fathers, Judaism is a vestigial anachronism, a "has been" whose purpose was that of *preparatio evangelica*, preparing the path for the good news of the advent of Christ. In the gospels of Matthew, Mark, and Luke, we read that on the day that Jesus died some forty years before the destruction of the Second Temple, the veil of the Temple was rent in twain from the top to the bottom. The Temple, the priests, the sacrificial system, and the authority of the Rabbis collapsed; the instruments for communion with God fell exclusively into the hands of the true believers in Christ crucified and resurrected.

It is noteworthy that the Christian Bible includes the Old Testament with the New Testament, but with a rearrangement of the order of the Old Testament books. The Jewish Bible (*Tanakh*) ends with the Writings, for instance, Proverbs, Psalms, and the concluding book of Chronicles, which contains a historical résumé of biblical history. The last verse in Chronicles II refers to Cyrus, King of Persia, who is charged by God to build His house in Jerusalem, that is, to rebuild the Temple. Cyrus, who in Isaiah 45:1 is referred to as Messiah—"anointed"—proclaims to the Jewish exiles: "Whoever is among you of His people, may the Lord be with him. Let him go up." In the Christian reordering of the Jewish Bible, the last books are from the Prophets, specifically the prophet Malachi. Here the last verse reads, "Lest I come and smite the earth with a curse." In this manner the Christian canonizer of the Old Testament has removed the hope of Jewish return to Zion and has replaced it with threat of Israel rejected. On that ordering of the testaments, Jesus succeeds and supplants the Hebrew prophets. With the reordering of the Hebrew texts, Israel's tragic destiny is scripturally foreshadowed. The old covenant is broken, and Israel depends for its redemption upon acceptance of the new covenant and the resurrected Savior.

And, the universal burden of original sin [is compounded for Jews by] the particular sin of deicide, the betrayal and killing of the son of God. The episode of the Roman procurator Pontius Pilate, washing his hands of the blood of the Jews to be crucified and the obdurate insistence of the mob of [Romans and] Jews crying "Crucify him!" is dramatized in Easter Passion plays and in such commercial dramas as *Godspell* and *Jesus Christ Superstar*. To the contagion of the original sin is added the culpability for the rejection and mortification of Jesus. The chilling words in Matthew 27:25 put into the mouths of the Jewish mob, "His blood be on us and on our children," augurs the history of contempt for "the perfidious Jew" so virulent in the hands of the mobs as to defy even the restraints of higher church officials.

Baptism and Circumcision

Sam and Peggy are oblivious to the theological, moral, and emotional contradiction in circumcision and baptism. For them, both are items of ritual choreography devoid of theological roots or psychological consequences. But baptism and circumcision are far from complementary dramas. Baptism is predicated upon an anthropological pessimism. Man is born in the womb of sin. Since there is nothing that a sinner can do in terms of works or reparation to expiate that innate and humanly ineradicable blemish, his sole recourse is to throw himself upon a supernatural Other who assumed the burden of suffering atonement for all others. For all others, the atonement is gained vicariously. As Luther expressed it, the believer becomes *velut paralyticum*, as one paralyzed, abandoning the conceit of his own deeds, utterly dependent on the self-sacrifices of the innocent lamb of God.

Circumcision is the initiation into the covenant with God and Abraham. The eight-day old child carries no baggage of sin with him into the world. He is no alien flung into the hands of demonic powers. The Christian infant prior to his baptism is a pagan; the Jewish child is Jewish even before or without the rite of circumcision. The Jewish child is born innocent, body and soul, created and sustained in God's image. He has no need to be saved because no Satan threatens him, no eternal damnation hovers over him. As a Jew he will be raised in a tradition that mandates him to save lives, not souls.

For Christianity, man sins because he is a sinner. For Judaism, man sins when he sins. Of course, he will sin—not because he enters the world condemned as a sinner, but because he is a fallible human being and "there is no righteous human being who has done good and does not transgress" (Ecclesiastes). The sin is his or hers, the choice is his or hers, and the reparation to be done is his or hers.

No one can sin for another, cry or die for another, or absolve another. No confessors, intercessors, surrogates, or substitutes can stand in for another's turning from sin. No one can shower, bathe, clean himself that the other shall be clean. "Wash yourself clean," Isaiah addresses the penitent. "Put away the evil doings from before Mine eyes; cease to do evil, learn to do well; seek judgment, relieve the oppressed, the fatherless; plead for the widow." Communion with God is without rabbinic or priestly mediation. "Blessed are you Israel. Before whom are you purified and who purifies you? Your Father who is in heaven" (*Yoma* 85b).

The divine-human connection in Judaism is unmediated. Moreover, whereas in Christianity the relationship between self and God is a vertical relationship, the Jewish connection with God is horizontal. The horizontal human transactions that call for reparation, forgiveness, and apology for the injuries of others cannot be skipped over by a vertical leap between the individual and God in heaven, ignoring the proper relationships with God's children on earth. The prophet Ezekiel makes it clear what the truly penitent is to do: "If the wicked one restores the pledge, gives back what he has robbed, walks in the statutes of life ... he shall surely live ... none of the sins he has committed shall be remembered against him" (Ezekiel 33:15-16).

Baptism emphasizes the paralysis of the human will, helpless without God combating Satan. The covenant of circumcision focuses on the competence of the human being to exercise control over his life. To the sulking Cain, depressed over his act of fratricide, the Torah counsels, "Sin crouches at the door but you may rule over it."

Salvation is not for Jews alone. In Judaism, those who do not believe our way or pray our way are not threatened with divine anathema. In rabbinic literature, heaven and earth are called to witness that "whether they be gentile or Jew, man or woman, slave or free man, the Divine Presence rests on each one according to his deeds" (*Yalkut Shimoni, Tanya Debei Elijah*). The people of Nineveh (in the Book of Jonah) are spared because of their deeds, not their conversion to Judaism; because of their turning from evil ways, not their acceptance of the Sabbath and festivals. Jews do not seek to convert the world to Judaism but to convert the world to righteousness, justice, and peace.

Sam and Peggy must be given to understand that circumcision is not baptism. They are not knife or water alternatives, but ritualized dramas of values, affecting their relationships to God, world, neighbor, and self. Baptism depends upon belief in a specific divine person who walked the face of the earth. In Judaism there are no such incarnate divine beings, whether clothed as patriarchs, priests, or prophets. There is no Jewish beatification or canonization of saints, no apotheosis of blood-and-flesh heroes, no doctrine or infallibility.

The heroes of Israel are magnificent, but not so special that they are to be obeyed without question.

Family Ties

Peggy spoke warmly of the Jewish family. Family is one of the consistent praises of Jewish life that rabbis hear from non-Jews. The primacy of family is not irrelevant to the horizontal theological frame of Judaism. The family and its friends are rooted in a tradition that does not tolerate the schism of love between humans and that between humans and God. Nowhere in Jewish religious literature could one find, even remotely, the approach to the family that Jesus expresses in the gospel in Luke and Matthew. "If any man comes to me and hates not his father and mother and wife and children and brothers and sisters—yea and his own life also, he cannot be my disciple" (Luke 14:26). In Judaism, Jews come to God through their families and friends, not through sacrifice of their relationship nor the sacrifice of self. Divinity yields its character not through the subtraction of humanity, not through the elimination of the self, but through the love and care of human others and self. Jesus declares, "For I have not come to bring peace on earth but a sword. For I have come to set man against his father and a daughter against her mother, and a daughter-in-law against her mother-in-law." For Jesus, the believer is confronted with a hard, exclusive disjunctive. Either heaven or earth, either Christ or family, either Jesus or self. "He who loves father or mother more than me is not worthy of me" (Matthew 10:34). In Christianity, one cannot come to the Father except through the Son. In Judaism, one cannot come to the Father except through the earthly sons and daughters of one's human family.

These are not easy instructions for Peggy and Sam to hear. But it is important that the difference in their birth traditions not be trivialized. The theological differences between Christianity and Judaism are likely to cast cultural and moral penumbra larger than they may have imagined. They may come to understand that genuine tolerance does not entail indiscriminate adoption of all faiths and that openness does not mean to reduce all traditions to sameness.

They may come to recognize conversation as not discrediting the other's faith but as flowing from an awareness of the profound dissonance between religious cultures. Their resolve to hold incompatible traditions in one household would not only distort the uniqueness of each faith civilization but compromise their own integrity. With the best of intentions, Peggy and Sam thought to offer their offspring the best of religion. But, to paraphrase Santayana, such is the attempt of those who would speak in general without using any language in particular. Judaism and Christianity are particular languages, with precious, unique syntaxes, which when thrown together produce a babble of tongues.

Sam and Peggy have important decisions to make. If they build their lives on the narrow edge of the Judeo-Christian hyphen, they offer their children the fate of Disraeli. He became the British Prime Minister of Queen Victoria, was converted to Christianity by his father, and yet held pridefully the glories of his Jewish ancestry. Queen Victoria is reported to have asked him, "What are you, Disraeli? Which Testament is yours?" He replied with sadness, "I am, dear Queen, the blank page between the Old and the New Testament."

Hopefully, Sam and Peggy will learn to recognize and respect the uniqueness and difference of the Jewish and Christian outlook and not lead their children to inherit the blank page of the Testaments. For all the commonality between Christianity and Judaism, the hyphen between the cross and the Star of David is no sign of identity.

Editors' note: The theological concepts discussed by Rabbi Schulweis— original sin, the value of good works, the age of baptism, the value of family ties, etc.—vary widely among different Christian denominations and even within certain Christian denominations. Rabbi Schulweis has selected representative interpretations of Christian thought to present an extremely broad overview.

Reprinted in Jewish Marital Status: A Hadassah Study, *Carol Diament, ed. (Northvale, NJ: Jason Aronson, 1989), pages 238-245. Originally published in the* Baltimore Jewish Times, *December 18, 1987.*

RABBI HAROLD M. SCHULWEIS of Valley Beth Shalom in Encino, California, is the author of Evil and the Morality of God *and* For Those Who Can't Believe: Overcoming the Obstacles to Faith.

PROGRAMMING IDEAS

AT HOME

Torah Table Talk   A discussion of Jewish thought and values with your family and/or friends. The emperor Napoleon Bonaparte was the first European ruler to grant Jews in his domain citizenship (although he did place limitations on Jews' rights). Emancipation of French Jews, however, was conditional. Jews could no longer declare themselves to be a separate nation within France, and they were bound to follow French law even when it conflicted with Jewish law.

Prior to granting French Jews citizenship, Napoleon convened an Assembly of Jewish Notables, who would declare France's Jews to be "Frenchmen" and "faithful subjects." These Notables, who were chosen by French officials, deliberated from July to August 1806, answering twelve questions on Jewish law. The following is the third question posed by Napoleon, along with the answer approved by the Assembly. Because the final answers of the Assembly did not seem sufficiently authoritative, the emperor then gathered together a more impressive council, called the "Great Sanhedrin," to approve and publicize the conclusions of the Assembly. The excerpt below is found in *Modern Jewish History: A Source Reader* (edited by Robert Chazan and Marc Lee Raphael [New York: Schocken, 1969], pages 20-21), and is reprinted from *Transactions of the Parisian Sanhedrin or Acts of the Assembly of Israelitish Deputies of France and Italy*, collected by Diogene Tama and translated by F. D. Kirwan (published in London in 1807).

Acts of the Assembly of Israelitish Deputies of France and Italy

Third Question: Can a Jewess marry a Christian, and a Jew a Christian woman? Or does the law allow the Jews to intermarry [marry] only among themselves?

Answer: The law does not say that a Jewess cannot marry a Christian, nor a Jew a Christian woman; nor does it state that the Jews can only intermarry among themselves.

The only marriages expressly forbidden by the law are those with the seven Canaanite nations, with Amon and Moab, and with the Egyptians. The prohibition is absolute concerning the seven Canaanite nations; with regard to Amon and Moab, it is limited, according to many Talmudists, to the men of those nations, and does not extend to the women; it is even thought that these last would have embraced the Jewish religion. As to Egyptians, the prohibition is limited to the third generation. The prohibition in general applies only to nations in idolatry. The Talmud declares formally that modern nations are not to be considered as such, since they worship, like us, the God of heaven and earth. And, accordingly, there has been, at several periods, intermarriage between Jews and Christians in France, in Spain, and in Germany; these marriages were sometimes tolerated and sometimes forbidden by the laws of those sovereigns who had received Jews into their dominions.

Unions of this kind are still found in France; but we cannot dissemble that the opinion of the rabbis is against these marriages. According to their doctrine, although the religion of Moses has not forbidden the Jews from intermarrying with nations not of their religion, yet as marriage, according to the Talmud, requires religious ceremonies called *kiddushin*, with the benediction used in such cases, no marriage can be *religiously* valid unless these ceremonies have been performed. This could not be done toward persons who would not both of them consider these ceremonies as sacred; and in that case the married couple could separate without the *religious* divorce; they would then be considered as married *civilly* but not *religiously*.

Such is the opinion of the rabbis, members of this assembly. In general they would be no more inclined to bless the union of a Jewess with a Christian, or of a Jew with a Christian woman, than Catholic priests themselves would be disposed to sanction unions of this kind.

Questions for Thought and Discussion

1. The Assembly of Notables, according to Professors Robert Chazan and Marc Lee Raphael, had greater difficulty answering Napoleon's third question than any other. And the answer, "which divided Jewish law into nonexistent categories, was unique in its historical importance as well as its ingenuity."

For the category of expressly forbidden marriage, the Assembly refers to Deuteronomy 7:1-4: "When the Lord your God brings you to the land that you are about to enter and possess, and He dislodges many nations before you—the Hittites, Girgashites, Amorites, Canaanites, Perizzites, Hivites, and Jebusites, seven nations much larger than you—and the Lord your God delivers them to you and you defeat them, you must doom them to destruction: grant them no terms and give them no quarter. You shall not intermarry with them: do not give your daughters to their sons or take their daughters for your sons. For they will turn your children away from Me to worship other gods, and the Lord's anger will blaze forth against you and He will promptly wipe you out."

What reason does the Bible give for the ban against marrying the seven nations of Canaan? What are the consequences for those who disobey God's word? How were the deputies of the Assembly able to use this passage to divide "Jewish law into nonexistent categories"?

2. The Assembly also differentiated between religiously valid marriage and civilly valid marriage. Today in America, categorization of marriage as either civil or religious is so accepted as to seem self-evident. However, prior to 1806, the non-religious civil marriage was an anomaly and an original conception. Discuss.

3. Professors Robert Chazan and Marc Lee Raphael state that an accommodation by the Deputies of the Assembly, allowing Jews to marry non-Jews "would ignore fifteen hundred years of clear Jewish legislation against intermarriage." What tactics did the Assembly use to avoid making such an accommodation and also to avoid clearly stating that Jewish law definitely forbids interfaith marriage?

4. What does the Assembly's answer say about Jewish-gentile relations in nineteenth-century France?

5. Historian Baruch Mevorah writes: "At first sight, it would appear that the drafters of the regulations subordinated Jewish law to that of the state, but in reality they did not undermine halakhic principles" ("Sanhedrin, French" in *Encyclopaedia Judaica*, volume 14, page 841). How were the rabbis and laymen of the French Sanhedrin able to interpret Jewish law to meet the demands of their time? What does this imply for today's halakhic authorities?

INTEREST/STUDY GROUPS

Hold a discussion based on the following questions:

1. Should each partner of an interfaith couple study the tenets and rituals of the other's religion? Why or why not? Should they give particular emphasis to the similarities and the differences between their religions? Why?

2. What are "the dual advantages of two religious civilizations" which the hypothetical Sam and Peggy wish to offer their children? What are the disadvantages of a two-religion household for children?

3. Rabbi Schulweis lists a number of differences between Judaism and Christianity: original sin; baptism versus circumcision; cleansing oneself of sin; and the role of family. Which difference do you find most significant? Why? What other theological differences would you add to Rabbi Schulweis's list?

4. Discuss guilt and sin in Jewish and Christian theology and in associated customs and ideas. (Note that in different Christian denominations, concepts of sin vary widely. For instance, the seventeenth-century Puritans strongly emphasized human sinfulness.) How is sin a women's issue? Consider that both

Jews and Christians trace the first sin back to Eve! How has Eve's disobedience affected both Christian and Jewish attitudes toward women? How does the Christian concept of original sin affect women?

5. Describe in writing a model for marriage and family life between a Jew and a non-Jew that most likely will not result in an inheritance of "the blank page between the Old and the New Testaments." When all study group members have completed this task, share your efforts.

MEETINGS

❖ Invite a professor of religion, a rabbi, or other scholar to explain basic theological differences between Judaism and Christianity, including differences between Jewish and Christian concepts of marriage and family. As part of the meeting, examine both a Jewish and a Christian calendar to point out how theological differences translate into different attitudes toward time, daily life, and sanctity. (Note differences between "high church" and "low church" calendars.) Follow the talk with a discussion session.

❖ Invite an ethnotherapist to discuss her or his work with interfaith couples. Ethnotherapy is counseling aimed at recognizing, confronting, and accepting the cultural and psychological differences between marital partners of two different ethnic backgrounds. How do Jews and Christians see themselves and each other? What are the cultural pressures? How are they affected by their differing ethnic heritages?

ANNUAL EVENTS

❖ Refer to the "Annual Events" section of "The Jewish Community in Crisis—Two Views of Intermarriage" to organize an Education Day on interfaith marriage, pages 136-137.

HANDS-ON

❖ Hold a panel discussion between members of your chapter or group and members of a Christian women's group. If possible, choose a women's group with a mission similar to Hadassah's—providing funds for medical care or for overseas educational aid or children's welfare.

ADVICE ON RAISING CHILDREN OF INTERMARRIAGE

Paul Cowan and Rachel Cowan

Think About Your Child's Jewish Status

This consideration is important for couples who decide to raise Jewish children. There are now two different working definitions of who is a Jew. According to *halakhah* (Jewish law), a child of a Jewish mother and gentile father is a Jew by birth, while the child of a Jewish father and gentile mother must be converted in order to be a Jew. The Orthodox and Conservative movements of Judaism adhere to that law. By contrast, Reform and Reconstructionist Jews assert that if either parent is a Jew, the child is a Jew if he or she is raised as one.

The distinction, which is hotly debated among rabbis and Jewish leaders, is very hard for many gentiles to understand. If the gentile mother has any doubts about raising Jewish children in the first place, the thought that they might have to be converted adds to her fear of separation. Many couples, even those who have decided they want their children to be Jewish, are not willing to grant Jewish law authority over their lives.

However, children who have not been converted often describe the pain and anger they feel when they are told they can't celebrate a bar or bat mitzvah in a Conservative synagogue, or join an Orthodox synagogue, or when the traditional Jew they love refuses to date them or marry them unless they become legally Jewish. We have met many people who have been angry at their parents for not making them halakhically

Jewish when they were young. They feel they would have been spared a lot of turmoil.

Think Carefully About The Neighborhood You'll Live In and the Schools You Choose For Your Children

If you want to raise your children as Jews, don't move into a predominantly Catholic or Protestant neighborhood. If you want to raise your children as Christians, don't move into a predominantly Jewish community. If you want to raise them without any religious affiliation, don't move into an area that is primarily populated by religiously observant people. Otherwise, they will feel like outsiders among their friends.

Be Aware of the Attitudes of Significant Relatives

Often grandparents, aunts, and uncles may be prejudiced against the person who has married their child or sibling, or may be troubled about their religion. Sometimes they see the grandchildren as their allies, and seek to communicate their biases, or to convert them to the religion that they believe is true. In the South we met many couples who were confused about how to handle relatives who were born-again Christians. They didn't want to prevent a child from seeing a grandparent. But how could they stop these fervent Christians from baptizing their youngsters in their eagerness to save them from going to hell? After long discussions in their workshops, several decided that they would invite their parents or siblings to their home to spend time with the children, but not let the children go off to visit them.

Some children of intermarriages recalled feeling wounded and jealous when they saw how obviously their Jewish grandparents favored their cousins who had two Jewish parents over them. The cousins would be invited for all the holidays, would get more presents, and would be hugged with much warmer embraces.

Be Careful How You Teach About The Holocaust

Many parents try to create a child's Jewish identity with stories about the Holocaust. No one is served if Judaism is presented as a religion of fear: a passport to the gas ovens.

Some intermarried Jewish parents tell their children that Hitler would have considered them Jewish and killed them along with all other Jews. The reminder is supposed to give them a sense a identity. Instead, it terrifies them. They are not given any other pathway into Jewish life. With no sense of a large, vibrant Jewish community, with no larger frame of reference, they imagine the Holocaust as the terrifying sum of Jewish history, as the sole content of Judaism.

Don't Suppress a Parent's Past

If the parent whose faith isn't practiced suppresses his or her ethnic background, a child can spend much of a lifetime trying to unearth it. For children idolize their parents. They fantasize about them, trying to imagine their childhoods, seeking to reconstruct important personal facts or marital bargains that seem to have been hidden.

That happened to me. From my boyhood until the day my father died, I was always aware of the fact that he had once been a Cohen and was now a Cowan, and that he had a father with a past that I wasn't permitted to know about. He and I had an unusually close relationship. We talked on the telephone several times a week, and met for lunch or supper at least once every two weeks. During the last ten years of his life, he was either bedridden or in the hospital for months at a stretch, and I visited him frequently. We always discussed political developments or trends in the arts, books he was reading or stories I was writing. But, even though he knew how curious I was about his father, he would never describe him or discuss the Jewish aspect of his childhood.

I didn't try to provoke him to talk. I respected the fact that the mere mention of Jake Cohen's name caused him a great deal of pain. But within weeks of my father's death I set out to discover his hidden past. As I learned about it, I began to alter my picture of the Judaism my parents had transmitted to me. But I wasn't forced to choose one parent's faith over another's, as I might have been if my mother was a gentile and my father had concealed his history in order to placate her.

Make Religion A Life Style, Not A Label

If a religion is no more than a family label, it is not likely to mean much to children. If it seems to signal that one partner has won a marital struggle, that the other's identity has been ripped at the seams, it may provoke turmoil.

It is prudent for parents to work out ways of embodying the religion of one without hiding the other's past. Those who choose to weave Judaism into their lives display tact and foresight if they visit the Christian in-laws at crucial moments of their religious and secular year. Most of all, it is important for the couple, as a unit, to remember that they are their children's primary role models. If they embody a grudging sense that one is acquiescing to the other, they convey a negative, hostile message to their children. If they display loving sensitivity to each other's spiritual sensibilities, they convey a positive, optimistic one.

Lisa Cowan is our daughter. In 1986, she entered college. When we asked if we could interview her for the book, she laughed and said, "I don't really think of myself as the child of people with two religious backgrounds."

But then she recalled that she did have one worry when she was younger—that Rachel's parents would feel rejected. She described the episode that assuaged that fear.

"Remember when we were visiting Maggie [Rachel's mother] one Easter when it was also Passover? We brought along enough *matzah* for all of us, but it was before we had completely given up eating bread during Passover. Maggie brought out a plate of warm hot cross buns for breakfast. Mom picked one up. She said, 'This is my heritage!' I remember the pride on her face when she said it. I'm not sure whether she ate the bun, but I was glad to see her show pride in her past. I didn't like the feeling that she had turned her back on her family."

"Does my conversion ever trouble you?" Rachel asked.

I was a little disappointed when we stopped celebrating Christmas. Who wouldn't be? I loved all the excitement. But now I think it would be wrong to have a Christmas tree. I don't mean morally wrong. It would just feel wrong.

"No! Judaism seems so normal to me that I don't quite understand people who belong to another religion. But then I think, what if Matt became a Buddhist? What if he stopped doing all the things we've been doing since we were little? No matter how much he explained it—or it helped him grow—I'd still think it was strange. So I was glad when Mom did something to show her parents that she was still proud of them and what they gave her."

When Lisa was in high school, she seldom came to synagogue with us except on the High Holy Days. But lighting candles on Friday night was special. That was a religious experience for her.

"Well, maybe not religious exactly. I don't know if I believe in God. But it was the purest form of family time I've ever known. It had a quality of ... wholeness, which is the same kind of feeling I get when I'm in direct communication with nature or feel in communication with myself."

Then she laughed a little self-consciously. "I hate to put these things into words. It sounds so totally corny. But when I feel it, I know it."

The sense of family tradition was important to her. "This year, when I stayed at school during Yom Kippur, I went to service. It's not that I like being in synagogue that much. But I feel like I'm linked to my family."

Although she is an agnostic, she made it clear that the religion her parents chose gives her a sense of place and of internal order.

"I was a little disappointed when we stopped celebrating Christmas. Who wouldn't be? I loved all the excitement. But now I think it would be wrong to have a Christmas tree. I don't mean morally wrong. It would just feel wrong. It's the same thing during Passover. I don't eat *hametz* [leavened foods]. It's a tradition I care about. It wouldn't feel right to eat bread. It would be like eating pork."

Toward the end of the interview, we told her that a great many children of intermarried couples resent their parents' thoughtlessness or indecisiveness. If she could give us retroactive advice about her religious upbringing, what would she say?

She began to laugh. "I don't know. I can't think of anything. You're both such different people, but you share the same values. Even though you had different religions when I was born, I don't feel like the child of an intermarriage. Judaism is a part of me."

Coda

Most intermarried people who choose to make religion a way of life and not a label begin by doing so for their children. But in fact they are untying a knot at the core of their marriage. For even if the child ultimately rejects their way of life—as some will—the husband and wife have resolved their own dilemma.

They have transformed the problem of an intermarriage into the opportunity to fashion a faith they can share for a lifetime.

Reprinted in Jewish Marital Status: A Hadassah Study, Carol Diament, ed. (Northvale, NJ: Jason Aronson, 1989), pages 253-260. Originally published in Paul Cowan with Rachel Cowan, Mixed Blessings: Marriage Between Jews and Christians (New York: Doubleday, 1987), excerpted from pages 245-266.

PAUL COWAN, journalist and author of An Orphan in History, died in 1988.

RACHEL COWAN converted to Judaism after fifteen years of marriage. While writing Mixed Blessings she was a rabbinical student. Rabbi Cowan currently serves as Director of the Jewish Life Program of the Nathan Cummings Foundation of New York.

PROGRAMMING IDEAS

AT HOME

Torah Table Talk   A discussion of Jewish thought and values with your family and/or friends. From 1906 onward, "A Bintel Brief" (a bundle of letters), the advice column in the Yiddish-language *Jewish Daily Forward*, was a voice of authority for bewildered and impoverished Yiddish-speaking immigrants trying to learn about their new country and build new lives. By mid-century, the letters to "A Bintel Brief" reflected new problems—and were frequently written in English.

The letter below, written during the seventies, is found in *A Bintel Brief: Letters to the Jewish Daily Forward, Volume 2: 1950-1980*, ed. Isaac Metzker (New York: Viking, 1981), pages 143-145.

Letter to the Jewish Daily Forward

Dear Editor:

Several times I have read in your paper about mixed marriages and each time I am reminded of our own experience because the same thing happened to us.

We have two children, a son and a daughter. We gave them a Jewish upbringing and we always observed Jewish tradition in our home. We are not Orthodox (my husband keeps the store open on Saturday), but I always kept a kosher kitchen and we go to synagogue on Rosh Hashanah and Yom Kippur. Our son has a fine Jewish wife, and they lead a life like ours. Our daughter, who is seven years younger than our son, fell in love with a Christian boy while she was in college, and we didn't know anything about it for a while.

Once when she made a party at home she also invited her Christian friend. Although my husband and I spent the whole evening in another room in order not to interfere with the young people, I noticed the blond young boy and realized that he was not Jewish. I also felt that my daughter was very interested in him. That night I didn't sleep, and the next morning I had a talk with my daughter. But neither my talking nor my husband's had any effect. Her answer was that she loved him. We couldn't tear her away from this young man, who is a professional, and in time they were married. They moved far away from us, and we didn't see them for a year. I missed my daughter very much, and then one day she came to see us unexpectedly to tell us she was expecting a child in a few months, that her husband was going to convert to Judaism, and that they wanted a Jewish name for their child.

In short, our son-in-law became a Jew. Our daughter gave birth to a daughter, and the child was given a Jewish name in the synagogue. I want to say that it is not a question of asking someone else for advice as how to act in these matters. One has to act as the heart dictates.

With respect,

Mrs. B. R.

Answer:

These days it is not news when children bring home non-Jewish sons- or daughters-in-law to their parents. To our regret, the number of mixed marriages is increasing. Jewish parents, even those who are not religious, do not approve of mixed marriages, but enough parents make peace with it in time because their love for their children is stronger than anything else.

    The fact that your son-in-law converted must make you very happy, and you were right not to get angry and to keep a close relationship with the couple. Your comment that one cannot ask advice from others in a matter of this sort is correct. It is a private family matter, and each one must handle it according to his or her feelings and principles.

Questions for Thought and Discussion

1. Mrs. B. R. says that when children marry, the parent "has to act as the heart dictates." Do you agree? What if the heart's dictates are confusing and contradictory?

2. Do you agree with the editor's response that a child's interfaith marriage is "a private family matter, and each one must handle it according to his feelings and principles"? Or does interfaith marriage involve the entire Jewish community? Both? In what ways?

3. Assuming that Mrs. B. R. is typical of Jewish parents of the seventies, discuss how reactions to interfaith marriage have changed over the last twenty years. How have they stayed the same?

4. For Mrs. B. R., her daughter's marriage ultimately has a happy outcome, as the daughter eventually establishes a Jewish home with her newly Jewish husband. Yet about two-thirds of all interfaith marriages today result in either a dual-faith household or an entirely Christian household. How would you react to this letter had the husband remained a non-Jew? How might Mrs. B. R. have reacted?

Additional At-Home Activities

❖ Discuss interfaith dating and marriage with your children. If you are sure of your feelings, you need to express your views and guide your child. If you are ambivalent, discuss the topic with people whose opinions you respect. This will help you to clarify your own views.

INTEREST/STUDY GROUPS

Hold a discussion based on the following questions:

1. Paul and Rachel Cowan offer six areas of advice for parents. Which do you think is the most important for the well-being of the child? Which do you think is the most important for the well-being of the parents? Which is the most important for the well-being of the family? What other advice would you offer?

(a) Think about your child's Jewish status.

(b) Think carefully about the neighborhood you'll live in and the school you choose for your children.

(c) Be aware of the attitudes of significant relatives.

(d) Be careful how you teach about the Holocaust.

(e) Don't suppress a parent's past.

(f) Make religion a life style, not a label.

2. Many interfaith couples ignore the question of family religious practices

until children are born, or until the children reach religious school age. What are the pluses and minuses of waiting to deal with religion until children are involved?

3. Brainstorm on ways "to make religion a life style and not merely a label." One person should write down "raw" ideas as they come to mind. When the list is complete—when no one can come up with any additional items—discuss what you have come up with, and possibly rank the suggestions according to their importance. The list, along with explanatory comments, could make a good article for your chapter or region bulletin!

MEETINGS

❖ Invite a rabbi and/or a child psychologist to discuss religious affiliation as part of the identity formation of a child. Can children be raised in two religions without conflict? How do children of interfaith couples regard their own identity during childhood, adolescence, and adulthood?

❖ Invite several adult children of interfaith marriages to participate in a panel discussion based on Paul and Rachel Cowan's "Advice on Raising Children of Intermarriage." Which aspects of the Cowans' advice do the panelists consider most important? What other advice would they offer? How did the panelists come to their current religious affiliations? (Refer to the panel discussion on interfaith marriage, page 137).

ANNUAL EVENTS

❖ Refer to the "Annual Events" section of "The Jewish Community in Crisis—Two Views of Intermarriage" to organize an Education Day on interfaith marriage, pages 136-137.

HANDS-ON

❖ Establish (or work with) a Training Wheels group to familiarize young families with Jewish life. Training Wheels/*Al Galgalim* offers a curriculum for nine monthly parent-and-child sessions that introduce families to Jewish holiday celebrations. No prior Jewish knowledge is assumed. A pre-school curriculum is available and an early grade school curriculum is currently being compiled. Call the National Hadassah Training Wheels Department at 1-800-391-3339 or 212-303-8284 for further details.

❖ Establish, or encourage young Jewish singles to establish, a Vanguard steering committee. Vanguard plans and holds lectures, dances, outings, and other events where Jewish singles can meet and get to know each other. Call Hadassah's National Membership Division at 212-303-8061 for more information on Vanguard.

RECOMMENDED READING

Sexuality and Judaism

Adler, Rachel. "Tumah and Taharah—Mikveh," in *The First Jewish Catalog*, ed. Richard Siegel, Michael Strassfeld, and Sharon Strassfeld. Philadelphia: Jewish Publication Society, 1973. Pages 167-171.

Beck, Evelyn Torton, ed. *Nice Jewish Girls: A Lesbian Anthology.* Boston: Beacon, 1989.

Biale, David. *Eros and the Jews: From Biblical Israel to Contemporary America.* New York: Basic Books, 1992.

Biale, Rachel. *Women and Jewish Law: An Exploration of Women's Issues in Halakhic Sources.* New York: Schocken, 1984.

Borowitz, Eugene. *Choosing a Sex Ethic.* New York: Schocken, 1969.

Brewer, Joan Scherer. *Sex and the Modern Jewish Woman: An Annotated Bibliography.* New York: Biblio, 1986.

Feldman, David. *Marital Relations, Birth Control and Abortion in Jewish Law.* New York: Schocken, 1974.

Gittelsohn, Roland B. *Love, Sex, and Marriage.* New York: UAHC, 1980.

Goldstein, Rabbi Elyse. "Take Back the Waters: A Feminist Re-Appropriation of Mikvah," *Lilith Magazine*, Summer 1986, pages 15-16.

Gordis, Robert. *Love and Sex: A Modern Jewish Perspective.* New York: Farrar Straus Giroux, 1978.

Greenberg, Blu. *On Women and Judaism: A View from Tradition.* Philadelphia: Jewish Publication Society, 1981.

Heschel, Susannah, ed. *On Being a Jewish Feminist.* New York: Schocken, 1983.

Koltun, Elizabeth, ed. *The Jewish Woman: New Perspectives.* New York: Schocken, 1976.

Schneider, Susan Weidman. *Jewish and Female.* New York: Simon & Schuster, 1984.

Mothers and Daughters in Fiction

Epstein, Seymour. *Leah.* Philadelphia: Jewish Publication Society, 1987.

Fishman, Sylvia Barack, ed. *Follow My Footprints: Changing Images of Women in Contemporary American Jewish Fiction*. Hanover and London: Brandeis University Press, 1992.

Gornick, Vivian. *Fierce Attachments*. New York: Touchstone, 1988.

Merkin, Daphne. *Enchantment*. San Diego: Harcourt Brace, 1986.

Ozick, Cynthia. *The Cannibal Galaxy*. New York: NAL/Dutton, 1984.

Paley, Grace. *Later the Same Day*. New York: Viking Penguin, 1986.

Potok, Chaim. *Davita's Harp*. New York: Knopf, 1985.

Roiphe, Anne. *Lovingkindness*. New York: Warner, 1989.

Wouk, Herman. *Marjorie Morningstar*. Reprint; New York: Little, Brown, 1992.

Yezierska, Anzia. *The Open Cage*. Reprint; New York: Persea, 1993.

Mothers and Daughters—Non-Fiction

Barker, Teresa. *The Mother-Daughter Book Club*. New York: Harper Perennial, 1997.

Bassoff, Evelyn. *Mothers and Daughters: Loving and Letting Go*. New York: NAL, 1988.

Jonas, Susan, and Nissenson, Marilyn. *Friends for Life: Enriching the Bond Between Mothers and Their Adult Daughters*. New York: William Morrow, 1997.

Lowinsky, Naomi. *The Motherline: Every Women's Journey to Find Her Female Roots*. Los Angeles: Jeremy P. Tarcher/Perigee, 1992.

McGoldrick, Monica, Anderson, Carol M., and Walsh, Froma, eds. *Women in Families*. New York: W. W. Norton, 1991.

Secunda, Victoria. *When You and Your Mother Can't Be Friends: Resolving the Most Complicated Relationship of Your Life*. New York: Dell, 1990.

Waterhouse, Debra. *Like Mother, Like Daughter: How Women Are Influenced by Their Mothers' Relationship with Food—and How to Break the Pattern*. New York: Hyperion, 1997.

Interfaith Marriage

Cowan, Paul, and Cowan, Rachel. *Mixed Blessings: Marriage Between Jews and Christians*. New York: Doubleday, 1987.

Dershowitz, Alan M. *The Vanishing American Jew: In Search of Jewish Identity for the Next Century*. New York: Little, Brown, 1997.

Diament, Carol, ed. *Jewish Marital Status*, Northvale, NJ: Jason Aronson, 1989. See "Intermarried," pages 221-260.

Jacobs, Sidney and Betty. *122 Clues for Jews Whose Children Intermarry*. Culver City, CA: Jacobs Ladder Publications, 1988.

King, Andrea. *If I'm Jewish and You're Christian, What Are the Kids? A Parenting Guide for Interfaith Families*. New York: UAHC, 1993.

Levin, Sunie. *Mingled Roots: A Guide for Jewish Parents of Interfaith Grandchildren*. Washington, DC: B'nai B'rith Women, 1992.

Mayer, Egon. *Love and Tradition: Marriage Between Jews and Christians*. New York: Plenum, 1985.

Petsonk, Judy, and Remsen, Jim. *The Intermarriage Handbook: A Guide for Jews and Christians*. New York: Arbor House/William Morrow, 1988.

Schneider, Susan Weidman. *Intermarriage: The Challenge of Living with Differences Between Jews and Christians*. New York: Free Press, 1989.

Winer, Mark L., and Meir, Aryeh. "Questions Jewish Parents Ask About Intermarriage." New York: American Jewish Committee, 1992.

Conversion to Judaism

Epstein, Lawrence J. *Conversion to Judaism: A Guidebook*. Northvale, NJ: Jason Aronson, 1994.

Kertzer, Rabbi Morris. (Revised by Dr. Lawrence Hoffman). *What Is a Jew?* New Jersey: Collier Books, 1993.

Kukoff, Lydia. *Choosing Judaism*. New York: UAHC, 1982.

Myrowitz, Catherine Hall. *Finding a Home for the Soul: Interviews with Converts to Judaism*. Northvale, NJ: Jason Aronson, 1995.

Romanoff, Lena. *Your People, My People: Finding Acceptance and Fulfillment As a Jew by Choice*. Philadelphia: Jewish Publication Society, 1990.

Silver, Abba Hillel. *Where Judaism Differed: An Inquiry into the Distinctiveness of Judaism*. Reprint; Northvale, NJ: Jason Aronson, 1987.

Marriage and Divorce

Bulka, Reuven P. *Jewish Divorce Ethics: The Right Way to Say Goodbye*. Ogdensburg, NY: Ivy League, 1992.

Bulka, Reuven P. *Jewish Marriage: A Halakhic Ethic*. Hoboken, NJ: Ktav, 1986.

Diament, Carol, ed. *Jewish Marital Status*. Northvale, NJ: Jason Aronson, 1989.

Fried, Jacob, ed. *Jews and Divorce*. Hoboken, NJ: Ktav, 1968.

Gittelsohn, Roland B. *The Extra Dimension: A Jewish View of Marriage*. New York: UAHC, 1983.

Goodman, Philip and Hanna. *The Jewish Marriage Anthology*. Philadelphia: Jewish Publication Society, 1965.

Haut, Irwin H. *Divorce in Jewish Law and Life*. New York: Sepher-Hermon, 1983.

Klagsbrun, Francine. *Married People: Staying Together in the Age of Divorce*. New York: Bantam, 1985.

Lamm, Maurice. *The Jewish Way in Love and Marriage*. New York, Harper & Row, 1982.

Raising Children/The Jewish Home

Bayme, Steven, and Rosen, Gladys, eds. *The Jewish Family and Jewish Continuity*. Hoboken, NJ: Ktav, 1994.

Bell, Roselyn, ed. *The Hadassah Magazine Jewish Parenting Book*. New York: Macmillan/Free Press, 1989.

Diamant, Anita, and Cooper, Howard. *Living a Jewish Life: Jewish Traditions, Customs and Values for Today's Families*. New York: HarperCollins, 1991.

Donin, Hayim Halevy. *To Raise a Jewish Child: A Guide for Parents*. New York: Basic Books, 1991.

Gold, Michael. *And Hannah Wept: Infertility, Adoption, and the Jewish Couple*. Philadelphia: Jewish Publication Society, 1988.

Greenberg, Blu. *How to Run a Traditional Jewish Household*. New York: Simon & Schuster, 1983.

Grishaver, Joel Lurie. *Ten Things That Tend to Turn Kids into Menschen*. Los Angeles: Alef Design, 1995.

Kurshan, Neil. *Raising Your Child to be a Mensch*. New York: Atheneum, 1987.

Kushner, Harold. *When Children Ask About God*. New York: Schocken, 1976.

Reuben, Steven Carr. *Raising Jewish Children in a Contemporary World*. Rockland, CA: Prima, 1992.

Strassfeld, Sharon, and Green, Kathy. *The Jewish Family Book*. New York: Bantam, 1981.

Syme, Daniel B. *The Jewish Home: A Guide for Jewish Living*. Northvale, NJ: Jason Aronson, 1992.

Wolpe, David J. *Teaching Your Children About God*. New York: HarperCollins, 1994.

WOMEN AND THE WORKPLACE

In the first article of Unit 3, "Jewish Women in the Workplace," Sylvia Barack Fishman states: "One of the most widely discussed transformations in American Jewish life centers around current patterns of lifelong labor force participation among Jewish women, including Jewish mothers of young children." The demographics of this extraordinary transformation

are presented in Dr. Fishman's article.

Interviews with Rela Geffen and Judith Lichtman show how Jewish women's labor force participation affects our attitudes toward Jewish communal organizations and toward Jewish family life. In the eighties, Dr. Geffen conducted a groundbreaking sociological study of American Jewish professional and business women. She found that successful Jewish career women differ from their non-Jewish counterparts. While non-Jewish professionals are likely to be single, Jewish professionals are likely to combine successful careers with marriage and childbearing. Her research also led Dr. Geffen to suggest new roles for American Jewish women's organizations, as increasing numbers of young Jewish women enter the labor force.

Judith Lichtman offers personal comments on what has come to be known as women's "second shift": Working women must perform their jobs from nine to five, and then must perform nearly all of the household and childcare duties in their homes in the evening and on weekends. Although husbands may take on added household responsibilities, their domestic tasks generally remain a small fraction of those performed by their wives.

The final article of Unit 3 focuses on sexual harassment. Dahlia Ravikovitch's short story, which was published in English translation for the first time in Hadassah's *Ribcage: Israeli Women's Fiction*, presents a young Israeli woman newly inducted into the army. She is bold, fearless, proud of her youth. "Soon enough I will inherit the best life has to offer," she tells herself. But then her superior, an army major, makes a sexual advance. Readers empathize as the protagonist copes with a harsh reality.

Jewish Women in the Workplace

Sylvia Barack Fishman

One of the most widely discussed transformations in American Jewish life centers around current patterns of lifelong labor force participation among Jewish women, including Jewish mothers of young children. While the prevalence of Jewish women working outside the home has been startling to some observers, Jewish women have historically worked at non-domestic chores both inside and outside the home in many other times and places.

European and immigrant American Jewish women frequently worked for pay. Unlike the prototype of the shy and sequestered "little woman" which held sway in some American and Western European settings, both middle class and impoverished Eastern European Jewish women participated in acquiring the *parnoseh*, the livelihood, for the household. Perhaps the most well-known such woman is Glückel of Hameln (1646-1724), an aggressive businesswoman and mother of thirteen. Glückel's Yiddish memoirs have supplied historians with one of the best pictures of the social, economic, and cultural life of Central European Jews during that time period.[1] Similar personalities are described by authors such as Bella Chagall, who recalls her middle-class, storekeeping mother in *Burning Lights*,[2] and by Chaim Grade, who elegizes his impoverished mother, feeding her children from the proceeds of selling baskets of withered fruit, in *My Mother's Sabbath Days*.[3]

Many American Jews can recall European-born grandmothers and great-aunts who worked as storekeepers or seamstresses, presided over orderly and hospitable homes, and dominated family life as well. Immigrant and second generation Jewish women became extremely active and influential in some American industries, especially the garment industry, partially because they possessed useful skills and enthusiastic attitudes. In the United States, Jewish women had more opportunity for secular education and regular employment than they previously had in their countries of origin. But, paradoxically, at the same time that opportunity beckoned and economic necessity pushed women toward employment, American social values pushed women away from it. Large numbers of Jewish women, especially unmarried women, did in fact opt for the world of education and work. However, though educational levels remained high, by the middle of the twentieth century most American Jewish women had adopted the American preference for full-time homemaking, and in the post-World War II years they overwhelmingly stopped working for pay when they started bearing and raising children.

Today's American Jewish women, in contrast, choose in large numbers to continue working for pay throughout their adult lives. The majority of them continue to work for pay outside the home throughout their childbearing and child-rearing years, and well over half of Jewish mothers of children under six years old are employed. Among married Jewish women today, one-quarter call themselves full-time homemakers, 56 percent work for pay (44 percent work part time and another 12 percent work full time), and 18 percent are unemployed or retired from labor force participation. Among American Jewish women ages 44 and under, only 17 percent are homemakers, 11 percent are students, 70 percent work for pay (59 percent work full time and another 11 percent work part time), and four percent are unemployed (1990 NJPS Jewish female respondents).

Part of the reason for their labor force participation can be found in their extraordinarily high levels of secular education. Contemporary American Jewish women have attained higher levels of secular education than women at any other time in Jewish history. Sixty-six percent of younger (ages 18-44) American Jewish women today have bachelor's or higher degrees. Of these, 38 percent have completed their education as far as the bachelor's degree. More than one-quarter have also earned degrees beyond the bachelor's: 20 percent have master's degrees and 8 percent have doctoral or professional degrees. Another 24 percent of younger American Jewish women have attended or are attending college but have not completed their degree. Only one in ten younger American Jewish women—compared to more than one-third in the older age groups—have not gone beyond high school.

Today's striking levels of higher education for Jewish women translate into shifting occupational profiles as well. Nearly 40 percent of contemporary wage-earning American Jewish women who fall into the following categories—childless women, mothers with children 18 or under, and women age 44 and under—are employed in professional capacities. Among younger women there has been a dramatic decline in employment in clerical and technical capacities and a corresponding increase in those employed in professional capacities. Employment in the generally more lucrative high status professions, which have been accessible to women for the shortest period of time (physicians and dentists, lawyers and judges, professors, senior systems analysts, executive positions, etc.), increases from only seven percent of women with children 19 and over to 11 percent of women with children 18 and under and 15 percent of women who have not yet had children. Employment in the helping professions (teachers below the college level, social workers, librarians, middle-level engineers and programmers, nurses, etc.), many of which require master's degrees but are not usually as lucrative as the high status professions, increases from 16 percent of women with children ages 19 and over to 28 percent of women with children ages 18 and under, and declines slightly among women with no children (24 percent); this decline may be significant, because teaching, social work, librarianship, and nursing have traditionally been considered "women's professions," and the first two especially have historically been favored by American Jewish women. While the percentages of women employed in managerial or service positions remain stable from one family grouping to another, women with children ages 19 or over are far more likely to be employed in clerical or technical positions—56 percent—than women with children ages 18 or under—37 percent.

Jewish women who earn an independent income are often drawn to Jewish philanthropy. In this, they follow the example set earlier in the century, when the working energies of American Jewish women frequently found expression in Jewish communal efforts.

Perceived economic need is probably the single most significant factor affecting the proportion of Jewish women who work outside the home. As has been widely demonstrated in the general American population, for middle class families today, two incomes are often needed in order to attain and maintain a middle class standard of living: that is, purchase of a single family home in a desirable location; relatively new automobiles and major appliances; attractive educational options for one's children, including college and possibly private school and/or graduate school; and summer camp and vacation options. It is also true that perceptions of what compromises a middle class life style have been significantly revised upward, so that more income is needed by "middle class" families.

Jewish women who earn an independent income are often drawn to Jewish philanthropy. In this, they follow the example set earlier in the century, when the working energies of American Jewish women frequently found expression in Jewish communal efforts. The volunteer organizational work of American Jewish women involved near-professional effort and time commitments. Women who volunteered for Hadassah, ORT, Na'amat, Jewish federations, synagogue sisterhoods, and scores of other local, national, and international Jewish organizations did indeed "work for" those organizations, though they received no financial remuneration for their efforts.

The volunteer organizational work of American Jewish women involved near-professional effort and time commitments.

In a 1993 article, Susan Weidman Schneider, the editor of *Lilith,* stated: "Because women were traditionally closed out of much of public religious life, community involvement through philanthropy became an alternative route to participation and empowerment in the Jewish community." Today, with less time for volunteer work than full-time homemakers, Jewish working women are more apt to donate money than to donate time in order to participate and feel connected to the Jewish community.

After interviewing Jewish women donors around the country, Schneider concluded that women's giving differs enormously from men's giving. Jewish men, she says, make charitable donations to amass prestige and influence; whereas Jewish women, who are eager to donate to causes in which they believe, make donations to help bring about social change. Schneider also found that the way in which men ask for money antagonizes many potential women philanthropists. When men solicit, they tell donors that a given amount of money is needed, that last year's contribution was not adequate, and that more money is needed this year. Women find this method of solicitation to be controlling and even intimidating. Such an approach repels women, who prefer to learn how their money will help a project they believe in, like a shelter for battered women, a feminist Seder program, or working toward women's equality in Israel.

In short, the Jewish working woman can be a significant asset to Jewish philanthropic efforts—but she won't open her checkbook unless she is persuaded that the money will make a difference.

The prevalence of working Jewish mothers was at one time condemned as "bad for the Jews"—and in some circles the working Jewish mother is still stigmatized. However, working outside the home is not the determining factor in a mother's level of Jewish observance—nor is it the determining factor of the Jewish values in her home. The majority of mothers who define themselves as Orthodox hold paying jobs, and national and local studies show that, across the denominational spectrum, employed mothers are as traditionally "Jewish" as the minority of mothers who stay home full time. Working mothers are just as likely to join synagogues and Jewish organizations, and just as likely to perform Jewish rituals in the home. In the Hadassah-sponsored "Voices for Change" focus groups, working Jewish mothers—who spoke of themselves as being forced to think through their priorities and to organize their time—revealed that they took quite seriously their own relationship with Judaism as the editors and transmitters of Judaism for their children. Many of them focused on enhancing their children's positive knowledge of and feelings about their Jewish heritage.

Moreover, despite widespread Jewish communal anxiety about the impact of higher education and careerism upon the communal activities of American Jewish women today and tomorrow, high levels of education and occupational accomplishment are certainly consonant with Jewish communal life. In fact, low levels of participation in Jewish communal causes, as members and as volunteers, are found among Jewish women who have generally weak ties to the Jewish community—and weak ties are more prevalent among those who lack higher education. (Joining and working for Jewish causes is also linked to level of Jewish education.) Contrary to the once popular belief that more education and higher career aspirations rob females of commitment to organized religions, Jewish women who hold post-baccalaureate degrees are proportionately more likely to volunteer for Jewish organizations than those who do not; similarly, Jewish women who have completed college are more likely to volunteer than those who have not.

Contemporary trends in education, occupational choices, and labor force participation have changed the behavior of American Jewish women. These changes show no signs of abating. But research shows that although the attitudes and behavior of American Jewish women at the end of the twentieth century are different than they were in the middle of the twentieth century, many American Jewish women continue to be involved in Jewish life, both on a familial and on a communal level. The community can make a difference, by committing itself wholeheartedly to extensive and intensive Jewish education for females and males, and by responding to the needs of the new Jewish family.

In pursuing occupational goals while raising Jewish families, contemporary American women are fulfilling the potential of work patterns established by previous generations of Jewish women in paid and unpaid employment outside the home. Jewish women at work today are a new incarnation of ancient and time-honored Jewish models of female competence and energy. They are contemporary women of valor.

"Jewish Women in the Workplace" was written in 1997 for Jewish Women Living the Challenge.

SYLVIA BARACK FISHMAN, Ph.D., is Assistant Professor of Contemporary Jewish Life and Associate Director of the new International Oral Research Institute on Jewish Women (sponsored by Hadassah) at Brandeis University. She is the author of A Breath of Life: Feminism in the American Jewish Community *and editor of* Follow My Footprints: Changing Images of Women in American Jewish Fiction.

PROGRAMMING IDEAS

AT HOME

Torah Table Talk #1   A discussion of Jewish thought and values with your family and/or friends. Glückel of Hameln (1646-1724) was an aggressive businesswoman, a mother of thirteen, and a pious Jew. Her memoirs have supplied historians with one of the best pictures of the social, economic, and cultural life of Central European Jews during the late seventeenth and early eighteenth century. This passage (from *The Memoirs of Glückel of Hameln*, translated by Marvin Lowenthal [New York, Schocken, 1977], pages 178-180) opens with an argument between Glückel and her grown son Loeb, an extremely poor businessman who was deeply in debt. Although his family had paid off his creditors in the past, he again required help from his mother and brothers.

The Memoirs of Glückel of Hameln

My full heart sank at [my son Loeb's] words, and I could not answer him for bitter tears. Presently I said to him: "How can you think of such a wrong? Well you know that your brothers have already come to grief through you, in truth they can no longer support their losses; and now when a bit of tear-stained money, alas, returns to them, you want to snatch it from their bitterly aching hearts."

And then, for an hour together, the both of us pitifully screamed and quarreled—until at length our words gave out.

Silently I gathered my Hamburger shawl about me, and with tears and bitter heart betook myself home. I said nothing of it to my children, but my son Loeb did not fail to send for them and kept at them with his prayers until, generous souls that they were, they promised to do his will.

So, in a short while, he came to an agreement with his creditors and returned to me in Hamburg. Quickly as his father-in-law heard of it, he dispatched his daughter, Loeb's wife, together with her child, likewise to my house, and gave his daughter two Reichsthalers a week for pin-money. There was naught for me to do save to take it all with the best mien I could.

At that time I was busied in the merchandise trade, selling every month to the amount of five or six hundred Reichsthalers. Further, I went twice a year to the Brunswick Fair and each time made my several thousands profit, so in all, had I been left in peace, I would have soon repaired the loss I suffered through my son.

My business prospered, I procured my wares from Holland, I bought nicely in Hamburg as well, and disposed of the goods in a store of my own. I never spared myself, summer and winter I was out on my travels, and I ran about the city the livelong day.

What is more, I maintained a lively trade in seed pearls. I bought them from all the Jews, selected and assorted them, and then resold them in towns where I knew they were in good demand.

My credit grew by leaps and bounds. If I had wanted 20,000 Reichsthalers *banko* during a session of the Bourse, it would have been mine.

"Yet all this availeth me nothing" [Esther 5:13]. I saw my son Loeb, a virtuous young man, pious and skilled in Talmud, going to pieces before my eyes.

One day I said to him, "Alas, I see nothing ahead of you. As for me, I have a big business, more indeed than I can manage. Come then, work for me in my business and I will give you two percent of all the sales."

My son Loeb accepted the proposal with great joy. Moreover, he set to work diligently, and he could soon have been on his feet had not his natural bent led him to his ruin. He became, through my customers, well known among the merchants, who placed great confidence in him. Nearly all my business lay in his hands.

Questions for Thought and Discussion

1. Do Glückel's concerns for her improvident, unsuccessful son and for her successful business in any way reflect your concerns for your family and career? How?

2. Glückel's detailed descriptions of her business dealings in this passage are typical of the concern for money which she shows throughout the memoirs. In the "Introduction" to the book, Richard Rosen states: "To those who profess scorn for what they perceive as Jewish materialism and middle-classness, the book reveals the roots of those qualities, reveals the life-and-death matters that built those traits into Jewish life. A limited economy forced Jews in Europe into certain business activities that were more frequently fraught with danger than they were profitable. A respect for money was vital for their physical survival: near-ruinous taxes were levied on Jewish communities and on Jews individually in connection with every aspect of their personal and business lives" (page xv). How do you react to Glückel's discussion of finances? What is your own attitude toward "materialism" and "middle-classness"?

3. Although Glückel is aware that her son is an inept money manager, she nonetheless invites him to work in her business. Why? What is your own experience of family businesses? Explore Glückel's feelings for Loeb—the quarrel that lasts an hour, her description of him as virtuous and pious, and her statement that "his natural bent led him to his ruin."

Torah Table Talk #2   The Talmud frequently discusses charity and "loving kindness," as in the passage below. Loving kindness is an approximate English translation of the Hebrew phrase *gemilut hasadim*; it is also translated as "acts (or practices) of kindness."

Babylonian Talmud (compiled between 200 and 500), Sukkah 49b

Rabbi Eleazar stated: Greater is one who performs charity than one who offers all the sacrifices, for it is said, "To do charity and justice is more acceptable to the Lord than sacrifice" (Proverbs 21:3).

Rabbi Eleazar further stated: Loving kindness is greater than charity, for it is said, "Sow to yourselves according to charity, but reap according to kindness" (Hosea 10:12). If you sow, it is doubtful whether you will eat [the harvest] or not, but when you reap, you will certainly eat. Rabbi Eleazar further stated: The reward of charity depends entirely upon the extent of the kindness in it, for it is said, "Sow to yourselves according to charity, but reap according to kindness."

Our Rabbis taught: In three respects is loving kindness superior to charity. Charity can be done only with one's money, but loving kindness can be done with one's person and one's money. Charity can be given only to the poor, loving kindness can be given both to the rich and the poor. Charity can be given to the living only, loving kindness can be done both to the living and to the dead.

Rabbi Eleazar further stated: One who executes charity and justice is regarded as one who had filled all the world with kindness, for it is said, "God loves charity and justice, the earth is full of the loving kindness of the Lord" (Psalms 33:5).

Questions for Thought and Discussion

1. The Hebrew word for charity is *tzedakah*. When this word is used in the Bible, it usually means "righteousness." However, over the course of time, *tzedakah* has come to mean "charity" as well. Judaism generally views the giving of charity as a necessary action, not as a freely offered choice. How does the idea of righteousness or of justice affect your idea of charity? In what ways is charitable giving a duty rather than a choice?

2. How would you characterize your own charitable practices? Do they include acts of kindness as well as monetary donations? What do you aim for? What do you achieve? Is your involvement with Hadassah an act of loving kindness?

3. In the recent past, women typically gave time and effort to charitable work, while men typically gave money. The Rabbis of the Talmud clearly placed greater emphasis on the female pattern of giving than on the male. What changes are likely today, as women increasingly participate in the work force and have less time for acts of loving kindness?

4. Rabbi Eleazar offers the biblical verse Hosea 10:12 as "proof" that acts of kindness are more important than donating money. (Note: The 1985

Jewish Publication Society translation of Hosea 10:12 is: "Sow righteousness for yourselves; Reap the fruits of goodness.") Rabbi Eleazar's style of reasoning is extremely common in the Talmud and in later Jewish texts. How would you characterize this sort of proof? Does Rabbi Eleazar's logic make sense to you?

Additional At-Home Activities

❖ Refer to "Additional At-Home Activities" section of "Thoughts on Jewish Women on the Way Up," page 184.

INTEREST/STUDY GROUPS

Hold a discussion based on the following questions:

1. Sylvia Barack Fishman notes some of the changes in employment patterns that have occurred over the past eighty years in the United States. How have these affected you and your family? Did your mother or grandmother hold a paying job prior to marriage? After marriage? How did their husbands react? What about you, your daughters, and your granddaughters?

2. What careers do you hope your granddaughters and great-granddaughters will choose? Why?

3. Professor Fishman notes Jewish women's "striking levels of higher education." Many explanations have been offered for this. What are some of the factors involved?

4. Professor Fishman reports that women who hold graduate degrees "are proportionately more likely to volunteer for Jewish organizations than those who do not; similarly, Jewish women who have completed college are more likely to volunteer than those who have not." Why? And why are popular perceptions in opposition to these research findings?

5. What can be done to encourage a volunteer spirit among your members and among the population at large? How can Hadassah work toward increased volunteerism?

6. How do you react to Jewish organizations soliciting philanthropic donations? Do you agree that men and women have different motives in giving money to charitable causes? Who makes the decisions about philanthropy in your family? Is this decision tied to income levels? To commitment to a cause?

7. What steps might Hadassah take to commit itself to "extensive and intensive Jewish education" and to respond "to the needs of the new Jewish family"?

MEETINGS

❖ Invite a guest speaker to discuss "Men And Women—Different Messages." What are the historic sex-based expectations, roles, and priorities for Jewish men and women? How have these changed in our century? How does the Jewish community support/not support Jewish women today? What messages do we give our children about sex-based roles and priorities? How can we teach our sons and grandsons to be respectful of women? How can we empower our daughters and granddaughters?

❖ Hold a panel discussion to explore the impact of new work force options on Jewish women's lives and their family's lives. Invite several panelists, for instance: a small business owner; a telecommuter; a freelancer; a full-time, nine-to-five employee; a full-time homemaker. Choose the panelists from several different fields. How has working for pay or not working for pay affected their participation in Jewish life? What types of child care arrangements have they made? How long have the panelists held their current positions? Do they expect to choose a different employment option in the future, for example, part-time to full-time employee as children grow, or paid worker to homemaker when children are born?

❖ Invite a rabbi or other scholar to discuss Jewish business and financial ethics. Concentrate on ethical questions relevant to the service professions, where Jewish women are overwhelmingly employed—from social workers to doctors to real estate agents. Also include the topic of women's philanthropy and teachings of the Jewish tradition.

❖ Hold a meeting on working women's philanthropy. Refer to the *Voices For Change Video Discussion Guide* for programming suggestions on women's ways of giving and the unique concerns of women and philanthropy. The *Voices for Change* videotape is based on interviews with young American Jewish women; they talk about their lives, views of Jewish organizations, and aspirations. To order a copy of the video and discussion guide, at $25 per set, contact the Hadassah National Video Department at 212-303-8165.

ANNUAL EVENTS

❖ Together with a local women's professional association or local Jewish family service agency, hold a symposium on "Women in the Workplace—Where We Are ... Where We Are Going." Topics to be addressed could include: flextime and job sharing; antisemitism in the work force; age discrimination; the "mommy" track hits the glass ceiling; planning for retirement; competitiveness with female colleagues; love in the workplace; small business ownership; telecommuting and freelancing; tensions between full-time homemakers and working mothers.

❖ Conduct an Education Day on recent changes in Jewish women's work force participation and the effects of those changes on Jewish family and communal life. The following schedule is from an Education Day sponsored by the Philadelphia Chapter of Hadassah in March 1985. Use it as a model, and adapt it to the expertise of Judaic scholars and feminists in your community.

Judaism and Feminism—Converging or Diverging?

9:15-10.00	Registration

10:00-11:00 **The Jewish Woman's Evolving Roles**
The crucial changes in women's status over the past century.
Susannah Heschel, Ph.D., editor of On Being a Jewish Feminist

11:15-12:15 *Select one session*

A. The Jewish Woman in the Family
Has Jewish family life suffered or been enhanced as increasing numbers of women work for pay outside the home? How do we struggle with changing family configurations?
Donna Pressman, director of the Jewish Family and Children's Agency

B. The Jewish Woman in Public Life
What does community life offer? How has volunteerism affected the community? How do working women manage to volunteer for communal work outside the home?
Norma F. Furst, Ph.D., president of Harcum Junior College

12:30-1:30 Lunch

1:30-2:30 **The Jewish Woman's Aspirations for the Future**
What are our expectations? Are they different from those of men? Specifically, in Jewish life what professions are available to women?
Judith Hauptman, Ph.D., professor of Talmud at the Jewish Theological Seminary, New York

HANDS-ON

❖ Organize a Hadassah mentor program. Ask established professionals to mentor young Jewish women just entering the work force (or to mentor older women returning to work after a child-rearing hiatus). Match up women according to their professions. Suggest that each pair meet about once a month to talk, and keep in touch over the phone more frequently if needed.

❖ Take your daughters or granddaughters to work on the yearly "Take Our Daughters To Work Day." If your employer does not participate in this event, speak to friends and relatives about programs at their workplaces. Many employers happily welcome extra girls. And, if you are self-employed or if your supervisor approves, bring your daughters (as well as your sons) for brief periods on some additional days each year.

❖ Work together with Hadassah leaders nationally to develop a business women's network. For details, call the Community Projects chair of the Hadassah National Membership Division at 212-303-8042.

---

1. *The Memoirs of Glückel of Hameln,* translated by Marvin Lowenthal (New York: Schocken, 1977). The memoirs were begun in 1690, and after a hiatus were completed in 1715. Glückel wrote in Yiddish, interspersed with many Hebrew phrases from the Bible, prayer book, and other sources.

2. Bella Chagall, *Burning Lights,* translated by Norbert Guterman (New York: Schocken Books, 1946).

3. Chaim Grade, *My Mother's Sabbath Days* (New York: Alfred A. Knopf, 1986, originally published in Yiddish as *Der Mames Shabbosim*, 1955).

Thoughts on Jewish Women on the Way Up

Interviews with Rela Mintz Geffen and Judith L. Lichtman

Jewish Women on the Way Up *was published in the mid-eighties. Dr. Rela Mintz Geffen, a noted sociologist and currently Coordinator of the programs in Jewish communal studies at Gratz College in Philadelphia, conducted the study to examine Jewish career women, their identity conflicts, and their attitudes toward Judaism. Dr. Geffen questioned approximately one thousand Jewish business and professional women, and she found that a majority of Jewish career women (unlike their non-Jewish counterparts) had managed to combine successful careers with marriage and childbearing.*

In addition, Dr. Geffen reported that:

❖ *A majority of Jewish business and professional women viewed their Jewish identity as an important source of their personal strength.*

❖ *More than half of the respondents felt that the Jewish community did not support women as they balanced their obligations as wives, mothers, and workers.*

❖ *Single women "had definite and often negative stereotypes about Jewish men." They saw them as more dependent and less sexy and macho than non-Jewish men. Yet, at the same time, respondents viewed Jewish men as caring, intelligent, and achieving, with good potential as fathers.*

Many who read Jewish Women on the Way Up *stressed the alienation* from the established Jewish community felt by many of the survey respondents—whether married, single, young, middle-aged, or older— whether strongly connected to Jewish life or only marginally affiliated. This alienation has been a serious challenge to the community, and over the last decade Jewish institutions have begun to change to meet that challenge.

Two interviews follow below. The first interview is with Dr. Rela Mintz Geffen, conducted by Dr. Efrat Levy, former National Director of Hadassah's Program Department.

The second interview is with Judith L. Lichtman, President of the Women's Legal Defense Fund, an "archtypical Jewish woman juggler." Lichtman was asked to comment—from a personal angle—on the findings of Dr. Geffen's research. This interview was part of a press conference given at the American Jewish Committee in December 1987 and was published in Textures, May 1988.

Many of Dr. Geffen's conclusions were again noted in 1995, in the published results of a Hadassah-Brandeis University survey. In 1994, Hadassah, through its Strategic Planning Department, commissioned a survey to examine Jewish women's attitudes, beliefs, and behaviors. The survey, conducted by the Maurice and Marilyn Cohen Center for Modern Jewish Studies at Brandeis University, involved fourteen focus groups, held across the United States. Participating in the focus groups were 152 American Jewish women from their late twenties through their early forties.

What did the 152 participants express? That Jewish women continue to lead complex lives that blend familial and professional obligations. Forty-six percent of adult Jewish women work full time outside the home, and this percentage reflects an increase from previous surveys. Time is precious for these women, as the following response indicates. The speaker is an Orthodox mother, but her words are typical for all Jewish working mothers, regardless of denominational affiliation.

"I get up at 6:00—the baby wakes me up. I shower and get myself together and make the baby's lunch. Around 6:30 my husband gets up and the other child gets up. I take care of the baby and he takes care of my other son. I feed him, make his lunch, make my own lunch, and get dressed. My husband takes our son to school so everyone is out of the kitchen by about 8:15. I take my son to the baby sitter and go to work. I am a guidance counselor in a high school. I have 90 emotionally disturbed children on my case load. I see each one once a week for 40 minutes.... I've heard it all, and a lot of it is very sad. Then I pick up my older son from school at 4:00 and bring him home and pick up my younger son right after that at 4:30. I play with them for about an hour and get supper at 5:30. Then they get baths and my husband comes home at 6:30 and everyone is happy. We run around and play for another hour. I put the one kid to bed at about 7:30 and *the other one will stay up till 9:30. Then my husband and I get a chance to talk."*

The survey also found that most American Jewish women are not affiliated with synagogues or with Jewish organizations. This lack of affiliation is due in part to their hectic schedules, and in part due to their lack of satisfaction with organized Jewish life today.

One cause of their dissatisfaction may be women's limited roles in the organized Jewish world. According to the 1990 Jewish Population Survey, conducted by the Council of Jewish Federations, women in the professional Jewish world reach a glass ceiling. While 61 percent of Jewish federation staff are women, only 18 percent are executive directors, and none of these directors is in a large city. Of all the national Jewish organizations (excluding all-women organizations such as Hadassah), only one has a woman at the helm.

There was always the pressure to get married and to have children. But now we raise our daughters to have that same push toward achievement in the professional world as well.

Interview with Rela Mintz Geffen

EFRAT LEVY
In your study you cite evidence that Jewish women want to combine marriage and childbearing with careers rather than choosing one over the other. Did you find an explanation for this?

RELA MINTZ GEFFEN
There is pressure on Jewish women to succeed in all the different areas of their lives. I recently saw a revival of "Funny Girl." No matter how successful Fanny Brice was, all her relatives and neighbors kept saying was, "she's not married." There was always the pressure to get married and to have children. But now we raise our daughters to have that same push toward achievement in the professional world as well.

EL
One of your most important findings was the degree to which women in the study felt alienated from the Jewish community.

RMG
They weren't really alienated from the community. In fact, many of them indicated a high level of personal involvement.

But many felt strongly that they should be able to get more satisfaction from the Jewish community. Some single women felt that the community was rejecting them. The married women, doing the balancing act, felt that the community was not fulfilling their needs, was not providing services that would make a real difference to their lives.

EL

What steps should be taken to address these concerns?

RMG

There are two arenas in which steps need to be taken. The first is what I would call ideology. Women need reassurance that the issues facing them are important to the Jewish community. The second arena is very pragmatic. It has to do with things such as day care or transportation to Hebrew school.

EL

So it's important for career women to take even more of an active role in the Jewish establishment?

RMG

Sure, I think that women have to fight for things. But they have to be in coalition with other people. We face two kinds of hostility. One is the people who say: "They should do it for themselves. Why should the Jewish community have to do it?" I answer, Yes, if they do it totally for themselves, they will find solutions, but it will probably mean that they won't see the Jewish community as an important part of their lives. The second attitude is expressed by people who say things like, "I think it's wrong that women have their children in day care centers." I'm not saying that all children should be in day care centers. What we're talking about is giving the best possible help to Jewish families who want and need it.

EL

How can an organization like Hadassah respond to these issues?

RMG

Organizations like Hadassah are a natural base of operations because you already have the women working together who care about each other and who care about these issues. It's absolutely essential in terms of attracting young women to speak to this agenda. Of course, it could be a grandmother's agenda as well as a granddaughter's.

Jewish women's organizations have not sufficiently looked after their own members' needs. They should be advocates *and* provide services, things like support groups, hotlines, or referral to child care services.

You can't assume anymore that members are either going to stay with you or come to you out of altruism. It's not evil to say that; it's recognizing the changing needs of American Jewish women. It used to be, when most women were at home, that their most important need was to get out of the house and do something for the Jewish community. But now, ironically, meeting the private needs of women may be the more important endeavor. Jewish women's organizations are a natural base for helping the Jewish community respond to these issues. This doesn't mean to give up other missions. It means you shouldn't feel you're compromising if you do something for yourselves.

Interview with Judith L. Lichtman

I am going to begin by telling an Ellen Goodman story—the quintessential superwoman story. Goodman's superwoman begins her day by making a nutritious breakfast for her children, then jumps into her Anne Klein suit and her nine-year-old Volvo, drops the kids at school, and goes downtown to her office. She has a two-martini business lunch with two men, and comes home to spend quality but not quantity time with her children. She prepares a gourmet dinner for her husband and jumps into bed about midnight, at which time she is expected to be multi-orgasmic.

The point of this story is that when I heard it in the late seventies, nobody laughed. Men were too embarrassed because Goodman said "orgasm"; women didn't think it was funny because it depicted their lives.

I am for all intents and purposes both a personal and a professional feminist. In other words, I get paid to live out my personal value system and that is wonderful. Still, it is often exhausting, a secret I tell only to my friends and colleagues.

The feminist revolution was really a revolution for both men and women. Roles have changed. Both men and women can speak eloquently about how family responsibilities differ in different households. But I was struck by Geffen's study because it talks about supportive husbands, not about the equality of job sharing in households. It talks about husbands helping wives, dads helping mothers. And I think that is a reality, probably because we wives and mothers bring to marriage what men bring, our own emotional baggage.

Simple things like arranging transportation for children to get from school to Hebrew school would be enormously helpful to working parents.

When I get angry with my husband, about the disproportionate things I do, he reminds me that I think of myself as the household manager. I delegate responsibilities to him but I keep control of the household. I am absolutely happy for him to do all those domestic things but I want them done my way. He is right to remind me. Yet, I am often struck by the way my husband's day and mine differ at work. They differ in that I watch my watch. I know where my kids are at any given hour. I know when they are home. If they don't call, I call them. It doesn't occur to my husband. His head is never half-way home. Even if I am out of town, his head isn't half-way home. He believes wholeheartedly that the children are fine. I believe they are fine but I just want to check. I don't believe this is genetic; I believe we have been socialized this way. I further believe my generation is socializing their children this way.

There isn't a lot of time for mothers of young children to participate in communal life. But what you find, and I'm not alone in my little peer group of Washington Jewish women lawyers, is that you can count on the people who are the busiest to squeeze in yet one more activity. I think it is because we have become comfortable with our juggling that we can allow ourselves to be active in Jewish communal life.

I think I do balance a lot. I have a wonderful life. I spend a lot of time thinking that I could use more sleep. I don't think about my life in very global terms. I live feeling fulfilled and in large measure very lucky. One of the things that interests me in the Geffen study is that there are really very concrete suggestions about the way the Jewish community could be supportive. I frankly never thought of it. Simple things like arranging transportation for children to get from school to Hebrew school would be enormously helpful to working parents. This and other recommendations are very thoughtful. I believe the study deserves wide circulation and I hope that it will stimulate purposeful action within the Jewish community.

From Textures, Hadassah National Jewish Studies Bulletin, *May 1988, vol. 6, no. 3.*

PROGRAMMING IDEAS

AT HOME

Torah Table Talk   A discussion of Jewish thought and values with your family and/or friends. In traditionally observant households, the husband sings or recites the Woman of Valor, or *Eishet Hayil*, verses to his wife every Friday night. The *Eishet Hayil* is an ideal wife whose value is prized above all material wealth.

Proverbs 31:10-31

What a rare find is a capable wife!
Her worth is far beyond that of rubies.
Her husband puts his confidence in her,
And lacks no good thing.
She is good to him, never bad,
All the days of her life.

She looks for wool and flax,
And sets her hand to them with a will.
She is like a merchant fleet,
Bringing her food from afar.
She rises while it is still night,
And supplies provisions for her household,
The daily fare of her maids.
She sets her mind on an estate and acquires it;
She plants a vineyard by her own labors.
She girds herself with strength,
And performs her tasks with vigor.
She sees that her business thrives;
Her lamp never goes out at night.
She sets her hand to the distaff;
Her fingers work the spindle.
She gives generously to the poor;
Her hands are stretched out to the needy.
She is not worried for her household because of snow.
For her whole household is dressed in crimson.
She makes covers for herself;
Her clothing is linen and purple.
Her husband is prominent in the gates,
As he sits among the elders of the land.
She makes cloth and sells it,
And offers a girdle to the merchant.
She is clothed with strength and splendor;
She looks to the future cheerfully.
Her mouth is full of wisdom,
Her tongue with kindly teaching.
She oversees the activities of her household
And never eats the bread of idleness.
Her children declare her happy;
Her husband praises her,
"Many women have done well,
But you surpass them all."
Grace is deceptive,
Beauty is illusory;
It is for her fear of the Lord
That a woman is to be praised.
Extol her for the fruit of her hand,
And let her works praise her in the gates.

Questions for Thought and Discussion

1. Do you identify with the Woman of Valor in any way? Why or why not? Do you aspire to live the life of the Women of Valor? Why or why not?

2. Compare the Woman of Valor, the ideal wife of biblical times, to the "superwoman" of modern times. How are these two idealized concepts of womanhood similar and how are they different?

3. Why do some laud this female ideal while others deplore it?

4. Murray Lichtenstein, a professor of Hebrew at Hunter College, writes in the January 1988 issue of *Textures*: "For a poem produced in a patriarchal culture, the husband's minimal role in household affairs takes us by surprise." Indeed, "the husband [is] conspicuous by his absence." Yet he "is prominent in the gates as he sits among the elders of the land," which means that he is involved in the public administration of communal justice—a male activity throughout the Bible. But the works of the wife are also praised "in the gates"; she is also to receive public acknowledgment of her deeds. Hence, Professor Lichtenstein notes: "Patriarchal dominance, often claimed to be a biblical legacy, is mitigated here in the poem of the *Eishet Hayil*." Would you agree that the *Eishet Hayil* achieves a measure of parity with her husband?

5. Professor Lichtenstein also explains that the Hebrew term *hayil*, which means soldier, connotes power, wealth, and excellence, so that Woman of Valor might be translated as "Woman of Substance." Do you regard the *Eishet Hayil* as powerful? As a woman of substance?

Additional At-Home Activities

❖ Create a modern Woman of Valor poem with your husband. Share it with each other every Shabbat.

❖ If you are a working woman seeking Jewish education, but cannot fit study group meetings or formal courses into your schedule, order Hadassah's Jewish Education Department publications to study on your own or with one study partner—your husband, daughter, mother, friend, etc. Consult the *Hadassah Resource Catalogue* for ordering information. Call the Hadassah National Order Department 1-800-880-9455 to obtain a copy. One good choice for home study is *Ribcage: Israeli Women's Fiction*, Carol Diament and Lily Rattok, eds. (New York: Hadassah, 1994). To purchase, call 1-800-880-9455. Order number: #R492. Cost: $10 for Hadassah members; $15 for non-members.

Or, participate in a Hadassah study group through teleconferencing. This option suits working women who can't spare the commuting time, but do have time for the study session itself. Teleconferencing also suits the working mother who has no access to childcare when the study group meets, but whose children do allow her to hold a telephone conversation!

❖ Working women who seek a Hadassah connection but have little time for Hadassah meetings are encouraged to explore the Hadassah website at http://www.hadassah.org. An opportunity to interact with others on Jewish women's issues is currently in the works: coming soon is a Jewish Education chat room where members can further discuss the topics raised in *Jewish Women Living the Challenge*.

INTEREST/STUDY GROUPS

Hold a discussion based on the following questions:

1. Rela Geffen, interviewed in 1988, noted Jewish women's dissatisfaction with organized Jewish communal life. How have Jewish organizations in your community changed since then? In what ways, if any, are they more responsive to working women's needs? In what ways could they become more responsive still?

2. Judith Lichtman points out the difference between a husband who helps and supports his wife and a husband who fulfills his share of household responsibilities. Is there more than a semantic issue at stake? Discuss division of labor in your members' households. In what ways are the issues raised by Lichtman valid for you?

3. Compare the portrait of Jewish working women provided ten years ago by Rela Geffen and Judith Lichtman to the recent *Voices for Change* study. (You can order a copy of *Voices for Change: Future Directions for American Jewish Women* through Hadassah's Strategic Planning Department. Call 212-303-8024. The price is $15.00.) What has changed? What hasn't? If Hadassah sponsors another survey ten years from now, what might the results be?

4. Rela Geffen states: "Jewish women's organizations have not sufficiently looked after their own members' needs. They should be advocates *and* provide services, things like support groups, hotlines, or referral to child care services." Do you agree that Hadassah should focus more on social issues, such as these issues of importance to working mothers? Why or why not? And if so, what action could your unit take?

MEETINGS

❖ Watch the *Voices for Change* video which, like the Hadassah-Brandeis study that preceded it, is based on interviews with young American Jewish women. In the video, women talk about their lives, feelings about Israel, views of Jewish organizations, and aspirations. An accompanying discussion guide suggests sixteen activities for Hadassah units. To order a copy of the video and discussion guide, at $25 per set, contact the Hadassah National Video Department at 212-303-8165.

❖ Invite an expert in time management to discuss "Getting Organized" with your members. Follow up with a discussion of organizational skills as they relate to running a Jewish household while holding a job. Is the Jewish "piece" an added pressure, an adaptive tool for stress relief, or both? How does Sabbath observance relate to time management?

ANNUAL EVENTS

Refer to the "Annual Events" section of "Jewish Women in the Workplace" by Sylvia Barack Fishman, pages 174-175.

HANDS-ON

❖ Establish a couples discussion group where both women and men can share ways to balance work and family responsibilities and can discuss difficulties together. Invite a Jewish family services counselor or other Jewish professional to lead.

❖ Create a list of local child care services and child care referral services. Provide the list to members who are mothers of young children. As a community service, post the list at pediatricians' offices, at playgrounds, etc., and on the Internet. (You must include a legal disclaimer: Hadassah does not endorse nor does it guarantee the services of the child care providers listed. Families who use the list must research the child care providers themselves before availing themselves of services. Hadassah provides the list only as information and does not recommend or validate any of the individuals or companies on the list, nor does it recommend or validate their work.)

❖ Organize a "buddy" system for working mothers. Match up women who have children of similar ages so that they can share advice and help each other with the logistical problems of running a household while holding a job.

❖ Join or establish a Training Wheels group to familiarize young families with Jewish life, and hold sessions on Sundays or early on weeknights to accommodate the schedules of working mothers and fathers. Training Wheels/*Al Galgalim* offers a curriculum for nine monthly parent-and-child sessions that focus on Jewish holiday celebrations. No prior Jewish knowledge is assumed, and sessions can be tailored to the needs of local families. Curricula for both the pre-school and the early grade school levels are available. Call the National Hadassah Training Wheels Department at 1-800-391-3339 or 212-303-8284 for details.

A SLIGHT DELAY

Dahlia Ravikovitch

A wicker fence. A wicker fence. Nettles from the first autumn rains. Then, two abandoned stalls of cold water showers. A row of books in a wooden case. A Japanese picture and a shadeless lamp. This was my room, and from here I was supposed to move into the office.

"Have you moved the bed into the office yet?"

"Did you take the blankets?"

"Did you bring the cakes from the kitchen?"

"You must be crazy walking around the camp in a housecoat like this!"

"I'll be back in half an hour. If there's a phone call for me...." Rachel, the Bombshell, threw the towel on her arm and left. She had a soft voluptuous body and fair hair, and she had the right attitude toward life. There was always someone whispering with her at night.

They said that there was a radio in the commanding officer's room. But it was forbidden to enter the commander's room and, in any event, any girl who entered there would have to dust the place. It was best not to go in. One of the officers lingered in the adjacent room; it was four or five in the afternoon on Friday. He had come from home on a bike. He was not planning to do any work.

"Why did you enter the commander's room, and how did you get the key?" Rachel asked resentfully, and her suitor chimed in, "Who gave you permission to turn on the radio?"

I examined the detailed map of Israel, the archeological shards, the carpet, and the enormous desk. This room retained the sunlight long after the sun had set. The commander had left his office long ago. A cascade of sunlight mixed with dust flooded the broad brown desk. It was five o'clock, and two Brandenburg concertos were playing on the radio. For a while I could not find a place for myself; then I settled in the deep chair and sat immobile across from the desk. It was as if I were asleep. I did not want to move a limb. I was thinking about the matriculation exams I had taken a few months earlier, and about the impatience and anxiety I had experienced before taking them. I remembered the first exam, and how I enjoyed myself once I realized what it was like. How powerful I became in my own eyes. A few days later, we went on a trip around the country, I and my boyfriend: we whistled in movie theaters and were uncharacteristically insolent. When all that was over, we were drafted into the army, and I despised myself because I felt so useless. The days and weeks passed, and most things fell into place. When the first concerto was over, my cheek was sticking to the desk. I shuddered when I realized how quickly the time had passed. The light in the room became brighter and whiter. The room looked hoary and no longer different from the other rooms. The concerto was over and I hastened to leave the room.

The sun had set, and I began to sing loudly. My own voice grated on my ears, but I continued to sing with gusto, all the while hoping for a change to take place in me so that my voice would sound different. After a while I distracted myself from thinking about my voice. While I was making my camp-bed, I accidentally knocked down a pile of Lost Equipment forms. Rachel peered at me. When I bent down to pick up the scattered forms, I was beset by mosquitoes. As I straightened up, I watched the receding paleness in the west. I started to plot and scheme how to use the phone despite the prohibition. The windows turned ink-blue a moment before darkness. I trusted I could find a way to use the phone without being punished.

When I came out of the room, Rachel, the Bombshell, said to me, "If you don't bring me food, I am leaving the office."

"She's screwed up," said Rachel, the Bombshell, to the man waiting for her outside. "You can't rely on her."

At eight, I went to the Recreation Room. In the big dilapidated armchair sat Barukh Shoshani. Although he was a refugee from the Second World War and never had a proper education, he managed to rise to the rank of sergeant, and even prepared himself for the equivalency matriculation exams. I was surprised to see him seated in that armchair, with its broken springs and gray oily edges visible from behind. This armchair may have been just as filthy on the day it was brought in with the rest of the spoils from Ramla. At any rate, the springs could certainly have been repaired, but we were not deemed worthy of the effort, being an indolent and low-class service unit.

As I was leafing through the weekend papers, I noticed the spider web between the legs of the chair underneath the radio. Only then did I realize that I had missed the PX yet again. I had a great craving for candy, particularly for those triangular chocolate-covered wafers. The Sabbath stretched before me so lean and emaciated, as if my very roster duty had caused it to be thus reduced. At least I'll be able to sleep late, and there won't be any parade. Saturday duties were rare; they were also meaningless and wasteful. I knew what I wanted. I wanted to be somewhere else altogether. A hefty mosquito circled near my arm, buzzing vociferously. I shuddered.

Rachel, the Bombshell, returned to the office, her hair wet from the shower. It looked thick even when wet. I offered her some of the raisins my family had sent me, because I was afraid of her. I had just started reading a serial when I heard a train. It was a late freight train that had been delayed until after Sabbath had started, and it now rumbled by stealthily and unlit. I thought to myself: Where is it going? How far is it going? I listened to it fade out of earshot.

Suddenly a round, ruddy head adorned with a faded gray mustache appeared in the door.

"Are you minding the phone?" Major Rosenblum asked. I waited for Rachel to answer.

"Yes, yes, I am here all the time," Rachel said.

"So am I."

"I'm expecting a call," Rosenblum said. "If they call, tell them I'll be back in half an hour."

"Major Rosenblum—" I pleaded.

"What is it?"

"Can I call home? ... Long distance," I hastened to add. I was not sure he had heard me.

"Where to?" he asked.

"To the Galilee." I sounded ridiculous to myself.

"We shall see," said the major. "I'll be back in half an hour. Maybe you'll be able to call from my office."

"Thanks," I called after him, but he had already left. A sense of joyous adventure filled me. I was going to call home against standard orders. The officer on duty had agreed immediately, I was lucky.

His room was brightly lit. There were three lamps: one hanging from the ceiling with a shade resembling an enamel plate, another perched on a spiral metal stem, and a third hung from a nail by a made up camp-bed. On the table were yeast-cakes streaked with threads of jam and a pot of coffee.

"I'll dial for you," Rosenblum said.

I sat, somewhat confused, on a footstool by the table. I was wearing a grayish-pink housecoat which I realized was not appropriate. I had no idea how to start a conversation. And anyway, conversation was superfluous. The major was a complete stranger to me. But he had done me a favor, and I was beholden to him. I hoped he would understand that I was still immature and lacking in social skills, and it was up to him to decide whether or not to strike up a conversation with me.

"The operator says it will take about twenty minutes," Rosenblum said, his cheeks puffed and rubicund.

"I can go back to the office," I said, but I was sleepy and slow to get up.

"What's the hurry?"

I kept silent and hunched.

"Have some coffee."

"I don't drink coffee at night."

"Then take a piece of cake."

"No, really," I said affectedly. "It's not out of politeness. I am full of cake already." I wanted to smoke but I had left my cigarettes at the office.

"How old are you?"

"Eighteen."

"I thought you were older."

"Everybody thinks so," I laughed. "But I had my birthday last Sunday." I was very proud to be so young. I felt an advantage over those older than me. Some, burdened with wife and children, had problems supporting their families, and were humiliated by their superiors. I thought to myself: What have they done with their lives? How have they wasted the years? From time to time, I was seized by fear that my youth would be frittered away. But in the meantime, I still had my youth and I was very careful with it. Every day I watched it and gave it serious consideration.

"Did you graduate from high school?"

"Three months ago," I said and thought: What an advantage!

"Do you have siblings? Older or younger?"

"I have a younger brother. He's smart as a whip, and handsome, too."

"No wonder, with such a sister."

I knew he was flattering me, but the frost around me was thawing.

"He writes me such funny letters that I roll on the floor with laughter." I decided to go and fetch my cigarettes after all.

"What's the rush? Have some coffee."

"No thanks." I felt resentment. Why does he keep harping on coffee when I have already told him?

His desk was close to the door. He got up. He was taller than me, and I felt him look down on me. He leaned against the threshold, and his hand touched my back, as if by accident. I recoiled a little. I was not quite sure he really meant it. The pinkish-gray housecoat was so obviously inappropriate. I felt as if I was wearing rags.

"Wait," he said, "why are you running?"

I stood a little shaken. "What are you afraid of?" He smiled. Suddenly the phone rang. His wedding ring was thick and crude. Everybody knew he had a seven-month-old baby.

"Mom," I cried into the phone. "How was your week? Can you imagine, I managed to call you tonight without any problems. Is Micah with you?"

My mother wanted to know if her package had arrived. I told her everything was all right with me. A complaint was lodged against me for disorderly appearance, but it was later dropped. I am beginning to get the hang of the work. Mother was very pleased.

"Have a nice Sabbath, and all the best," Mother said, and before hanging up she added, "Who stayed with you this weekend? Do you have a nice roommate?"

He leaned against the threshold, and his hand touched my back, as if by accident. I recoiled a little.

"What does it matter?" I answered. "I have a book to read, and I am still translating those poems. I feel great here in the office. It beats the four-hour guard shift everyone else has to do."

"Why didn't you add regards from me?" Rosenblum said in a rasping voice. "After all, I let you make the phone call."

"It's really wonderful of you."

He grabbed my arm near the shoulder. There was neither grace nor affection in his movement. I was startled and pulled my arm back forcefully.

"Stupid girl. Are you afraid?"

"No."

"What then?" He was still holding my arm.

"I am not afraid." All the pleasantries were now drained out of me. "I am not afraid at all. I simply don't want to."

He let go of me and looked at me coldly. I remained standing there.

"Okay, leave."

When I entered the room, Rachel was still standing in the window, talking to her suitor, and the room was swarming with mosquitoes. Rachel had smeared herself with mosquito repellent and was unaffected by them. The light was too poor for reading and my sadness was too overwhelming. I still had not fully grasped what had happened to me. That's why I found it hard to concentrate. There were numerous preparations before sleep, and they took forever. I filled out the duty roster and hung it on a hook. Later, I lay down on the camp-bed and rifled through old letters. Tranquillity descended on me, and it seemed as if it all had happened many months before and was already forgotten. My old thoughts surfaced and clustered together. I thought to myself that I was, indeed, eighteen, and it was an age to be proud of. I will be careful and not let this age slip away from me. Soon enough I will inherit the best life has to offer. Soon I will fall asleep and enjoy the bliss of dreaming. Thus I am preparing myself for life, and life will follow.

Perhaps the coming year will be the best ever. Winter will be here soon, and the mosquitoes will disappear. Whatever I am looking for will be given to me in spades. Maybe it won't happen exactly as I plan it, maybe not even in the manner I envisage it, but I am sure I will lack for nothing. The heat started mounting from my feet up. I filled up the entire bed. It's just a slight delay, I laughed. Even my brother used to mock me in his letters. But my brother will soon change his attitude. No doubt he, too, will love me when my wishes come true. I rubbed against the sheets. I stroked my shoulder with my hand. I will get my heart's desire in spades, I thought. And then some. It's just that everything will be slightly delayed.

Translated by Marganit Weinberger-Rotman

From Ribcage: Israeli Women's Fiction, *ed. Carol Diament and Lily Rattok (New York: Hadassah, 1994), pages 151-159.*

DAHLIA RAVIKOVITCH has written six volumes of poetry, a book of short stories, and two children's books. She is the recipient of many of Israel's literary awards, including the Shlonsky, Brenner, Ussishkin, and Bialik Prizes. She currently lives in Tel Aviv. "A Slight Delay" was written in 1965.

PROGRAMMING IDEAS

AT HOME

Torah Table Talk   A discussion of Jewish thought and values with your family and/or friends. For this article, discuss rape in the Bible by comparing two accounts: the rapes of Dinah (Genesis 34) and Tamar (2 Samuel 13). This *Torah Table Talk* is not appropriate for families with young children. Hold this discussion only with adults and mature adolescents.

Genesis 34: 1-19, 24-31

Now Dinah, the daughter whom Leah had borne to Jacob, went out to visit the daughters of the land. Shechem, son of Hamor the Hivite, chief of the country, saw her, and took her and lay with her by force. Being strongly drawn to Dinah daughter of Jacob, and in love with the maiden, he spoke to the maiden tenderly. So Shechem said to his father Hamor, "Get me this girl as a wife."

Jacob heard that he had defiled his daughter Dinah; but since his sons were in the field with his cattle, Jacob kept silent until they came home. Then Shechem's father Hamor came out to Jacob to speak with him. Meanwhile Jacob's sons, having heard the news, came in from the field. The men were distressed and very angry, because he had committed an outrage in Israel by lying with Jacob's daughter—a thing not to be done.

And Hamor spoke with them, saying, "My son Shechem longs for your daughter. Please give her to him in marriage. Intermarry with us: give your daughters to us, and take our daughters for yourselves. You will dwell among us, and the land will be open before you; settle, move about, and acquire holdings in it." Then Shechem said to her father and brothers, "Do me this favor, and I will pay whatever you tell me. Ask of me a bride-price ever so high, as well as gifts, and I will pay what you tell me; only give the maiden for a wife."

Jacob's sons answered Shechem and his father Hamor—speaking with guile because he had defiled their sister Dinah—and said to them, "We cannot do this thing, to give our sister to a man who is uncircumcised, for that is a disgrace among us. Only on this condition will we agree with you; that you will become like us in that every male among you is circumcised. Then we will give our daughters to you and take your daughters to ourselves; and we will dwell among you and become as one kindred. But if you will not listen to us and become circumcised, we will take our daughter and go."

Their words pleased Hamor and Hamor's son Shechem. And the youth lost no time in doing the thing, for he wanted Jacob's daughter ... and all males, all those who went out of the gate of his town, were circumcised.

On the third day, when they were in pain, Simeon and Levi, two of Jacob's sons, brothers of Dinah, took each his sword, came upon the city unmolested, and slew all the males. They put Hamor and his son Shechem to the sword, took Dinah out of Shechem's house, and went away. The other sons of Jacob came upon the slain and plundered the town, because their sister had been defiled. They seized all their flocks and herds and asses, all that was inside the town and outside; all their wealth, all their children, and all their wives. All that was in the houses, they took as captives and booty.

Jacob said to Simeon and Levi, "You have brought trouble on me, making me odious among the inhabitants of the land, the Canaanites and the Perizzites; my men are few in number, so that if they unite against me and attack me, I and my house will be destroyed." But they answered, "Should our sister be treated like a whore?"

2 Samuel 13

Absalom son of David had a beautiful sister named Tamar, and Amnon son of David became infatuated with her. Amnon was so distraught because of his [half-] sister Tamar that he became sick; for she was a virgin, and it seemed impossible to Amnon to do anything to her....

Amnon lay down and pretended to be sick. The king came to see him, and

Amnon said to the king, "Let my sister Tamar come and prepare a couple of cakes in front of me, and let her bring them to me." David sent a message to Tamar in the palace, "Please go to the house of your brother Amnon and prepare some food for him." Tamar went to the house of her brother Amnon, who was in bed. She took dough and kneaded it into cakes in front of him, and cooked the cakes. She took the pan and set out [the cakes], but Amnon refused to eat and ordered everyone to withdraw. After everyone had withdrawn, Amnon said to Tamar, "Bring the food inside and feed me." Tamar took the cakes she had made and brought them to her brother inside. But when she served them to him, he caught hold of her and said to her, "Come lie with me, sister." But she said to him, "Don't brother. Don't force me. Such things are not done in Israel! Don't do such a vile thing!" ... But he would not listen to her; he overpowered her and lay with her by force.

Then Amnon felt a very great loathing for her; indeed, his loathing for her was greater than the passion he had felt for her. And Amnon said to her, "Get out!" ... When King David heard about all this, he was greatly upset. Absalom didn't utter a word to Amnon, good or bad; but Absalom hated Amnon because he had violated his sister Tamar.

Two years later, when Absalom was having his flocks sheared at Baalhazor near Ephraim, Absalom invited all the king's sons.... Now Absalom gave his attendants these orders: "Watch, and when Amnon is merry with wine and I tell you to strike down Amnon, kill him!" ... Absalom's attendants did to Amnon as Absalom had ordered....

Absalom, who had fled to Geshur, remained there three years. And King David was pining away for Absalom, for [the king] had gotten over Amnon's death.

Questions for Thought and Discussion

1. What is the difference between the two rapes and the ways they are carried out?

2. How do the biblical accounts characterize Dinah and Tamar? Create a list of adjectives. Are they active or passive? How does each fight against her aggressor?

3. How do Shechem and Amnon regard Dinah and Tamar before the rape and then after the rape?

4. How are Tamar and Dinah treated by those around them? When does Dinah go to Shechem's home?

5. How do Tamar and Dinah feel? Does the Bible tell us? Why or why not?

6. In "Attitudes Toward Rape in Traditional Jewish Sources" (*Textures*, May 1994), Rachel Biale states, "Jewish traditional sources, while imbued with a world view in which women are dependent on and secondary to men, nevertheless recognize and protect a woman's legal autonomy over her body and control of her sexuality." How does the Bible make clear that women have autonomy over their bodies and control over their sexuality?

INTEREST/STUDY GROUPS

Hold a discussion based on the following questions:

1. What is your reaction to the narrator's statement, "[My boyfriend and I] were drafted into the army, and I despised myself because I felt so useless"? How is the statement typical of any new army recruit, and how does it apply more particularly to Israeli women recruits?

2. The 18-year-old narrator, although initially confused, realizes that Major Rosenblum is making a sexual advance. She then unhesitatingly rejects him, without considering the consequences (and a hostile superior officer would definitely have negative consequences). Consider similar situations in your experience, either as a teenager or as an older woman. Is the narrator typical in her initial confusion? Is she typical in being able to tell a man "I simply don't want to"?

3. In reflecting on the harassment, the narrator at first is unable to "grasp what had happened." After taking care of her tasks, however, she looks on the incident as something that happened long ago, and is able to comfort herself with optimistic slogans. Compare your own reactions to terrible events. Consider as well the sadness of this passage—the brother who "no doubt … will love me when my wishes come true" and the vagueness of the narrator's hopes. Nonetheless, these reflections following sexual harassment are remarkably free from shame. Comment.

4. The narrator says that Rachel "had the right attitude toward life. There was always someone whispering with her at night." Is this said ironically? Or does the narrator believe that always having a man is evidence of the right attitude?

5. Compare this narrative of sexual harassment with the biblical stories of the rapes of Dinah and Tamar. (Refer to the "At Home" section, pages 192-194.

6. Is rape an instance of sexual harassment taken to its most extreme degree? In other words, are sexual harassment and rape fundamentally similar acts or are they fundamentally different acts? Why?

7. In "Attitudes Toward Rape in Traditional Jewish Sources" (*Textures*, May 1994), Rachel Biale states: "Rape is a unique crime, a physical assault that violates both body and spirit." Yet our spirit is violated when we are violently assaulted in other ways or even in non-violent crimes, for example, when our house is burglarized. What makes rape unique?

8. The *New Republic* of February 24, 1997 reports on a 1996 talk given by Captain Cornelia de Groot Whitehead, a naval officer. She states that forty percent of new recruits have been "victims of serious physical or sexual abuse." Furthermore, accounts of sexual harassment in the American military routinely appear in newspapers, magazines, and television. Compare harassment in the military to harassment at the corporate office, the university, or the clinic. Also, if any study group members are knowledgeable about the Israeli Defense Forces, compare American and Israeli women's experiences as soldiers.

MEETINGS

❖ Invite a speaker, such as a therapist or a human resources professional, to discuss sexual harassment in the workplace. Use role playing and/or hold group discussions on how to handle different situations.

❖ Invite an Israeli woman to speak to the study group about her army service. Note that Israeli women do not serve in combat units. What is the effect on a female soldier of spending two years "in an indolent and low-class service unit"? Of knowing that any female soldier who enters the commander's room will "have to dust the place"? Does army duty foster the ideal of women's service to men, or does it merely reflect conditions that are pervasive within Israeli society as a whole? What aspects of women's service in the Israeli Defense Forces are repeated throughout Israeli women's work lives?

❖ View and discuss the film *To Be a Woman Soldier* (color, 50 minutes, Hebrew with English subtitles). This documentary on the realities of army service explodes the myth that Israeli women fight side by side with Israeli men. The videotape is available for $34.95 from Ergo Media in Teaneck, NJ, 1-800-695-3746. Order #225.

ANNUAL EVENTS

❖ Organize an Education Day on sexual harassment and rape. Invite a Judaic scholar to discuss rape and sexual harassment in Jewish texts, and a lawyer or feminist activist to discuss recent legislative activity on sexual harassment in the workplace. Divide the day into a morning of lectures and an afternoon of participatory workshops. Workshop sessions might include a "speak-out" by participants on their personal experiences with harassment; discussion with a psychologist or social worker on how to help rape victims; and discussion with human services professionals from major corporations on policies and procedures that prove effective in the workplace.

HANDS-ON

❖ Enroll in a self-defense course, or have your chapter or group sponsor a self-defense course for your members. Before the course begins, meet briefly and have each group member explain why she wants to take the course. After the course has ended, meet for a wrap-up session. How does each member now feel when she commutes to and from work? When she works late? Has her identity as a Jewish woman altered? What role models does Jewish history offer?

RECOMMENDED READING

Balancing Work and Family

Apter, T. E. *Working Women Don't Have Wives: Professional Success in the 1990s*. New York: St. Martin's, 1994.

Barnett, Rosalind, and Rivers, Caryl. *She Works/He Works: How Two-Income Families are Happier, Healthier, and Better-Off*. San Francisco: HarperSanFrancisco, 1996.

Berry, Mary Frances. *The Politics of Parenthood: Child Care, Women's Rights, and the Myth of the Good Mother*. New York: Viking, 1993.

Blakely, Mary Kay. *Wake Me When It's Over: A Journey to the Edge and Back*. New York: Times Books, 1989.

Bravo, Ellen. *The Job/Family Challenge: A 9 to 5 Guide*. New York: Wiley, 1995.

Chagall, Bella. *Burning Lights*. Translated by Norbert Guterman. New York: Schocken, 1946.

Eyer, Diane. *Motherguilt: How Our Culture Blames Mothers for What's Wrong with Society*. New York: Times Books, 1996.

Fishman, Sylvia Barack. "Working, Volunteering, and Jewish Living." In *A Breath of Life: Feminism in the American Jewish Community*. Hanover and London: Brandeis University Press, 1993. Pages 65-94.

Goldman, Katherine Wyse. *My Mother Worked and I Turned Out Okay*. New York: Villard, 1993.

Mahony, Rhona. *Kidding Ourselves: Breadwinning, Babies, and Bargaining Power*. New York: Basic Books, 1995.

Women and Jewish Philanthropy

Quint, Ellen Deutsch. "Women in Leadership Roles in Federations: An Historic Review," *Journal of Jewish Communal Service*, Fall/Winter 1995/96, volume 72, number 1/2, pages 96-101.

Schneider, Susan Weidman. "Jewish Women's Philanthropy: What Do We Need to Know?" *Lilith*, Winter 1993, pages 6-12, 29, 38-39. Part one of two-part series.

Schneider, Susan Weidman. "Feminist Philanthropy," *Lilith*, Fall 1993, pages 14-17. Part two of two-part series.

Tobin, Gary A. *Trends In American Jewish Philanthropy: Market Research Analysis*. Waltham, MA: Brandeis University Center for Modern Jewish Studies, 1992. Prepared for the United Jewish Appeal.

Sexual Harassment

Bravo, Ellen. *The 9 to 5 Guide to Combating Sexual Harassment: Candid Advice from 9 to 5, the National Association of Working Women*. New York: Wiley, 1992.

NiCarthy, Ginny. *You Don't Have to Take It! A Woman's Guide to Confronting Emotional Abuse at Work*. Seattle: Seal, 1993.

Rutter, Peter. *Sex, Power, and Boundaries: Understanding and Preventing Sexual Harassment*. New York: Bantam, 1996.

US Department of Defense, Office of the Inspector General. *The Tailhook Report: The Official Inquiry into the Events of Tailhook '91*. New York: St. Martin's, 1993.

Warshaw, Robin. *I Never Called It Rape: The Ms. Report on Recognizing, Fighting, and Surviving Date and Acquaintance Rape*. New York: Harper & Row, 1988.

Zimmerman, Jean. *Tailspin: Women at War in the Wake of Tailhook*. New York: Doubleday, 1995.

Unit

SOCIAL ACTION

We present three questions of women's rights within Judaism, along with the Jewish approaches to insure justice. The first case is of Zelophehad's daughters, from the biblical Book of Numbers. Zelophehad had died leaving no male heir who could inherit his property. However, he had five daughters, who as women were unable to inherit property. They appealed

to Moses, who brought their case before God. As a result, a new law was decreed: When no male heir exists, daughters inherit their father's estate. This story is the first recorded instance of Jewish women demanding justice, a demand that has continued throughout Jewish history and that reverberates throughout the Jewish world today.

The second issue is abortion. In "Abortion and Jewish Law," Rachel Biale explains abortion from the standpoint of *halakhah* (Jewish law). Most Orthodox Jews believe that a woman does not have the right to choose to terminate a pregnancy. They hold that abortion is allowed only when the mother is likely to suffer severe or near-fatal injury as a result of pregnancy or birth. A minority of contemporary Orthodox rabbis, however, have ruled that a pregnancy may be terminated when the mother is likely to suffer severe psychological injury. Rachel Biale's article spells out what is acceptable under Jewish law. According to Biale, Judaism is, at its foundation, pro-choice. The Bible does not treat the fetus as a living person, and later commentators give rulings that, in certain circumstances, specifically make abortion permissible.

Our third article explores the status of women in Israeli society. Even though Israel's near-mythical past would seem to insure equal rights for women—women fought alongside men in the war for statehood, women worked alongside men in making the desert bloom, and so on—Alice Shalvi demonstrates that Israeli women today are relegated to pink-collar occupations in the workplace and to second-class status within the family.

THE STORY OF ZELOPHEHAD'S DAUGHTERS

David Epstein and Suzanne Singer Stutman

David Epstein and Suzanne Singer Stutman, in Torah With Love, *encourage parents to study Torah together with their children. They show how Jewish values are strengthened as families discuss stories from the Bible, focusing on the moral, ethical, and spiritual questions raised. In this article, the authors use the daughters of Zelophehad to illustrate how "ten universal questions" can be used to initiate and to deepen a conversation about a Torah passage.*

A petition was presented by the daughters of Zelophehad, son of Hefer, son of Gilead, son of Makhir, son of Manasseh, of the family of Joseph's son Manasseh. The names of these daughters were Mahlah, Noa, Haglah, Milkah, and Tirtzah. They now stood before Moses, Eleazar the priest, the princes, and the entire community at the Communion Tent entrance with the following petition:

"Our father died in the desert. He was not among the members of Korah's party who protested against God, but he died because of his own sin without leaving any sons. Why should our father's name be disadvantaged in his family merely because he did not have a son? Give us a portion of land along with our father's brothers."[1]

Moses brought their case before God. God spoke to Moses, saying, "The daughters of Zelophehad have a just claim. Give them a hereditary portion of land alongside their father's brothers. Let their father's hereditary property thus pass over to them."

"Speak to the Israelites and tell them that if a man dies and has no son, his hereditary property shall pass over to his daughter. If he has no daughter, then his hereditary property shall be given to his brothers. If he has no brothers, you shall give his property to his father's brothers. If his father has no brothers, then you shall give his property to the closest relative in his family, who shall then be his heir."

This was the decreed law for the Israelites, as God had commanded Moses (Numbers 27:1-11).

The tribes protested God's decision to award the inheritance to Zelophehad's daughters, saying: "The tribe of Joseph's descendants have a just claim. This is the word that God has commanded regarding Zelophehad's daughters—You may marry anyone you wish as long as you marry within your father's tribe. The hereditary property of the Israelites will thus not be transferred from one tribe to another, and each person among the Israelites will remain attached to the hereditary property of his father's tribe" (Numbers 36:5-7).

*G*od spoke to Moses, saying, "The daughters of Zelophehad have a just claim. Give them a hereditary portion of land alongside their father's brothers."

Ten Universal Questions

1. Who is in the predicament?
The five daughters of Zelophehad: Mahlah, Noa, Haglah, Milkah, and Tirtzah; also, Moses, Eleazar the priest, the princes, and the entire community.

2. What is the predicament?
The daughters are challenging the inequity of the proposed distribution of land among the sons of the tribes and the exclusion of female inheritance.

3. What is the relationship between the people?
Their father, Zelophehad, was a descendant of Manasseh, the son of Joseph. While each of Joseph's eleven brothers formed a separate tribe, Joseph's was especially recognized. Instead of the creation of a single tribe of Joseph, two half tribes were formed by his sons, Ephraim and Manasseh.

4. Is God involved?
God decides the merits of the claim and gives precise instructions on the inheritance laws among the Israelites.

5. How is the predicament resolved?
Through God's intervention.

6. How does the community affect the predicament?
The community, the elders of the tribes of Manasseh, requests and

receives an amendment to God's ruling that the daughters are permitted to inherit the land. Daughters are permitted to inherit the land only if they marry a man within their tribe, thereby avoiding the possibility that the land would go to a member of another tribe. The latter would occur if the daughters married men from other tribes, and their children, taking their father's tribal affiliation, would own land that once belonged to Manasseh and is within its territorial boundaries. The community interest is a strong element of the resolution of the predicament. (Numbers 36:1-12.)

7. Does the predicament illuminate our contemporary life?

At its most obvious level, this story deals with distinctions made on the basis of gender; also, the process of making a moral argument as a reason for changing a law. A law may on the whole be good, but in its application, in particular unanticipated circumstances, may have consequences that are unjust.

8. What ethical and moral principles are posed by the manner in which the predicament occurred or is resolved?

The community is dealing with its moral obligation to the individual. A person who is aggrieved may petition for a consideration of her rights. The daughters do not evidence any fear or need of restraint in challenging the proposed conduct of Moses and the other leaders.

The daughters effectively present a petition for personal justice. They argue that the community's land distribution limited to male heirs will be disadvantageous to their family line. They acknowledge that sinful conduct by a father can cause a loss of inheritance, and distinguish between sins that might justify disinheritance and sins that do not.

Rebellion against God may justifiably cause disinheritance to the family line.

The daughters do admit that their father committed a personal sin, which caused his death. The community appears aware of the circumstances of the father's death, although it is not described in the episode. A personal sin is apparently not the basis for disallowing an inheritance for sons. Therefore, the daughters argue that their father's sin and resulting death should not disinherit them. The only reason for disinheriting them is because they are women, and this they challenge. God hears them and commands a general rule to include women within the rights of inheritance.

9. Does the individuals' "free will" permit any other course of conduct?

The women had the choice of accepting or challenging the custom of the community. We do not know how Moses and the leaders would have resolved the issue, because Moses brought the issue to God.

10. How can you retell the story?

The daughters' petition to Moses and the elders is similar to persuading a legislature to change a law that is having unjust results. Assign participants to serve as principal characters. Hold hearings to discuss reasons for existing law and the requested changes.

Reprinted in Textures, Hadassah National Studies Bulletin, *March 1987, vol. 5, no. 3. Originally published in David Epstein and Suzanne Singer Stutman,* Torah with Love: A Guide for Strengthening Jewish Values Within the Family *(New York: Prentice Hall/Simon & Schuster, 1986), pages 75–78.*

DAVID EPSTEIN is a trial attorney in Washington, DC and an adjunct professor at Georgetown University Law Center.

SUZANNE SINGER STUTMAN is a psychotherapist in Washington, DC. She is also executive director of the Institute for Mental Health Initiatives, which promotes mental health through innovative public health campaigns.

PROGRAMMING IDEAS

AT HOME

❖ Use Epstein and Singer's article to spur a discussion on Jewish values of social justice around your family's table. Friday night Shabbat dinner and Jewish holiday dinners are wonderful times to hold family talks on Jewish themes. In your *Torah Table Talk,* ask family members to think of other Jewish women and men who confronted authority and righted injustice.

A man came to Menahem Mendel of Kotzk and asked how he could make his sons [and daughters] devote themselves to the Torah.

Menahem Mendel answered:

"If you really want them to do this, then you yourself must spend time over the Torah, and they will do as you do. Otherwise, they will not devote themselves to the Torah but will tell their sons [and daughters] to do it. And so it will go on.

"If you yourself forget the Torah, your sons [and daughters] will also forget it, only urging their sons [and daughters] to know it. And no one will ever know the Torah."

❖ Read about and discuss twentieth-century Jewish women who have sought justice for themselves and others. Refer to the list of biographies in "Recommended Reading" at the end of Unit 4, pages 224-226.

❖ Think about and discuss ways in which your family works for social justice. How does your work for Hadassah follow in the path of Zelophehad's daughters? What projects are your children involved in? Are there projects in which you participate as a family?

INTEREST/STUDY GROUPS

Hold a discussion based on the following questions:

1. Jewish women avidly read the Bible and later Jewish texts for role models, and Zelophehad's daughters have been a particular favorite of feminists for much of the twentieth century. How is their story inspirational for women today, and how does it reflect the patriarchal society of ancient Israel?

2. Zelophehad's daughters approach Moses and the elders of Israel with a personal demand, yet their demand ultimately benefits all women. How do we know when to make such demands on our own behalf?

3. Judith S. Antonelli explains that the term "inherit" in the Bible is misleading. Although daughters could only inherit if no sons were alive, the sons were obligated to support the daughters (and the widow) in the style to which they had been accustomed. This support, which the Talmud calls maintenance, would today be called an inheritance. In cases where the estate is small, the female survivors are actually favored, because their maintenance is mandatory, while the males must support themselves through other means. Judith Antonelli continues:

"A feminist is likely to think that equality would be better for women than favoritism. That sounds fine in theory, but in practice it would be devastating, because it presumes a basis of economic equality that simply did not exist—either then *or* now. 'No-fault divorce' is a modern example of this. Treating men and women as equals under divorce law has only enriched the men and impoverished the women, for without alimony, a so-called 'privilege,' a divorced woman's income declines by 73 percent in the first year while that of a divorced man increases by 42 percent" (*In the Image of God: A Feminist Commentary on the Torah* [Northvale, NJ: Jason Aronson, 1995], page 380).

Discuss this explanation. Are there other cases where theoretical equality results in real-life hardship to women?

❖ Create a study group on the Jewish woman in history and literature. Refer to the 13-session syllabus written by Paula Hyman, professor of Jewish history at Yale University and printed in the Fall 1987 issue of *Bat Kol*, Hadassah's Jewish Education Guide. Call 212-303-8167 for a photocopy of the syllabus. (This course was prepared on audiocassette tapes for the Jewish People's University of the Air, but these tapes of Professor Hyman's lectures are no longer available.)

MEETINGS

❖ Focus on the struggle for sexual equality, beginning your meeting with the biblical story of the daughters of Zelophehad. Summarize the story and read excerpts from the Book of Numbers, 27:1-11 and 36:1-11. Discuss the following: Even though the five daughters advocate for their rights and are granted their father's inheritance, their options remain restricted. (Daughters can only inherit if no sons are alive; daughters must marry within the tribe so that the inheritance will remain intact.) Bring this problem up-to-date. What are the sex-role-based restrictions we place on our daughters (and sons)? Consider conditions on inheritance, as well as conditions on both financial and emotional support for marriages and weddings, college education and graduate schools, the raising of grandchildren, and life cycle events. How many of these conditions are spoken? How many are unspoken?

❖ Invite an Orthodox feminist (one of your members or a guest speaker) to report on the first International Conference on Feminism and Orthodoxy, held in 1997. The conference explored the impact of feminist values on traditional Jewish women's lives. Orthodox women increasingly play important roles in communal affairs of a secular nature, and they are currently aiming for a greater role in religious life as well. Discuss recent struggles.

ANNUAL EVENTS

❖ Organize a Women's Symposium together with a university in your area to address issues of concern to Jewish women today. The Women's Symposium is a full-day event sponsored jointly by a Hadassah region or chapter and the Jewish studies department of a local college or university. After an opening plenary session, participants choose from a variety of workshops. Each participant attends three workshops, with luncheon providing a break between them. Topics will vary based on the expertise of Judaic scholars, Hadassah volunteers, and rabbis in your community. Workshops at previous symposia have addressed: "Jewish Continuity and Feminism on the College Campus," "Empowering Women in the Jewish Communal World," "Religious Traditions and Feminist Trans-formations," "The Contemporary American Jewish Woman in Literature," "The Single Jewish Woman of All Ages," "Issues in Family Economics for the 21st Century," and "The Glass Ceiling," among many others. The symposium ends with a closing plenary session. For information on planning a symposium, call 212-303-8112 or 212-303-8132.

❖ As part of an Education Day or Evening, invite a multi-generational panel of Jewish women to discuss sexual equality in the American Jewish family and in society at large. How did parental restrictions, based on sex roles, affect the participants? What restrictions have the participants placed (will they place) on their children? How have societal expectations influenced the participants' choices of family status, educational achievements, and career? How have changes in women's roles over the past twenty years affected each participant? How have these changes affected the participants' parents and children?

HANDS-ON

❖ Begin a weekly Torah discussion group together with a small group of families and/or friends. Read the weekly Torah passage and discuss it together over Friday night Shabbat dinners or on Shabbat afternoons. Ellen Frankel's *The Five Books of Miriam—A Woman's Commentary on the Torah* will give you a woman's "read" of each *parashah* (weekly passage).

❖ Work together with the American Affairs/Domestic Policy chair of your Hadassah unit on issues of importance to women. (One such issue is ending domestic violence against women. Hadassah has advocated for passage and full funding of the Violence Against Women Act. See the article "A *Mezuzah* Does Not Ward Off Domestic Violence" by Rabbi Julie Ringold Spitzer and accompanying Programming Ideas, pages 119-125. Call the National American Affairs/Domestic Policy Department at 212-303-8136 for more information.)

---

1. All biblical citations are from *The Living Torah* (New York: Maznaim, 1981).

ABORTION IN JEWISH LAW

Rachel Biale

Jewish law *(halakhah)* has no monolithic position on abortion and throughout the ages there have been legal authorities who permitted abortion under certain circumstances, while others were less lenient.

Abortion appears in biblical legislation only in the case of an accidental miscarriage caused by an assault: "When two men fight and one of them pushes a pregnant woman and a miscarriage results, but no other harm ensues, the one responsible shall be fined according as the woman's husband may exact from him" (Exodus 21:22). Accidentally induced abortion is treated as a civil matter and the husband is compensated for loss of the fetus as a loss of property. In other words, the destruction of the fetus is not considered a capital crime, and therefore, later sources conclude, a fetus is not considered a living person *(nefesh)*. In fact the fetus is defined as a part of its mother's body: *ubar yerekh immo* "a fetus is [like] its mother's thigh"—(Babylonian Talmud, *Hulin* 58a, *Gittin* 23b).

Since the fetus has no independent rights it may be destroyed to save the mother's life, even as late as in the birth process itself: "If a woman is having difficulty giving birth, one cuts up the fetus within her and takes it out limb by limb because her life takes precedence over its life. Once its greater part has emerged, you do not touch it, because you may not set aside one life for another" (Babylonian Talmud, *Oholot* 7:6).

Though the fetus' life is inferior to that of the mother until it is born, it is nevertheless valued as *potential* life and one may violate the law in order to save its life (Babylonian Talmud, *Yoma* 85b). Thus, even those halakhic authorities who base their view of abortion strictly on the principle that a fetus is not a person, allow abortion only in grave circumstances.

The talmudic halakhah provides the "pro-choice" position with a clearly stated principle that the fetus is not a person, not just until the end of the second trimester of pregnancy but until the actual moment of birth.

In the twelfth century, Moses Maimonides introduced a new idea, arguing that the fetus is a "pursuer" (*rodef*), who, like a murderer pursuing a victim, may be killed to save the life of the pursued (that is, the mother) (*Mishneh Torah*, Laws Concerning Murderers and the Preservation of Life 1:9). Maimonides' ruling that the fetus is a "pursuer" implicitly undermines the argument that a fetus is not a person. Although Maimonides favored abortion when the mother's life is in danger, later authorities used his "pursuer" argument to oppose abortion. For instance, in the nineteenth century, Rabbi Hayyim Soloveitchik wrote: "The reason for the opinion of Maimonides here ... is that he believed that the fetus falls into the general category of *piku'ah nefesh* (protecting life) in the Torah since the fetus, too, is considered a *nefesh* and is not put aside for the life of others" *(Hiddushei Rabbi Hayyim Soloveitchik to Mishneh Torah).*

The Talmud cites another, quite bizarre situation when abortion is permitted that introduces a different principle: "If a woman is about to be executed, one does not wait for her until she gives birth ... one strikes her against her womb so that the child may die first, to avoid her being disgraced" (Babylonian Talmud, *Arakhin* 7a-b). The case is theoretical since capital punishment was no longer practiced in the time of the Talmud. But the principle is important: the dignity of a condemned woman takes precedence over the life of the fetus, as does the mental anguish she would experience if she were to wait for the execution in order to complete the pregnancy. The implication of this ruling for the more permissive legal authorities is that abortion may be actively sought and induced in order to save a woman from great suffering, even if it is only psychological. Thus, Jacob Emden in the eighteenth century allowed a woman who conceived a child through adultery to have an abortion because of her anguish at "the thought of giving birth to a *mamzer* (bastard)" (*She'elat Ya'avetz* No. 43).

Similarly, Rabbi Yehiel Jacob Weinberg in Switzerland permitted abortion of a fetus conceived by a woman infected with rubella, and Rabbi Eliezer Waldenberg in Israel ruled that, in theory, a Tay-Sachs fetus may be aborted. These halakhists do not justify their rulings on account of the expected suffering of the baby, a halakhically unacceptable argument, but on the mother's anguish at the prospect of bearing a fatally ill or deformed child, for "psychological suffering is in many ways much greater than the suffering of the flesh" (*Responsa Tzitz Eliezer*, Part 13, No. 102). Despite these rulings, however, even lenient halakhists generally allow abortion only when there is a *physical* (not psychological) hazard to the mother, short of an actual threat to her life.

What are the implications of Jewish law for today's debate on abortion? The talmudic *halakhah* provides the "pro-choice" position with a clearly stated principle that the fetus is not a person, not just until the end of the second trimester of pregnancy but until the actual moment of birth. Yet, the principles of protecting potential life, and the justification of abortion on the grounds of the fetus' status as "pursuer," limit abortion to circumstances of grave physical or psychological threat to the mother.

The *halakhah* also implicitly assumes that a woman has an inalienable right to determine her own fate and future of her pregnancy in its insistence on exempting women from the legal duty of procreation. While men are bound by the *mitzvah* (commandment) of procreation (based on Genesis 1:28, "Be fruitful and multiply," and Genesis 9:7), the Rabbis deliberately exempted women from that duty (Babylonian Talmud, *Yevamot* 65b). I believe they did this for reasons similar to those of today's pro-choice movement.

From Textures: Hadassah National Jewish Studies Bulletin, *May 1990, vol. 8, no. 2.*

RACHEL BIALE is the author of Women and Jewish Law: An Exploration of Women's Issues in Halakhic Sources, *first published in 1984 and reissued in 1995. She has lectured widely throughout the United States, Israel, and Europe on Jewish women. She holds an MSW degree and currently works as a senior clinician with Jewish Family and Children's Services of the East Bay in Berkeley, California.*

PROGRAMMING IDEAS

AT HOME

Torah Table Talk   A discussion of Jewish thought and values with your family and/or friends. The circumstances under which Jewish law permits abortion are subject to much discussion. The Talmud allows abortion to save the life of the mother, because, as Rashi explains, the fetus is not a living person. However, Maimonides explains that abortion to save the mother's life is permitted for a different reason: because the fetus pursues the mother and will kill her unless it is killed. According to this explanation, the fetus is a living being. Subsequent Jewish legal authorities have tried to accommodate both Maimonides and the Talmud as interpreted by Rashi.

Mishnah (compiled approximately 200), Oholot 7:6

If a woman is having difficulty giving birth, one cuts up the fetus within her and takes it out limb by limb, because her life takes precedence over its life. Once its greater part has emerged, you do not touch it, because you may not set aside one life for another.

Babylonian Talmud (compiled between 200 and 500), Gittin 23b and Hulin 58a

A fetus is [as] its mother's thigh.

Rashi (1040-1105), explicating Babylonian Talmud, Sanhedrin 72b

For as long as it has not yet emerged into the world, it is not a *nefesh* (living person) and one may kill it to save its mother.

Maimonides (1135-1204), Mishneh Torah, *Laws Relating to Murder and the Preservation of Life 1:9*

This is ... a negative commandment, that we have no pity on the life of the pursuer (*rodef*). Consequently the Sages have ruled that if a woman with child is having difficulty in giving birth, the child inside her may be taken out, either by drugs or by surgery, because it is regarded as one pursuing her and trying to kill her. But once its head has appeared, it must not be touched, for we may not set aside one human life to save another human life; and what is happening is the course of nature.

Rabbi Yehezkel Landau (eighteenth century), Noda bi'Yehudah (2nd ed.), *Hoshen Mishpat number 59*

And the difficulty in the ruling of Maimonides is that he considers the fetus before its head emerges to be a pursuer, and after its head emerges he does not consider him a pursuer for that is "the course of nature." And this is peculiar since before the head emerges it is also "the course of nature"! Unfortunately, this matter has not been clarified for me and I find no clear way to explain it, and to explain it away with excuses—that has already been done in previous generations.[1]

Rabbi Shneor Zalman (Freiken) of Lublin (died 1902), responsa *Torat Hesed 2:42*

[He compares therapeutic abortion to the case of a ship that is about to sink at sea, when we are permitted to throw the cargo overboard.] In such circumstances the cargo is the reason for the danger to life and is therefore called a pursuer. Even though there is no crime in the cargo that is on the boat at all, and the excess weight is caused equally by the people (*nefashot*) as by the cargo, nevertheless the cargo is considered a pursuer and it is sacrificed to save the people.

Rabbi Hayyim Soloveitchik (died 1918), Hiddushei to Mishneh Torah, Laws Relating to Murder and the Preservation of Life 1:9

The reason for the opinion of Maimonides here, namely, that the fetus is like a pursuer pursuing her in order to kill her, is that he believed that a fetus falls into the general law of *piku'ah nefesh* (avoiding hazard to life) in the Torah since a fetus, too, is considered a *nefesh* and is not put aside for the life of others. And if we intend to save [her] life through the life of the fetus and he were not a pursuer, the law would pertain that you do not save one *nefesh* through [sacrificing] another. Therefore, if we were to judge this case according to the general rule of *piku'ah nefesh* in the Torah we would not push aside the fetus's life for the mother's life. And it is only because of the law of saving the one who is pursued that there is the ruling that the fetus's life is put aside to save the mother's life.

Questions for Thought and Discussion

1. What are the consequences of considering the fetus as a *nefesh*, a living person?

2. How does Rabbi Shneor Zalman of Lublin reconcile Rashi's and Maimonides's opinions?

3. The method for aborting the fetus described by the Talmud and Maimonides seems similar to the method known today as partial birth abortion. What are the differences and similarities? Why does the Mishnah permit this method?

4. Orthodox authorities today generally permit abortion only under extraordinary circumstances. Explain why.

5. With reliable prenatal diagnosis available for certain conditions (Tay-Sachs disease, Down's syndrome), abortion to prevent a lifetime of suffering is now possible. However, Jewish law does not recognize this as a valid reason for abortion. Only when the birth of such an infant is likely to threaten the mother's life is abortion permissible. What is your reaction?

INTEREST/STUDY GROUPS

Hold a discussion based on the following questions:

1. How does the Jewish perspective on abortion, as presented by Rachel Biale, fit into America's abortion debate? Can a Jewish perspective in any way affect the deadlock between the two factions, pro-choice and pro-life?

2. Rachel Biale states: "The *halakhah* [Jewish law] implicitly assumes that a woman has an inalienable right to determine her own fate and the future of her pregnancy in its insistence on exempting women from the duty of procreation." Yet Jewish law forbids a woman to determine the fate of her own body by, for instance, cutting off a limb (unless removing the limb is necessary to save her life)

or even putting on a tattoo. These restrictions hold true for men as well. Discuss in connection with Biale's statement and in connection with the abortion question in American society.

MEETINGS

❖ Invite a guest speaker to discuss Jewish outlooks on abortion. If possible, ask the speaker to give an overview of the teachings of Jewish law and to summarize the opinions of the different Jewish denominations today. Coordinate the meeting with your American Affairs chair, and include information on Hadassah's work to protect reproductive rights. Call the National American Affairs/Domestic Policy Department at 212-303-8136 for information.

ANNUAL EVENTS

❖ Participate as a Hadassah unit in a pro-choice rally. Coordinate with your American Affairs/Domestic Policy chair and with other women's organizations in your community.

❖ As part of an Education Day or Evening, include guest speakers on abortion. Ask a Judaic scholar to present an overview of the teachings of Jewish law, and ask a Jewish feminist activist to discuss the history of abortion in the United States and the impact made by and felt by American Jews. What were the dangers of illegal abortion in the decades prior to *Roe v. Wade*? What are the physical and psychological implications of abortion today? What current legal battles are emerging? Provide participants with Hadassah's issue card "Protect Reproductive Choice" to provoke thought and to promote interest in membership. (Call the National Order Department at 1-800-880-9455. Order number: #R654a. Minimum order: 500 cards. Cost: $5.00 for 500.)

HANDS-ON

❖ Support Hadassah's pro-choice efforts. Call the National American Affairs/Domestic Policy Department at 212-303-8136 for assistance and information.

❖ Work in collaboration with synagogues and Jewish organizations in your community to support local abortion and family planning clinics.

1. Translations of the writings of Yehezkel Landau, Shneor Zalman (Freiken) of Lublin, and Hayyim Soloveitchik are from Rachel Biale, *Women and Jewish Law: An Exploration of Women's Issues in Halakhic Sources* (New York: Schocken, 1984), pages 231, 233, 232.

WOMEN AND SOCIETY IN ISRAEL

Alice Shalvi

In November 1989, the Jewish Education Department first published Alice Shalvi's essay on women's position in Israeli society. Sadly, the inequity that Shalvi reported then remains true today—and some would say it has intensified. In her 1995 book, Jewish Women/Jewish Men: The Legacy of Patriarchy in Jewish Life, *Aviva Cantor observes that Israeli women are second-class citizens in the economic arena. Despite Israel's 1964 equal employment law, she notes that women earn only 69 percent of the wages of men, and that discrimination exists in all job sectors. Furthermore, in 1992 the Israel Women's Network estimated that ten rapes take place every day in Israel and that ten percent of Israeli women are regularly battered. In the essay below, statistics have been updated whenever possible.*

Until recently, it was widely held—both in Israel and abroad—that Israel was a state in which women had achieved a greater degree of equality than in the vast majority of even Western countries, with the possible exception of Scandinavia. Many factors gave rise to this view: women's marked presence among the pioneers who resettled the land early in the twentieth century; women's participation in the armed struggle for independence reflected today in conscription of young women into the Israeli Defense Forces; the kibbutz way of life, with its concept of equality among all members; the powerful women's organizations and their role in providing health and educational services; women's involvement in politics, reaching its climax in the figure of Golda Meir, one of the very few women in the world to head a government; and the universally-held view of the Jewish *materfamilias* as a major power within the Jewish family and community.

Yet the reality is far removed from the ideal. Women in Israel, as in most countries, are engaged primarily in "pink-collar" occupations. According to 1987 findings from the Central Bureau of Statistics, three quarters of Israeli women are employed in "women's" jobs—secretary, teacher, seamstress, child care worker, etc. A mere two percent are employed in senior executive or management posts.

How can one explain the substantial gap between old ideals and the starker reality?

Three factors contribute to the regression from the ideals of 1948 and earlier; all three confirm traditional notions regarding women's primary role as helpmate, mother, wife, and homemaker. The three are *halakhah* (Jewish rabbinical law) and Jewish tradition, modern legislation, and received opinion or social convention.

Halakhah presupposes that women are married homemakers; thus they are excluded from public roles in the community, the synagogue, and the *beit midrash* (place of Torah study).

Modern legislation, like Jewish tradition and Jewish law, conceives of woman as different from man, specifically as regards her marital duties and her maternal role. As wife and mother, she receives special treatment, but it is a treatment that perpetuates the stereotype of woman as spouse and homemaker rather than as equal partner in the economy, government, or defense.

Precisely the same picture emerges when one surveys the grey area of social convention and received opinion—because this third factor is less easily defined, analyzed, and summarized than either Jewish law or Knesset legislation. Social convention and received opinion will be the focus of this article. Perhaps they are even more critical than *halakhah* or modern legislation in determining the state of things.

Two aspects of Israeli life are of vital importance where the status of women is concerned: family and security. Israel is a family-centered society. Recent statistics indicate that 25.1 is the average marriage age for women, 28.1 for men. Only 3 percent of Israeli women never marry. The average number of children per couple (2.38) is high by comparison with other developed countries, many of which have gone beyond zero population growth to a negative population balance; divorce rates are comparatively low; 9.2 out of every 1,000 Israeli women ages 15 to 49 became divorced in 1994 (the most recent year for which statistics are available).

These statistics in themselves are indicative of nothing save the average Israeli's adherence to traditional Jewish values of permanence and stability in family life. What must concern us is that the average Israeli "family" is invariably interpreted as being a social unit comprised of a male income earner (usually older, and possibly better educated than his spouse), customarily employed outside the home; a female whose primary functions are those of homemaker; and children, the care of whom is primarily the duty of the woman-wife-mother.

Because this stereotype is widely accepted even by women and because it is reinforced by both Jewish and secular law, the percentage of women in the work force has, until the mid-nineties, been low. As of 1996, 46 percent of Israeli women were gainfully employed, and, of those employed outside the home, 43 percent worked part time, to enable them to cope with the duties of homemaking. Even today, the majority of working women are employed in those lower-paying occupations that demand a lower degree of personal responsibility, and less need to work after hours. The unfortunate result is that few women are in management or high-ranking, high-income-earning positions.

Though there are many women doctors, only a handful teach at the country's medical schools. Over half of government-employed lawyers are women, but that is partly because their male counterparts prefer lucrative private practice and are impervious to the fact that civil service employment implies fixed hours more compatible with family life.

Denied equal participation in the defense of the country, women are also denied membership in what is undoubtedly Israel's most wide-ranging and effective Old Boys' Network. Women have no organized framework in which to acquire "buddies" and none in which to accumulate "*protekzia*" or powerful influence in achieving desired social or economic goals. Men who serve in the Israeli Defence Fund, particularly those who attain senior rank in the regular army, acquire—at no personal financial cost—invaluable managerial skills which can hardly be attained by women of comparable age. No wonder so many senior officers, upon retiring from service at the comparatively early age of 45 or 50, have gone straight into top managerial positions or, even more significantly, into key political positions in the Knesset or in the cabinet itself. Yigal Allon, Moshe Dayan, Yigael Yadin, Yitzhak Rabin, Ariel Sharon, Ezer Weizmann, Haim Bar-Lev, and Raphael Eytan are some of the names that spring to mind. What, after all, is more natural than that a former Chief-of-Staff or corps commander should become Minister of Defense? And if Defense, why not also Minister of Education, of Finance, of Trade and Industry, or *anything*?

So the "protective" measure of keeping women safe at home, out of range of enemy weapons, ultimately boomerangs against them in

The voice of one-half of Israel's population remains unheard. Israel is not yet the ideal land of equal opportunity, reward, and status which Herzl, the early pioneers, and even the founders of modern Israel envisioned.

civilian life. Considered as unable to meet the military demands of the country, they are, in turn, perceived as unable to meet the demands of social administration, industrial management, political decision-making. On the rare occasions when a woman does rise to the occasion, as Golda Meir did, she is paid the ultimate compliment of being termed "the only man in the cabinet," with its attendant derogatory description of "unfeminine," overly forceful, etc.

Thus Israeli women today find themselves relegated to secondary social status. The subsequent loss is not only women's; the social fabric of Israel as a whole is damaged because women are unable to make the contribution that they could if social attitudes and institutions were to encourage them to do so. The voice of one-half of Israel's population remains unheard. Israel is not yet the ideal land of equal opportunity, reward, and status which Herzl, the early pioneers, and even the founders of modern Israel envisioned.

But as the great visionary of modern Zionism said, "If you will it, it is not a dream." Israeli women are increasingly becoming aware of their disabilities and of the discrimination to which they are subjected, wittingly or unwittingly. Increasingly, they are displaying their determination to bring about significant reforms. Feminist grassroots movements are proliferating, while the well-established women's organizations are becoming more feminist in orientation and action. Women's will, combined with increased education, resourcefulness, initiative, inventiveness, and compromise may well bring about what *halakhah* and Knesset legislation have failed to produce and may, in the not-too-distant future, turn dream into reality.

From Textures, Hadassah National Jewish Studies Bulletin, *November 1989, vol. 8, no. 1. Adapted.*

ALICE SHALVI, Ph.D., founding Chairwoman of the Israel Women's Network, was on the faculty of the Hebrew University of Jerusalem from 1950 to 1990. From 1975 to 1990 she also served as principal of Pelech, Religious Experimental High School for Girls.

P R O G R A M M I N G   I D E A S

AT HOME

Torah Table Talk A discussion of Jewish thought and values with your family and/or friends. "Clockwork Doll" was first published in Israel in 1959. The translation below, by Arieh Sachs, is from *The Modern Hebrew Poem Itself*, edited by Stanley Burnshaw, T. Carmi, and Ezra Spicehandler (Cambridge, MA: Harvard University Press, 1989), pages 186-187.

Dahlia Ravikovitch, "Clockwork Doll"

That night I was a clockwork doll
And I turned to the right and to the left, in all directions,
And I fell on my face to the ground and was broken to bits.
And they tried to join my broken bits expertly.

And after that I became again a complete doll,
And my whole manner was balanced and obedient,
But then I was already a doll of a second type
Like an injured twig held by a tendril.

And afterwards I went to dance at the ball,
But they put me in the company of cats and dogs
Whereas all my steps were measured and rhythmical.

And I had golden hair and I had blue eyes
And I had a dress the color of flowers in the garden
And I had a hat of straw with a cherry ornament.

Questions for Thought and Discussion

1. The speaker's identification with a mechanical doll is complete. She goes beyond dreaming about or imagining herself as a doll, and instead has become lifeless and inhuman. What effect does this loss of self have upon you? Can you empathize with the speaker's feeling of mechanization? How would you classify this feeling? Is it a condition of modernity? Of womanhood? Of living in Israel?

2. Consider the images of vulnerability and alienation in "Clockwork Doll." For instance, the toy is "broken to bits," is then compared to "an injured twig held by a tendril," and at the dance is "put in the company of cats and dogs." How do these images particularly reflect women's lives? How do they particularly reflect life in Israel?

3. The poem ends without giving readers any feeling of closure. Arieh Sachs calls this "a conclusion in which nothing is concluded." How does this non-closure affect you? How does the child-like yet remote quality affect you? How do these lines on appearance particularly speak to women in Israel and America?

Additional At-Home Activities

❖ Read recent Israeli women's writings in *Ribcage: Israeli Women's Fiction*, a collection of 16 short stories, edited by Carol Diament and Lily Rattok (New York: Hadassah, 1994). To purchase, call the Hadassah National Order Department

1-800-880-9455. Order number: #R492. Cost: $10 for Hadassah members; $15 for non-members.

❖ Correspond with an Israeli pen-pal, either through the mail or the Internet. Refer to the "Hands-On" section, page 221.

❖ Listen to Israeli women's music. Judaica stores and synagogue shops frequently carry CD's and cassettes of Israeli music; or contact Tara Publications for information, 29 Derby Avenue, Cedarhurst, NY 11516; phone 516-295-2290.

INTEREST/STUDY GROUPS

Hold a discussion based on the following questions:

1. Why does the myth of sexual equality in Israel continue despite evidence to the contrary? In particular, discuss the myths of sexual equality on the kibbutz and in the war for independence.

2. Of the three factors that contribute to sexual inequality—*halakhah*, legislation, and social convention—which does the most harm? If you could work on improving only one area, which would you choose? Why?

3. Discuss the possibility of women's and men's equal participation in the Israeli armed forces. What are the advantages and disadvantages to women sharing defense duties equally with men?

4. Hadassah, as an organization, provides medical care and other services to Israeli men and women, yet it generally avoids involvement in Israeli politics. Nonetheless, Hadassah has taken a stand in support of the Women of the Wall, a group of women who defy Israeli law by holding prayer services at the Western Wall in Jerusalem. In your opinion, what sort of involvement should Hadassah, as an American Zionist organization, have in Israeli women's struggle for greater equality? To what extent should we separate volunteer work from politics?

5. Part of Hadassah's mission is strengthening ties between American and Israeli Jews. Is Professor Shalvi's article likely to build bridges between Israeli and American Jewish women or to alienate Americans from Israelis?

MEETINGS

❖ Ask Israeli women living in your area to speak to your group, and read selections from *Networking for Women*, the newsletter of the Israeli Women's Network, to initiate discussion on issues of importance to women in Israel. (For information on ordering the newsletter, write to: Friends of Israel Women's Network Inc., PO Box 559, Union, NJ 07083.) How do these issues differ from American Jewish women's issues? Ask participants how their lives as women differ in America and Israel, what issues most concern Israeli women activists, and how religion affects women's issues in Israel and in America. Have participants' attitudes toward feminism and toward Judaism changed since coming to America? How?

ANNUAL EVENTS

❖ Organize an Education Day or Evening on Israeli and American Jewish women, our differences and similarities. Invite both an American Jewish and an Israeli scholar to hold a dialogue on women's concerns. Prior to the event, discuss with your guest speakers the questions that you would like them to address. Depending on their areas of expertise, focus on one or two topics in addition to a general overview of women's concerns, for example: Jewish women's literature; the impact of feminism on Jewish religion; women and Jewish law; demographic issues and their impact on women in Israel and the United States.

HANDS-ON

❖ Support Israeli feminists in their efforts to bring about sexual equality in Israel. US-Israel Women to Women promotes dialogue between our two countries. Write to: 275 Seventh Avenue, 8th floor, New York, NY 10001 (phone 212-206-8057; fax 212-206-7031). The International Committee for Women of the Wall (ICWOW) seeks to aid women who hold prayer services at the Western Wall. To assist in fundraising, public relations, etc., write to Vanessa Ochs, Associate Director, ICWOW, 57 Fairmount Avenue, Morristown, NJ 07960.

❖ Start a dialogue with one Hadassah-Israel chapter through letter writing. Write to Hadassah-Israel at 24 Straus Street, POB 5031, Jerusalem 91050, and ask for the address of a chapter seeking American correspondents. In the near future, you will have an opportunity use the Internet to share your interests and concerns with Hadassah-Israel members. Check the Hadassah web page (http://www.hadassah.org).

❖ Organize an Israeli dance course for your chapter or group. Or join an Israeli dance class on your own.

❖ Learn Hebrew, the language of Israel. Join or start an *Ivrit la Hadassah* class in your community. Call the National Hebrew Studies Department of Hadassah for details, 212-303-8164.

RECOMMENDED READING

Women's Equality and Jewish Feminism

Baker, Adrienne. *The Jewish Woman in Contemporary Society: Transitions and Traditions.* New York: New York University Press, 1993.

Baum, Charlotte, Hyman, Paula, and Michel, Sonya. *The Jewish Woman in America.* New York: Dial, 1976.

Berkovits, Eliezer. *Jewish Women in Time and Torah.* Hoboken, NJ: Ktav, 1990.

Biale, Rachel. *Women and Jewish Law: An Exploration of Women's Issues in Halakhic Sources.* New York: Schocken, 1984.

Cantor, Aviva. *Jewish Women/Jewish Men: The Legacy of Patriarchy in Jewish Life.* San Francisco: HarperSanFrancisco, 1995.

Cohen, Marcia. *The Sisterhood: The True Story of the Women Who Led the Women's Movement.* New York: Simon & Schuster, 1988.

Faludi, Susan. *Backlash: The Undeclared War Against American Women.* New York: Crown, 1991.

Fausto-Sterling, Anne. *Myths of Gender: Biological Theories About Women and Men.* New York: Basic Books, 1985.

Fishman, Sylvia Barack. *A Breath of Life: Feminism in the American Jewish Community.* Hanover, NH: Brandeis University Press/University Press of New England, 1993.

Greenberg, Blu. *On Women and Judaism: A View from Tradition.* Philadelphia: Jewish Publication Society, 1981.

Heschel, Susannah, ed. *On Being a Jewish Feminist.* New York: Schocken, 1983.

Kaye/Kantrowitz, Melanie, and Klepfisz, Irene, eds. *The Tribe of Dina: A Jewish Women's Anthology.* Boston: Beacon, 1989.

Koltun, Elizabeth, ed. *The Jewish Woman: New Perspectives.* New York: Schocken, 1976.

Morgan, Robin. *Sisterhood Is Powerful: An Anthology of Writings From the Women's Liberation Movement.* New York: Random House, 1970.

Schneider, Susan Weidman. *Jewish and Female.* New York: Simon & Schuster, 1984.

Steinem, Gloria. *Outrageous Acts and Everyday Rebellions.* New York: Dutton, 1986.

Abortion

Chalker, Rebecca, and Downer, Carol. *A Woman's Book of Choices: Abortion, Menstrual Extraction, RU486*. New York: Four Walls Eight Windows, 1992.

Chesler, Ellen. *Woman of Valor: Margaret Sanger and the Birth Control Movement in America*. New York: Doubleday, 1992.

Feldman, David. *Marital Relations, Birth Control and Abortion in Jewish Law*. New York: Schocken, 1974.

Kaplan, Laura. *The Story of Jane*. New York: Pantheon, 1995. Jane was the name of an underground, women-led, abortion provider service in Chicago in the years before *Roe v. Wade*.

Poppema, Suzanne. *Why I Am an Abortion Doctor*. Amherst, NY: Prometheus Books, 1996.

Women in Israel

Diament, Carol, and Rattok, Lily, eds. *Ribcage: Israeli Women's Fiction*. New York: Hadassah, 1994.

Hazelton, Lesley. *Israeli Women: The Reality Behind the Myths*. New York: Simon & Schuster, 1977.

Israel Information Center, *Women in Israel*. New York: Israel Information Center, 1996. (Write to: 800 Second Avenue, New York, NY 10017.)

Rein, Natalie. *Daughters of Rachel: Women in Israel*. New York: Penguin, 1980.

Sered, Susan Starr. *Women As Ritual Experts: The Religious Lives of Elderly Jewish Women in Jerusalem*. New York: Oxford University Press, 1992.

Shamgar-Handelman, Lea. *Israeli War Widows: Beyond the Glory of Heroism*. South Hadley, MA: Begin & Garvey, 1986.

Spiro, Melford. *Gender and Culture: Kibbutz Women Revisited*. Durham, NC: Duke University Press, 1979.

Stein, Geraldine. *Israeli Women Speak Out*. Philadelphia: Lippincott, 1979.

Swirski, Barbara, and Safir, Marilyn P., eds. *Calling the Equality Bluff: Women in Israel*. New York: Macmillan, 1991.

Biographies of 20th-Century Women Social Activists

Badt-Strauss, Bertha. *White Fire: The Life and Works of Jessie Sampter*. 1956; reprint, Wyncote, PA: Ayer, 1977.

Ben-Zvi, Rachel Yanait. *Before Golda: Manya Shochat*. Translated from Hebrew by Sandra Shurin. Reprint, New York: Biblio, 1989.

Dash, Joan. *Summoned to Jerusalem: The Life of Henrietta Szold*. New York: Harper & Row, 1979.

Davidson, Margaret. *The Golda Meir Story*. New York: Charles Scribner's Sons, 1976.

Fineman, Irving. *Woman of Valor: The Story of Henrietta Szold*. New York: Simon & Schuster, 1961.

Fink, Greta. *Great Jewish Women: Profiles of Courageous Women from the Maccabean Period to the Present*. New York: Menorah, 1978.

Freund-Rosenthal, Miriam. *In My Lifetime: Family, Community, Zion*. Chestnut Ridge, NY: Town House, 1989.

Goldman, Emma. *Living My Life*, 2 vols. 1930; reprint, New York: Dover, 1971.

Greenberg, Marian G. *There Is Hope for Your Children: Youth Aliyah, Henrietta Szold and Hadassah*. New York: Hadassah, 1986.

Gruber, Ruth. *Raquela: A Woman of Israel*. 1978; reprint, New York: Biblio, 1993 (special Hadassah edition).

Hay, Peter. *Ordinary Heroes: Chana Szenes and the Dream of Zion*. New York: G. P. Putnam's Sons, 1986.

Henry, Sondra, and Taitz, Emily. *Remarkable Jewish Women: Rebels, Rabbis, and Other Women from Biblical Times to the Present*. Philadelphia: Jewish Publication Society, 1996.

Krantz, Hazel. *Daughter of My People: Henrietta Szold and Hadassah*, 1987; reprint, Northvale, NJ: Jason Aronson, 1995.

Levin, Alexandra Lee. *The Szolds of Lombard Street*. Philadelphia: Jewish Publication Society, 1960.

Levin, Marlin. *Balm in Gilead*, revised ed. New York: Schocken, 1997.

Lowenthal, Marvin. *Henrietta Szold: Life and Letters*. New York: Viking, 1942.

Masters, Anthony. *The Summer That Bled: The Biography of Hannah Senesh*. New York: St. Martin's, 1972.

Meed, Vladka. *On Both Sides of the Wall: Memoirs from the Warsaw Ghetto*. Washington, DC: Holocaust Publications, 1979.

Meir, Golda. *My Life*. New York: G. P. Putnam's Sons, 1975.

Merriam, Eve. *Emma Lazarus—Woman with a Torch*. New York: Citadel, 1956.

Meyer, Annie Nathan. *It's Been Fun*. New York: Henry Shuman, 1954.

Pogrebin, Letty Cottin. *Deborah, Golda and Me: Being Jewish and Female in America*. New York: Crown, 1991.

Rogow, Sally. *Lillian Wald: The Nurse in Blue*. Philadelphia: Jewish Publication Society, 1971.

Senesh, Hannah. *Hannah Senesh: Her Life & Diary*. Introduction by Abba Eban. New York: Schocken, 1972.

Senesh, Hannah. *Letters, Diary, Poems*. New York: Herzl Press, 1972.

Shulman, Alix Kates. *To the Barricades: The Anarchist Life of Emma Goldman*. New York: Crowell, 1971.

Solomon, Hannah G. *Fabric of My Life: Autobiography of a Social Pioneer*. New York: Bloch, 1946.

Suhl, Yuri. *Ernestine Rose and the Battle for Human Rights*. 1959; reprint, New York: Biblio, 1990.

Syrkin, Marie. *Blessed Is the Match*. Philadelphia: Jewish Publication Society, 1947.

Wald, Lillian. *The House on Henry Street*. New York: Henry Holt, 1915.

SPIRITUALITY

For centuries, roles for men and women in Judaism were clear-cut: Women were responsible for the domestic sphere—home and children. Men were responsible for the theological sphere—Torah study and synagogue worship. But for many Jewish women and men today, these sex roles no longer hold true. Indeed, Jewish women have proven that both men

and women gain when women actively participate in theological life.

Vanessa Ochs remarks on Jewish women's spiritual history, and she chronicles the changes in Jewish women's religious lives today. When Henrietta Szold's mother died in the early years of our century, Szold publicly recited *Kaddish*, the mourner's sanctification of God's name, a tradition from which women had previously been excluded. In our time, Jewish women have fought for equality in all aspects of religious practice. Women in the Reform and Conservative denominations have demanded and won rabbinical ordination. Prayer books for these denominations have included the matriarchs where previously only the patriarchs were named. Naming ceremonies for baby girls have been created. And among Orthodox women, separate women's prayer groups that adhere to *halakhah* have been established throughout America.

Some of the new rituals created by women may seem far-fetched or unrelated to Jewish tradition—such as the menstruation ritual described by Tamara Cohen in "Contemporary Jewish Women's Rituals." But as Cohen demonstrates, innovation does not threaten Judaism. The new women's rituals work because they wed Jewish tradition with genuine spiritual meaning.

In "On Blessing," the feminist poet Marcia Falk shares her creative processes with readers as she composes Jewish blessings that incorporate feminine imagery. She argues that traditional masculine images of God as lord and king "no longer functioned metaphorically but had become instead an idolatrous name." Rather than replacing standard masculine images with new, soon-to-be standard feminine images, she proposes "a process of ongoing naming, which would point to the diversity of our experiences."

The fiction writer Nessa Rapoport describes how she came to compose *A Woman's Book of Grieving* in the article "On Sorrow and Solace." Like Gail Katz Meller in Unit 1, Rapoport explores how we grieve, and how grief changes us. Until very recently, Jewish rituals for grieving had been written by men, and they spoke primarily to men's needs. Nessa Rapoport's poetry, in contrast, speaks specifically to women.

THE FUTURE FOR JEWISH WOMEN

Vanessa L. Ochs

Women are revisioning Judaism from within. The future for women in Judaism will be shaped by the ways Jewish women see themselves, their potential, their responsibilities and rights as Jews.

Two major changes influencing the future for Jewish women in America have already happened. Not to take advantage of these changes is to miss a real opportunity.

The first change has been theological. Women have recognized that they have not had equal status in Jewish law and life. Women have acknowledged that this inequality is inconsistent with the ethics of contemporary life and, more crucially, they have recognized that such inequality is inconsistent with the central teachings of Torah. The second change has been a practical change, reflecting an adjustment in Jewish life and in Jewish law, giving more equitable consideration and responsibilities to women.

There was a time when Jewish women hesitated to blurt out the obvious: aspects of Jewish life, abuses of Jewish law, and limiting interpretations of sacred texts oppressed women. Women couldn't believe what they saw with their own eyes and experienced in their own souls. Why? Because it didn't look good to non-Jews? Because fathers and husbands would take it personally? Because Jewish women were good daughters and did not make waves?

As the greatest of Jewish feminists wrote in 1903, "To the Jew, accustomed from time immemorial to regard Jewish women as symbols of loyalty, a daughter's insubordination is nothing short of a catastrophe." The speaker was none other than Henrietta Szold, who proclaimed, "The time has passed when the argument holds: So your forefathers did, so I do, so you must do."

A poignant example of Szold's commitment to change is revealed in a letter she wrote to Hayyim Peretz, a family friend who offered to say *Kaddish* for Szold's mother, a woman who had eight daughters and no son. She thanked Peretz profusely and refused his offer. Szold, who knew the sacred texts from her studies with her father and from her studies at the Jewish Theological Seminary (where she was the first female student), explained that while women were not obligated to say *Kaddish*, Jewish law didn't prohibit women from saying *Kaddish* if they were capable of doing so. A woman's recital of *Kaddish*, she judged, was valid—God heard and accepted a woman's prayer of praise and sanctification. Moreover, a woman who recited *Kaddish* addressed her own important personal spiritual needs. As Szold wrote in her polite letter of refusal, "The *Kaddish* means to me that the survivor publicly and markedly manifests his wish and intention to assume the relationship to the Jewish community which his parents had, and that so the chain of tradition remains unbroken from generation to generation, each adding its own link. You can do that for the generations of your family, I must do that for the generations of my family." Jewish women are committed, as Szold named it, "to the regeneration of a whole people."

Women will have to determine the changes that are necessary and women will have to do whatever is necessary to make effective changes. To achieve this, they must give themselves authorization. Had young, trained women in the Conservative movement not demanded to be ordained, and had they not proved themselves to be intellectually and spiritually prepared for the rabbinate, would an august body of Conservative rabbis have thought to sit and debate women's ordination as an intellectual lark? If women wait for invitations or permission slips, they will never come.

Jewish women acted and men followed their lead. If men were suspicious at first, and if men were angry, their reactions made sense. It is not pleasant to yield power, to acknowledge that women had been hurt and ignored. Such an acknowledgment causes agitation and guilt. But much of that initial fear and resistance has turned to an acceptance of women as full-fledged Jews, because acceptance of women is becoming the status quo. Today, when one thinks of Jewish theologians and scholars who speak for women—Professors Judith Plaskow, Susannah Heschel, Ellen Umansky, Judith Baskin, Aviva Zornberg—one may also consider Rabbi Emanuel Rackman, Rabbi Eliezer Berkovits, Rabbi Yitz Greenberg, Rabbi Avi Weiss, and Rabbi Shlomo Riskin, who are all involved with major theological work concerning Jewish women—and who have all paid, in various ways, for the stances they've taken. Why have these rabbis been criticized? Because many Jews, generally the less educated (NOT the more observant), persist in believing that some place in Torah explicitly states that God has ordained domesticity for women and public worship and study for men. A rudimentary knowledge of sacred texts would reveal that such beliefs reflect only social mores within Jewish communities and not Jewish law.

The second, practical change in Judaism has been the increased effort to take women's lives and experiences into consideration. In progressive movements, this practical change has meant ordaining women, including women in public worship, and choosing women as community and synagogue leaders. It has also meant making changes in sermons to reflect the Jews who are women. When rabbis now speak about female personalities in Torah, they no longer emphasize only their nurturing, self-sacrificing traits—they point out a woman's persistence of faith, her leadership, her fearlessness, her relationship to God. This practical change in Judaism has resulted in changes in liturgy. It no longer sounds radical to pray to the God of Abraham *and* Sarah. The practical change in Judaism has resulted in ritual changes as well. Naming ceremonies for baby girls are now ubiquitous. Other ceremonies are less well known and have no standard formula—but they exist as women create Jewish rituals to mark major events in their lives.

Practical changes have also been made in traditional Judaism, where sexual separation is accepted and endorsed by women, because it is said to foster pride, self-reliance, initiative, and group cohesiveness. While these changes have been dramatic, they are clearly of a different nature from the changes in Conservative and Reform Judaism because of the community's adherence to *halakhah*. For instance, communities have made installing *eruvim* (symbolic boundary markers) a priority so women with small children can carry or wheel them to synagogue on Shabbat. Women have created institutions so that they can teach and study sacred texts at the highest levels. The idea of educating women to be sophisticated Jews would no longer be considered, as it was in Szold's time, like a dangerous dalliance with the "custom of the gentiles."

Women's prayer groups have been created within the last 15 years, enabling women to—in the words of one participant—"recognize the importance of addressing God directly, collectively, and out loud so that we can hear ourselves in each other's [female] voices, as well as develop spiritual skills as active participants, not as passive or invisible onlookers."

The battles have been waged and, in large part, won. It's been a decade since anyone argued that Jewish women who took their spiritual needs or Jewish communal responsibilities seriously compromised their ability to maintain Jewish homes and raise Jewish children. Problems, of course, remain. Just because women are being ordained does not mean that they are being hired for major pulpits. On February 27, 1991, the Israeli Supreme Court heard the case against the women who wished to pray at the Wall in strictest accordance with an Orthodox interpretation of law. Among the comments by the experts cited in the state's brief against the women, there were a few characteristic ones like that of the late and highly respected Rabbi Moshe Feinstein. Rabbi Feinstein stated, "Women's nature is more suited to raising children and therefore God did not obligate them to study Torah and to keep time-bound *mitzvot,* and no fighting about this will change it. Women who are stubborn and wish to fight and to make changes are considered heretics who do not have a share in the world to come." This comment raises women's ire, and shows that there is work still to be done, but the major work for women to do now is to acknowledge those changes that have already been made, and through them, thoroughly remold the female and male attitudes that will shape the future.

If Jews are to accept women rabbis, they must rethink what it means to be a rabbi, free of all gender associations. People will have to think about how female spiritual leadership might be different and advantageous.

Ridding people of their sex-role stereotypes will not be an easy task. If Jews are to accept women rabbis, they must rethink what it means to be a rabbi, free of all gender associations. People will have to think about how female spiritual leadership might be different and advantageous. Jews will be more accepting of women in the rabbinate only when women have been in the rabbinate longer and have made adjustments and transformations. New roles have to be lived; they have to be internalized. To accept the authority of women rabbis, Jews will have to accustom themselves to pray with them, to study with them, and to receive personal and spiritual guidance from them. Adjusting to change is not easy for anyone, even for those who endorse it.

Jewish culture, by and large, has been male determined. *Zakhor* means remember. From the same Hebrew root we have *zakhar*, male. What written record, what oral law is there of women's memory? Women will have to create new memory. The Hebrew for female is *nekeivah*; from the same root we get *nakav*: to perforate, punch, pierce; we get orifice, tunnel. But *nakav* also can mean to specify, to name, to distinguish, to state. Women shouldn't be blinded by an affectionate respect for tradition; they shouldn't deny themselves permission to be innovative. Women must continue to open up tradition, altering it as Jewish sages have always done. That is why Torah refers to both the words received by Moses at Sinai as well as to the teachings of our sages today. Women can and will alter tradition so that it reflects a female voice and female concerns, so that future Jews are molded in the light of this new consciousness. These changes will have to be made without worrying that irrevocable harm is being done. Mistakes will fade away—while the changes that are authentically Jewish will remain. Once Jews learn to distinguish between the ideas and practices that contaminate and abuse Torah and those that spread Torah, the new, more equitable changes will permit Jewish life to flourish.

From Textures, Hadassah National Jewish Studies Bulletin, *May 1992, vol. 10, no. 2.*

VANESSA L. OCHS is a senior fellow at the National Jewish Center for Learning And Leadership (CLAL). She has written Words on Fire: One Woman's Journey into the Sacred *and* Safe and Sound: Protecting Your Child in an Unpredictable World. *Vanessa Ochs is also Associate Director of the International Committee for Women of the Wall (ICWOW).*

PROGRAMMING IDEAS

AT HOME

Torah Table Talk A discussion of Jewish thought and values with your family and/or friends. The selections below are from the first two chapters of the First Book of Samuel, and they tell the story of Hannah, mother of Samuel.

In an essay on "Women and the Ancient Synagogue," Hannah Safrai writes: "As recorded in the Babylonian Talmud (*Berakhot* 31a-b), the tradition of public prayer [that is, synagogue prayer] proudly reaffirms and emphasizes that the prayer of a woman, Hannah, is the model for the order of Jewish prayer. The nine blessings in the Rosh Hashanah *amidah* are ordered after the nine times Hannah mentioned the name of God in her prayer; Hannah originated the term *Tzva'ot* (Lord of Hosts) in her prayer; Hannah invented the silent prayer; Hannah stood to pray, from which the *amidah* prayers derive (*amidah* means "standing"); and Hannah determined the structure of prayers within the *amidah*, beginning with praise of God, followed by petitions, and ending with thanksgiving." (In *Daughters of the King: Women and the Synagogue*, Susan Grossman and Rivka Haut, eds. [Philadelphia: Jewish Publication Society, 1992], page 47.)

I Samuel 1:1-28, 2:1-10

There was a man from Ramathaim of the Zuphites, in the hill country of Ephraim, whose name was Elkanah son of Jeroham son of Elihu son of Tohu son of Zuph, an Ephraimite. He had two wives, one named Hannah and the other Peninnah; Peninnah had children, but Hannah was childless. This man used to go up from his town every year to worship and to offer sacrifice to the Lord of Hosts at

Shiloh.—Hophni and Phinehas, the two sons of Eli, were priests of the Lord there.

One such day, Elkanah offered a sacrifice. He used to give portions to his wife Peninnah and to all her sons and daughters; but to Hannah he would give one portion only—though Hannah was his favorite—for the Lord had closed her womb. Moreover, her rival, to make her miserable, would taunt her that the Lord had closed her womb. This happened year after year: Every time she went up to the House of the Lord, the other would taunt her, so that she wept and would not eat. Her husband Elkanah said to her, "Hannah, why are you crying and why aren't you eating? Why are you so sad? Am I not more devoted to you than ten sons?"

After they had eaten and drunk at Shiloh, Hannah rose.—The priest Eli was sitting on the seat near the doorpost of the temple of the Lord.—In her wretchedness, she prayed to the Lord, weeping all the while. And she made this vow: "O Lord of Hosts, if You will look upon the suffering of Your maidservant and will remember me and not forget Your maidservant, and if You will grant Your maidservant a male child, I will dedicate him to the Lord for all the days of his life; and no razor shall ever touch his head."

As she kept on praying before the Lord, Eli watched her mouth. Now Hannah was praying in her heart; only her lips moved, but her voice could not be heard. So Eli thought she was drunk. Eli said to her, "How long will you make a drunken spectacle of yourself? Sober up!" And Hannah replied, "Oh no, my Lord! I am a very unhappy woman. I have drunk no wine or other strong drink, but I have been pouring out my heart to the Lord. Do not take your maidservant for a worthless woman; I have only been speaking all this time out of my great anguish and distress." "Then go in peace," said Eli, "and may the God of Israel grant you what you have asked Him." She answered, "You are most kind to your handmaid." So the woman left, and she ate, and was no longer downcast. Early next morning they bowed low before the Lord, and they went back home to Ramah.

Elkanah knew his wife Hannah and the Lord remembered her. Hannah conceived, and at the turn of the year bore a son. She named him Samuel, meaning, "I asked the Lord for him." And when the man Elkanah and all his household were going up to offer to the Lord the annual sacrifice and his votive sacrifice, Hannah did not go up. She said to her husband, "When the child is weaned, I will bring him. For when he has appeared before the Lord, he must remain there for good." Her husband Elkanah said to her, "Do as you think best. Stay home until you have weaned him. May the Lord fulfill His word." So the woman stayed home and nursed her son until she weaned him.

When she had weaned him, she took him up with her, along with three bulls, one ephah of flour, and a jar of wine. And though the boy was still very young, she brought him to the House of the Lord at Shiloh. After slaughtering the bull, they brought the boy to Eli. She said, "Please, my Lord! I am the woman who stood here beside you and prayed to the Lord. It was this boy I prayed for; and the Lord has granted me what I asked of Him. I, in turn, hereby lend him to the Lord. For as long as he lives he is lent to the Lord." And they bowed low there before the Lord.

And Hannah prayed:

My heart exults in the Lord; I have triumphed through the Lord. I gloat over my enemies; I rejoice in Your deliverance.

There is no holy one like the Lord,
Truly there is none beside You;
There is no rock like our God.

Talk no more with lofty pride,
Let no arrogance cross your lips!
For the Lord is an all-knowing God;
By Him actions are measured.

The bows of the mighty are broken,
And the faltering are girded with strength.
Men once sated must hire out for bread;
Men once hungry hunger no more.
While the barren woman bears seven,
The mother of many is forlorn.
The Lord deals death and gives life,
Casts down into Sheol and raises up.
The Lord makes poor and makes rich;
He casts down, He also lifts high.
He raises the poor from the dust,
Lifts up the needy from the dunghill,
Setting them with nobles,
Granting them seats of honor.
For the pillars of the earth are the Lord's;
He has set the world upon them.
He guards the steps of His faithful,
But the wicked perish in darkness—
For not by strength shall man prevail.

The foes of the Lord shall be shattered;
He will thunder against them in the heavens.
The Lord will judge the ends of the earth.
He will give power to His king,
And triumph to His anointed one.

Questions for Thought and Discussion

1. Contemporary feminist scholars note Hannah's mixture of feminist and patriarchal values. In what way is Hannah a revolutionary in her male-dominated society? In what way does she adhere to her society's patriarchal values?

2. Is Hannah's second prayer (I Samuel 2:1-10) particularly feminine? In what ways does her prayer reflect her personal experience, and in what ways

does the prayer reflect her knowledge of the world? Does Hannah's prayer affect you personally? What is most meaningful? Why?

3. Hannah presents the first example in the Bible of personal prayer occurring in a sanctuary or Temple. In earlier biblical accounts, Temple worship had consisted of sacrifices and priestly rituals. The rabbis of the Talmud, in fact, trace the development of synagogue prayer to Hannah. Describe Hannah's method of praying. How is it similar to or different from prayer in synagogues and temples today? How is it similar to your own method of praying? When have your personal prayers resembled Hannah's first prayer of supplication, and when have your personal prayers resembled her second prayer of thanks?

4. Nehama Aschkenasy and Cynthia Ozick believe that Elkanah is an early feminist, because he values Hannah as a person rather than as an instrument; in other words, he loves her for her character rather than her child-bearing ability. Marcia Falk, however, criticizes Elkanah for failing to respect Hannah's suffering. Rather than offering Hannah sympathy when she cries, Elkanah stresses his own worth. What is your opinion?

5. Comment on Hannah's vow and on the fulfillment of that vow. What sorts of vows do you make to God, and do you fulfill them as Hannah did?

6. Hannah's story is read at the synagogue every year on the first day of Rosh Hashanah. Why?

7. In "Reflections on Hannah's Prayer," Marcia Falk laments that Hannah is misunderstood both by her husband and by the priest, and she notes that Hannah's prayer as she beseeches God for a son is inaudible. Falk writes: "We might ... ask what it would be like to create a community of empathy, where silent pain is given a voice. What, indeed, would it be like to have a truly inclusive spiritual community, a community of equals, where all could pray together in the language of the heart? What might communal prayer sound like if it included everyone's voice?" (In *Out of the Garden: Women Writers on the Bible*, Christine Buchmann and Celina Spiegel, eds. [New York: Fawcett Columbine/Ballantine, 1994], page 100.) How might you answer Falk's questions? Describe the communal prayer that she envisions.

Additional At-Home Activities

❖ Find a prayer book, a translation of the Hebrew Bible, or a book on Jewish spirituality that speaks to you. Daily, or a few times per week, read a selection from the book and keep a journal of your responses to what you have read. If possible, include as well your reactions to Jewish events and to spiritual experiences as they occur in your life.

❖ Jewish women's music offers a wonderful way to connect to spiritual themes. Listen to tapes or CD's of artists such as Debbie Friedman, Julie Silver, Margie Rosenthal, Ilene Safyan, and Vocolot, a Jewish women's a capella group. Judaica stores and synagogue shops frequently carry a selection of music; or contact Tara Publications for information, 29 Derby Avenue, Cedarhurst, NY 11516; phone 516-295-2290.

INTEREST/STUDY GROUPS

Hold a discussion based on the following questions:

1. Vanessa Ochs states, "The major work for women to do now is to acknowledge those changes that have already been made, and through them, thoroughly remold the female and male attitudes that will shape the future." Have you acknowledged the changes that have already been made? How? Have your attitudes toward Jewish female and male roles changed as a result of these changes? How?

2. Can a traditional liturgy created exclusively by men, replete with masculine imagery for God, express the religious sensibilities of women?

3. Should traditional Judaism be threatened by Jewish feminist theology? What strategies for synthesis and compromise could be used for the benefit of both?

4. How does spirituality intersect with social action in your life? Are there behaviors or actions that enhance you spiritually? How can you incorporate *mitzvot* (commandments) and *gemilut hasadim* (acts of loving-kindness) into daily life?

5. Jewish feminists have devoted great energy to reclaiming the matriarchs and other biblical women. As Vanessa Ochs states, we "no longer emphasize only their nurturing, self-sacrificing traits"; today we "point out a woman's persistence of faith, her leadership, her fearlessness, her relationship to God." Have each participant choose a biblical figure and write a monologue, stream-of-consciousness memoir, or poem in that woman's voice.

6. What are the benefits and the dangers to religious life that come with radical changes in observance patterns, such as the changes in Jewish life brought about by the women's movement?

7. How does volunteer work enrich women spiritually? As Jewish women take on increasingly larger roles in synagogue life and religious ritual performance, will organizations like Hadassah suffer or be enriched? How has working for Hadassah affected you on a personal, spiritual level?

MEETINGS

❖ Ask a woman rabbi to address your Hadassah unit on the changing role of women in Judaism. How have the Conservative, Reconstructionist, and Reform denominations changed over the past century? What precludes Orthodox Jews from including women in an egalitarian way? How has your speaker struggled in joining the rabbinate, a field that, until the seventies, was completely male? Does she see her role as different from a male rabbi's role? In what ways? Does she bring a special perspective to the rabbinate? How?

❖ Invite a feminist Orthodox speaker to address your Hadassah chapter or group on women's prayer groups and the bitter controversy they have sparked within the Orthodox community. Separate prayer groups offer Orthodox women the opportunity to see and touch the Torah scroll, to read from the Torah and

Haftorah, and even to lead prayers. Because Orthodox women's prayer groups recite only those prayers that do not require a *minyan* (quorum of ten; in Orthodox Judaism all ten must be men), they do not violate Jewish law. However, nearly every rabbinical authority who has been consulted has condemned women's prayer groups, and those Orthodox rabbis who defend women's groups have themselves been denounced. (Refer to writings of Rabbis Emanuel Rackman, Eliezer Berkovits, Irving Greenberg, Avi Weiss, and Shlomo Riskin.)

❖ View and discuss the 1989 film *Half the Kingdom* (color, 59 minutes), which explores the lives of seven feminists in the process of discovering their place within Judaism. Central to the film is the movement of Jewish women from observers to active participants. The videotape is available through Direct Cinema, PO Box 10003, Santa Monica, CA 90410; phone 1-800-525-0000. The cost is $150 for purchase and shipping, and $75 for rental and shipping. In Canada, write for information to the National Film Board of Canada, P.O. Box 6100, Station A, Montreal, Quebec H3C 3H5 (order number: C 0189 099).

ANNUAL EVENTS

❖ Participate in a conference on women's spirituality in coalition with synagogues or Jewish women's groups.

❖ Hold an Education Day or Evening on Jewish women's spirituality. Invite speakers on several topics, such as: women in the rabbinate, sociological and spiritual dimensions; reclaiming the *mikvah* (ritual bath); women's three *mitzvot* and women's performance of time-based *mitzvot*; praying in gender-free language; history of women's spirituality—from biblical times to medieval *tekhines* (Yiddish prayers for women); women in *halakhah*—current controversies.

HANDS-ON

❖ Compile a list of local opportunities for women's involvement in Jewish spiritual experiences. Print the list in your bulletin or newsletter. Also include out-of-town opportunities for women's Jewish study and spirituality, such as multi-day conferences and symposia.

❖ Participate in Hadassah's adult bat mitzvah program, and become a bat mitzvah at National Convention. Call the National Jewish Education Department for details, 212-303-8112 or 212-303-8167.

❖ Create a Rosh Hodesh study group, developing your own prayers and rituals to complement the traditional Jewish liturgy. Use the articles contained here in *Jewish Women Living the Challenge* for study.

❖ For your Rosh Hodesh group or for a women's prayer group, create a *parokhet* (curtain) to cover the ark or create a Torah mantle. Write to the

Women's League for Conservative Judaism for instructions: 48 East 74th Street, New York, NY 10021.

❖ Organize a class on *simhah* dancing for your chapter or group. These dances are line dances performed at Orthodox celebrations (weddings, bar mitzvah parties, etc.) by separate groups of Jewish men and Jewish women. Some of the dances are complex, and some are extremely unrestrained. A number of Orthodox women (and men) find *simhah* dancing to be a means of spiritual expression.

❖ Print selections from members' spiritual journals (see "Additional At-Home Activities," page 236) in your unit's bulletin.

CONTEMPORARY JEWISH WOMEN'S RITUALS

Tamara Cohen

The police arrived, curious about what a group of women could possibly be doing after dark in a small park off the main road in Englewood, New Jersey. A thin sliver of moon shone through the tree branches as Morissa's mother assured the officers that we were safe and would be leaving shortly. The rest of us continued listening to the voice of a fifty-year-old woman as she described the day on which she first reported the blood on her underwear and her mother slapped her.

As a twelve-year-old, I had been to baby naming ceremonies, and the bat mitzvah season was just beginning, but a ceremony for getting your period? It was weird—not something I was sure I wanted to share with my mother, as Morissa did with hers. But I was curious enough to join her. There we sat, in a circle in the dark, listening to the voices of older Jewish women as they talked about their first periods and what menstruation meant to them. I didn't fully understand. The small brook, cold and deep, looked nothing like any *mikvah* I had ever imagined.

Yet something crucial became clear to me that night—there was a place within Judaism where women could talk about their lives. There was some connection between the intensity with which I was preparing for my bat mitzvah and the intensity with which I was experiencing my body's maturation. Living Jewishly meant more than studying Torah, going to synagogue, and eating holiday meals.

I already had learned, like the rabbi in *Fiddler on the Roof*, that "there

241

is a blessing for everything." What I realized that night, and what countless Jewish women creating and experiencing new rituals have realized, is that every blessing has not necessarily already been written. This certainly is true for the lives of contemporary Jewish women, and for the lives of many contemporary Jewish men as well.

When I did begin to menstruate, my mother gave me a card and a pile of books—a volume of Marge Piercy's poetry, Esther Broner's *The Weave of Women*, a teen version of *Our Bodies Ourselves*, and a book containing photographs of women around the world. This was our way of marking the event. When my sisters' periods arrived we both gave them books (by then *The Tribe of Dina* had been published). I gave perfume, along with the books, as a way of affirming our right to feel beautiful as well as intelligent.

We too had created a menstruation ritual. It was not a communal one like Morissa's, but a private family ritual, celebrating the onset of menses as our entrance into the world of adult Jewish womanhood in body, spirit, and mind. Thus, I learned my second lesson about ritual from my mother; it has to feel authentic to those involved.

Different forms of ritual will appeal to different women at different occasions within their lives. A ritual to heal a survivor of rape will differ from one that celebrates a commitment of love, and a twelve-year-old girl will observe ritual differently from a woman of sixty. Realizing that rituals can add to these experiences and these lives is the first step; figuring out what ritual is appropriate and meaningful is the next.

When women began to create celebrations of these life cycle events, traditional rituals became transformed.

Originally, rituals for Jewish women arose by examining the traditional Jewish life-cycle rituals for men and attempting to recreate them for women. Boys had bar mitzvahs, so girls would have bat mitzvahs. The birth of a boy was celebrated with a *brit milah*, so the birth of a girl would be celebrated with a *brit bat tzion* or a *simhat bat*.

When women began to create celebrations of these life-cycle events, traditional rituals became transformed. My youngest sister's *simhat bat* took place during the morning service on Rosh Hodesh. My parents were called to the Torah to name her. In addition, I read a poem that I had written, my grandmothers each received *aliyot* for the first time, and we recited some new blessings and provided explanations of the baby's name.

These new elements, in turn, influence the way boys in the community are brought into the Covenant. What began as a way to include girls in the existing ritual of *brit milah* ended up enriching the ceremony for boys as well.

Women also have transformed ritual by rewriting the formerly limited role prescribed to them within existing rituals. Many women have created wedding ceremonies that better fit the kinds of marriages and partnerships they want to sanctify. Some have rewritten the *ketubah* or have changed the imagery in the *sheva brakhot* to include feminine God language. Some couples have included contracts not only between the two partners, but between the partners and their friends, their community, and the world.

Another good example of transformed ritual is the proliferation of women's Passover Seders. Some Seders present an opportunity for women to share contemporary experiences of bondage and freedom in a world with oppressions very different from those inflicted by Pharaoh. Other women retell the story of the Exodus, highlighting the roles of Shifra and Puah (the midwives who saved Jewish babies) and Miriam. Others use the Seder as a framework for honoring women's roles throughout Jewish history. Many add to or replace Elijah's cup with a cup for Miriam. Some pour out ten drops of wine for modern plagues that afflict women, from AIDS to poverty.

For me, the most exciting aspect of new rituals for women lies in the terrain completely untraveled until recently. I am referring to the many events that make up our adult lives—expected changes and unexpected changes connected with our families, friends, communities, careers, and bodies. To celebrate these events, women have held adult bat mitzvahs in synagogues, lesbian coming-out ceremonies among friends, and *semahot hokhmah* (celebrations of the wisdom that comes with age, usually held on one's sixtieth birthday). Women also have created healing rituals. Rituals for healing from rape or other sexual violence often include immersion in a *mikvah*. This connects the healing process with a traditional site of women's ritual while transforming it into a site of spiritual renewal, thus rejecting the concept of the body's physical impurity.

Women all over the country gather to celebrate Rosh Hodesh with ritual and song, bringing to life a traditional connection between women and the new moon that had been almost completely suppressed. Rosh Hodesh has been used as an opportunity to mark life-cycle events, to discuss the change of seasons, to celebrate upcoming holidays, or as a chance to study text, learn from Jewish feminist scholars, share poetry, and learn new songs.

In an era in which established circles within the Jewish community worry about continuity, the explosion of new rituals for Jewish women seems a powerful statement that innovation does not threaten tradition, but rather, is a key to maintaining it. Yet many remain hesitant to embrace new ritual; women themselves are often cautious about writing, performing, or asking others to help them plan rituals.

In order to have access to new ritual, Jewish women need basic Judaic skills. Some women don't have these skills and they need comfortable environments in which to gain them. But I think most women do have enough skill, Jewish memory, and a basic, internal sense of ritual to begin the process of creating meaningful and authentic ceremonies. This does not always translate into the confidence necessary to write or orchestrate rituals, because women are not encouraged to draw attention to themselves and their life struggles. We often feel that our experiences are not important enough to merit public recognition. Also, many of us live in Jewish communities in which we rely on rabbis to do our rituals for us. Jewish feminists must be committed to empowering lay women at the same time as educating our rabbinate, male and female alike.

Some women worry that they might create a ritual that isn't Jewish in some basic sense. Yet, if we think about some of the basic rituals that we perform or that we remember our mothers or grandmothers performing, we can identify key elements of traditional Jewish rituals and incorporate them into new ones.

A few months ago, I wrote a ritual for a class taught by Esther Broner and Rabbi Sue Levi Elwell. When I sat down to write, I recognized the demons that stand in the way of creating new ritual. How was I to balance my need to create something comfortable yet profound, something sufficiently based in Judaic sources yet fully contemporary? Did my situation merit a ceremony?

As I wrote, I drew upon my internal sense of the kind of healing that I needed, upon my deep attachment to traditional symbols, and upon my knowledge of the ways in which women have always comforted each other. Most of all, I drew upon the lessons I learned over ten years ago from Morissa's mother and my own.

That night, under the new moon, I was given a gift—the feeling that these rituals are my right as a modern Jewish woman; that they are an authentic and integral expression of Judaism; and that we women have the power, the skills, and even the obligation, to continue to create them for ourselves and for our daughters.

From Textures, Hadassah National Jewish Studies Bulletin, *December 1994, vol. 13, no. 1.*

TAMARA COHEN is the program coordinator of Ma'yan: The Jewish Women's Project at the Jewish Community Center on the Upper West Side in New York City.

PROGRAMMING IDEAS

AT HOME

Torah Table Talk   A discussion of Jewish thought and values with your family and/or friends. This passage from the Midrash is the source for all later associations between women and the holiday of Rosh Hodesh.

Midrash, **Pirkei DeRabbi Eliezer,** *Chapter 45 (c. eighth century)*

The women heard about the construction of the golden calf and refused to submit their jewelry to their husbands. Instead they said to them, "You want to construct an idol and mask which is an abomination and has no power of redemption? We won't listen to you." And the Holy One, Blessed be He, rewarded them in this world in that they would observe the New Moons more than men, and in the next world in that they are destined to be renewed like the New Moon.

Questions for Thought and Discussion

1. Why might the New Month have been given to women as a reward for refusing to construct the golden calf? How is refusing to worship the calf related to celebrating the New Month?

2. Refusing to worship the calf implies that the Israelite women were more spirituality aware than the men. In fact, some Orthodox rabbis have explained women's exemption from time-bound *mitzvot* by asserting that women occupy a higher spiritual plane than men, therefore women do not require the *mitzvot* as men do! This outlook is in accord with Western European traditions dating from the nineteenth century, which picture the wife as the angel in the house. Even when the image of women is not specifically religious, women are seen as fragile, impractical, artistic, and sensitive. However, such an outlook is a minority opinion throughout Jewish history. In general, the Jewish tradition depicts women as more earthy, more practical, and less spiritual than men. In your estimation, are women today more or less spiritual than men? Is this true among both Jews and non-Jews? Discuss masculine and feminine images of spirituality.

3. Speculate on the meaning of "in the next world ... they are destined to be renewed like the New Moon." What will this renewal entail?

4. The menstrual cycle is often compared to the cycles of the moon. What is your reaction?

Additional At-Home Activities

❖ Make a timeline of significant events in your life, remembering important moments and anticipating future milestones. Anything you deem noteworthy may be included. You might want to frame your timeline and hang it up. (Consider also a family timeline.) How have these events enabled you to grow spiritually and Jewishly?

❖ Design a ritual to celebrate a significant event in your life. Remember, rituals are more than blessings; they involve *doing* something as well as saying a prayer. For more information on Jewish women's rituals, read *Lifecycles,* edited by Debra Orenstein, or *Miriam's Well,* by Penina Adelman (see "Recommended Reading," pages 267-268), or contact the Jewish Women's Resource Center at 212-535-5900, or Ma'yan: The Jewish Women's Project at 212-580-0099.

❖ To enhance your new ritual and to have a keepsake, make or purchase new ritual objects for the occasion. Refer to the "Hands-On" section for more details (page 247).

INTEREST/STUDY GROUPS

Hold a discussion based on the following questions:

1. Choose a holiday or a life-cycle ceremony that is meaningful to you. Why is it meaningful? What makes it Jewish? What elements does it share with other rituals (Jewish or non-Jewish)? Where is the ritual performed and how does the space and the audience affect it? Does the ritual speak to you as a woman? If not, what would make the ritual more meaningful to you as a woman?

2. Think of a significant event in your past that went unmarked or think of a significant event that is coming up. Who should share the event with you? What would you gain by marking the event with a ritual? What kind of ceremony would be meaningful to you?

3. What was your initial reaction to the ritual described in the opening section of this article? Did your reaction change as you read the rest of the article?

4. Why does women's involvement in religion spark such controversy?

MEETINGS

❖ Celebrate Rosh Hodesh together. Consult a *siddur* (prayer book) for the traditional blessings. *Miriam's Well: Rituals for Jewish Women Around the Year*, 2nd ed., by Penina V. Adelman (New York: Biblio, 1990) provides a complete program of additional rituals for women's Rosh Hodesh groups.

❖ Invite a guest speaker—perhaps a woman rabbi or professor of Jewish religion—to discuss modern women's rituals. How have today's bat mitzvah and *simhat bat* celebrations evolved from the traditional rituals for boys? What are some of the current rituals that have been developed for first menstruation, menopause, pregnancy, childbirth, miscarriage, divorce, and so on?

❖ View and discuss the video *Miriam's Daughters Now* produced by Lilly Rivlin in the eighties. In addition to portraying Jewish women's rituals, it addresses single parenting and other marital status issues and in the past has prompted heated discussion. To obtain a copy, write to Lilly Rivlin at: 463 West Street, Apt. 510A, New York, NY 10014; or phone: 212-242-0327.

❖ Celebrate Shabbat together. Attend a synagogue together as a unit, and then hold a Hadassah dinner, *kiddush*, or luncheon. As an alternative, you could adapt the Friday night or Saturday morning service for your members, and hold a special Hadassah prayer service. (This would require more planning!) The National Program Department has suggestions that will enrich a Hadassah Shabbat experience. Call 212-303-8027 for details.

ANNUAL EVENTS

❖ Create a ceremony that celebrates the founding of your unit. Spend the first portion of the program learning about rituals—what ritual entails, its significance, how to create new rituals. Spend the second portion of the program creating your own ceremony. Then use the rituals that you have created in the final portion of the program. The Hadassah National Programming Department's *Mishpahah* program includes guidelines for recording your new rituals and the history of your unit. Contact the National Programming Department at 212-303-8027 for information on obtaining this program.

❖ Host a women's Seder for your community. For information and assistance, call Ma'yan: The Jewish Women's Project at 212-580-0099.

❖ Host a women's Sukkot dinner. Invite biblical women and other Jewish women of the past into your *sukkah*, and discuss how they have nurtured your own spirituality. What makes each of these women a role model for us today—persistence of faith, leadership, fearlessness, wisdom, relationship to God? How have these women been portrayed throughout history? Are these the qualities that we admire today?

HANDS-ON

❖ Design a ritual to celebrate a significant event in your life. This can be an individual, small group, or large group project. Print an outline of the new ritual in your unit's bulletin. (Refer also to "Additional At-Home Activities," page 245).

❖ To enhance your new ritual and to have a keepsake, make or purchase new ritual objects for the occasion—a *kiddush* cup, *hallah* cover, *hallah* knife, tablecloth, candlesticks, etc. For creating your own, write to the Women's League for Conservative Judaism, 48 East 74th Street, New York, NY 10021, for a listing of crafts instructions. Or consult *The Jewish Party Book: A Contemporary Guide to Customs, Crafts, and Foods* by Mae Shafter Rockland (New York: Schocken, 1978) or *The First Jewish Catalog*, edited by Richard Siegel, Michael Strassfeld, and Sharon Strassfeld (Philadelphia: Jewish Publication Society, 1973).

❖ Incorporate music and movement into your new ritual, or use new music or new movement to enhance a ritual that is already important to you. Compose music, or adapt music, that would be appropriate for your ritual. Use dance as part of a celebration, or incorporate symbolic actions into a ritual (as when we circle the Shabbat candles with our hands after lighting them).

ON BLESSING

Marcia Falk

If you are looking for the heart and soul and bones of Jewish prayer, you will find them all in the blessing. A blessing—in Hebrew, *brakhah*—is an event; a blessing is also that which turns a moment into an event. Blessings intensify life by focusing our attention on our actions, increasing our awareness of the present moment. As a poet, I have long been drawn to the lyric intensity of the blessing, and for the past twelve years, I have been composing new blessings in Hebrew and English, as vehicles for new visions, steps toward creating Jewish feminist theology and practice. Over the course of that time, my own theology has taken many turns, all of which became part of the creative process. Because I never completely turned away from any place on the journey—never rejected my early blessings in favor of new ones, just kept moving on to create more—what I find today, as I compile my blessings into a new prayer book, is a variegated and layered collection.

The first blessings I wrote were actually based quite closely on the traditional *brakhot*; they exhorted the community to bless, praise, or seek out the divine presence in relation to specific occasions, such as beginning a meal or ushering in a holiday. Yet they departed sharply from the traditional blessings in offering new images for divinity—images that called into question the rabbinic depiction of God as lord and king. Because my theological metaphors were specifically created to resonate with the particular occasions being marked, and because all my language and imagery were rooted in biblical, rabbinic, and payyetanic[1] sources, my blessings could be read as a kind of *midrash*, or commentary, on the tradition:

Blessing Over Wine for New Holidays

Let us bless the wellspring of life
that nurtures fruit on the vine
as we weave the branches of our lives
into the tradition.

קִדּוּשׁ לְחַגִּים חֲדָשִׁים

נְבָרֵךְ אֶת עֵין הַחַיִּים
מַצְמִיחַת פְּרִי הַגֶּפֶן
וְנִשְׁזֹר אֶת שָׂרִיגֵי חַיֵּינוּ
בְּמָסֹרֶת הַדּוֹרוֹת.

My early blessings caught on especially quickly; they circulated informally around the country, where a range of communities—including Reconstructionist, Reform, Conservative, *havurah*-style, feminist, and unaffiliated groups—began using them. It was not long before people were extrapolating from my blessings to write new blessings of their own. This was gratifying, in that it meant the work was standing the test of use. Yet the results were often disturbing to me. I had thought of my early blessings as starting points in the creative process. I had never intended them to become archetypes, in the sense of blueprints for later compositions.

I was surprised and dismayed to hear people talk about my image *ein hahayyim*, "the wellspring, or fountain, or source, of life," as though it were my substitution for *Adonai Eloheinu, melekh ha'olam*, "the Lord, our God, king of the world." I believed that the image of God as lord and king was a dead metaphor—that is, an image of divinity that no longer functioned metaphorically but had become instead an idolatrous name for the unnamable, reinforcing patriarchal power and male privilege within society. Yet I did not believe that the alternative to this image was a new name or image for divinity, since all names and images are necessarily partial. Rather, I had proposed that we set in motion a process of ongoing naming, which would point to the diversity of our experiences and reach toward a greater inclusivity within the monotheistic framework. I believed it was important to do this liturgical work in Hebrew, our sacred tongue. As an example of what I was calling for, I began offering several new images of my own—among them, *ein hahayyim*.

I was even more concerned when it seemed that the opening of my blessings over bread and wine, *nevareikh et ein hahayyim*, "Let us bless the source of life," was being seen as a new prayer formula, intended to substitute for the opening of the traditional blessing. Just as I had never advocated a substitute name for the divine, the creation of new prayer formulas was very far from my intent. Such a project contradicted my core convictions about what constitutes authentic prayer—convictions I had tried to embody early on in my work.

For example, in my new *havdalah* ritual—which was among my earliest liturgical compositions—I had offered two new theological images: *nishmat kol hai*, literally, "the soul, or breath, of all living things," and *nitzotzot hanefesh*, literally, "the sparks of the spirit, or soul." As *ein hahayyim* was an image of water drawn from the earth, so *nishmat kol hai* and *nitzotzot hanefesh* were images of air and fire. Taken together, I thought that these three metaphors might begin to suggest the presence of divinity in the whole of creation; no image taken alone could evoke that awareness in the same way. My *havdalah* also introduced two variations for the verb *nevareikh*, "let us bless": *nehalel*, "let us praise, or celebrate" and *nevakeish*, "let us seek." For it struck me that just as divinity could be imaged in a myriad of ways, so prayerful action could take a great variety of forms—and the search for these, too, became part of my poetic process.

Indeed, each variation led to further ones. As I continued composing blessings, I experimented with a range of forms, probing the potential of lyric expression to evoke spiritual awareness. Thus I found myself varying not just words and images but whole syntactic formations. The creative process replicated the spiritual journey—or perhaps I should say that it *was* a spiritual journey, rich with the gifts of discovery and of surprise. So too, I wanted the products of my labor to evoke discovery and surprise in the reader, the pray-er. As I moved further away from the exhortative syntax of my original blessings, I found myself attempting to suggest the presence of the divine in less obvious and less predictable ways— until, at a certain stage, I found I was no longer using images to point toward divinity directly.

Thus many kinds of blessings appear side by side in *The Book of Blessings*—along with poetry and meditations that supplement the blessings and themselves form other kinds of prayer. Among the different blessings are quite a few that contain no specific reference to the divine, although they evoke the experience of the sacred. For example, my morning and evening blessings focus on a spiritual state of gratitude, deliberately leaving open the object of the emotion. My hand washing blessings make reference to holiness, seeking to bring about heightened awareness of the interrelationship of body and spirit. My blessing for the children echoes words spoken by the biblical God to suggest divinity within the human self; my blessing of the beloved adapts lines from the biblical Song of Songs to convey reciprocal human love. My new blessings of commandment embed a sense of the sacred within human actions. My blessings for circles of time—such as the new week and the new month—bestow good wishes upon others or seek goodness for one's self or one's community. And my

My morning and evening blessings focus on a spiritual state of gratitude, deliberately leaving open the object of the emotion. My hand washing blessings make reference to holiness, seeking to bring about heightened awareness of the interrelationship of body and spirit.

251

new *birkat halevanah*, blessing of the moon, takes the form of an extended personal reverie, a contemplation of the redemptive state.

Where is the divine in these? Nowhere in particular—yet, potentially, everywhere that attention is brought to bear. If the divine is everywhere, as many monotheists believe—or, if everything is capable of being made holy, as rabbinic Judaism seems to teach with its scrupulous attention to the many details of ordinary life—then surely we needn't worry about localizing divinity in a single apt word *or* phrase. We may find it wherever our hearts and minds, our blood and bones are stirred.

Here is my new evening blessing, with which I close each day:

Blessing Before Going to Sleep	בְּרָכָה לִקְרַאת הַשֵּׁנָה
Sleep descending, on my lids, on my limbs,	חֶבְלֵי שֵׁנָה עַל עֵינַי וּתְנוּמָה עַל עַפְעַפָּי,
I call to mind the gifts of the day—	מָלְאָה נַפְשִׁי הוֹדָיָה עַל מַתְּנוֹת הַיּוֹם,
the gift of this day— and give thanks.	מָלְאָה נַפְשִׁי הוֹדָיָה עַל מַתַּת הַיּוֹם.

From Textures, Hadassah National Jewish Studies Bulletin, *December 1994, vol. 13, no. 1.*

MARCIA FALK, Ph.D., is a well-known poet and author. Her recent books include The Book of Blessings: New Jewish Prayers for Daily Life, the Sabbath, and the New Moon Festival; With Teeth in the Earth: Selected Poems of Malka Heifetz Tussman; *and* The Song of Songs: A New Translation and Interpretation. *Marcia Falk conducts workshops around the country on spirituality and prayer.*

PROGRAMMING IDEAS

AT HOME

Torah Table Talk   A discussion of Jewish thought and values with your family and/or friends. Compare Marcia Falk's blessing over wine with the traditional blessing.

Traditional Blessing Over Wine (Mishnah Berakhot 6:1, compiled c. 200)

Praised are You *Adonai*, our God,
sovereign of the universe,
creator of the fruit of the vine.

בָּרוּךְ אַתָּה ה' אֱלוֹהֵינוּ
מֶלֶךְ הָעוֹלָם, בּוֹרֵא פְּרִי הַגָּפֶן.

Marcia Falk, "Blessing Over Wine for New Holidays"

Let us bless the wellspring of life
that nurtures fruit on the vine
as we weave the branches of our lives
into the tradition.

נְבָרֵךְ אֶת עֵין הַחַיִּים
מַצְמִיחַת פְּרִי הַגָּפֶן
וְנִשְׁזֹר אֶת שָׂרִיגֵי חַיֵּינוּ
בְּמָסֹרֶת הַדּוֹרוֹת.

Questions for Thought and Discussion

1. The Hebrew language differentiates between masculine and feminine word forms. In the traditional blessing, the nouns *Attah* (You), *melekh* (sovereign), and *borei* (creator) are all grammatically masculine. However, in Marcia Falk's blessing, the noun *ein* (wellspring) is feminine. In addition, the verb *barukh* (praised), referring to the word "You," is masculine in the traditional blessing, whereas in Falk's blessing *nevareikh* (let us bless) is neutral and *matzmihat* (nurtures), referring to the word "wellspring," is feminine. How do you react to the feminine grammatical usage in Marcia Falk's poem? Does it enhance your experience of the divine? Does it seem strange and foreign?

2. In addition to the grammatical differences between masculine and feminine words, the imagery of the two blessings differ sharply. Consider how the masculine image of the "sovereign of the universe" contrasts with the feminine image of the "wellspring of life." In what other ways does the imagery hold masculine and feminine connotations?

3. The standard prayer uses the second person singular (addressing God as You), whereas Marcia Falk writes in the first person plural (we). She may have chosen to use the first person plural voice, because it is the only verb form in Hebrew that does not differentiate between masculine and feminine. However, the use of "we" adds meanings of its own. Consider, for example, the Yom Kippur prayer when "we" as a group confess to many wrong deeds. How are you affected by addressing God as "You" in standard Hebrew prayer, and how are you affected when you say "let us bless"? How might God be affected?

4. For holidays (as for Shabbat), the blessing over wine is one part of the *kiddush*—the blessing that marks the festival day itself. Read, for example, the *kiddush* for Sukkot, and discuss how its emphasis differs from Falk's emphasis.

> Praised are You, *Adonai* our God, sovereign of the universe, who has chosen us from all the nations, and exalted us from all languages, by making us holy with Your commandments. And in your love, *Adonai* our God, You have given us this festival of Sukkot, the season of our gladness, to unite in prayer and

remember the exodus from Egypt. For you have chosen us and have set us apart for Your service from among all the people, and You have caused us to inherit Your holy festivals in joy and gladness. Praised are You, *Adonai*, who adds holiness to Israel and the festival seasons.

Additional At-Home Activities

❖ Obtain a *siddur* (prayer book), and read in English the prayers with which you are most familiar. List on paper each time God is referred to in male terms (father, king), and write down which attribute is highlighted. List as well each time God is referred to in neutral terms (redeemer, rock) or female terms (mostly in recent prayers, such as Marcia Falk's), and which attribute is highlighted there. If your prayer book is entirely gender-neutral, compare it with the prayers that you heard as a girl or with a traditional prayer book.

❖ Write your own prayer (concerning, for example, interpersonal relationships, beginning a job, traveling, health, children, nature). Compare your prayer to a traditional prayer. What elements have you altered, and why? How does saying a prayer at an appropriate occasion make a difference? What occasions in your life have been enhanced by blessings? What occasions would deserve a blessing in the future?

❖ Create your own ceremonial prayer shawl or other religious objects. Refer to the "Hands-On" section (page 255) for further details.

INTEREST/STUDY GROUPS

Hold a discussion based on the following questions:

1. What do you expect to experience by reciting a blessing? Do the words of traditional blessings fulfill your expectations? What needs, if any, are not met by traditional prayers? How can you fulfill these needs, both as an individual and as a community?

2. Do we need to invoke a divine presence in order to pray?

3. Marcia Falk states that calling God "king of the world" had become "an image of divinity that no longer functioned metaphorically but had become instead an idolatrous name for the unnamable, reinforcing patriarchal power and male privilege within society." Discuss your reactions to the established masculine metaphors for God (king, lord, father, etc.) and to the currently-used feminine metaphors for God (for example, source of life). In what ways are names of God idolatrous?

4. A number of traditionally observant Jews accuse Marcia Falk (and other Jewish feminists) of pantheism. They claim that a prayer addressed to, for instance, the "source of life" or the "breath of all living things" constitutes worship of an additional deity. Other detractors accuse Marcia Falk of atheism, arguing

that she has entirely eliminated God from her prayers. Although these criticisms are not specifically addressed in "On Blessing," the article does reveal Marcia Falk's viewpoint. How would she answer her critics? In this debate on new feminist Jewish prayers, which side do you take?

5. Why do we recite blessings over specific events in our lives? Marcia Falk believes that a blessing "turns a moment into an event. Blessings intensify life by focusing our attention on our actions, increasing our awareness of the present moment." Discuss. How do we grow spiritually by increasing our awareness of the present moment?

MEETINGS

❖ Ask participants who have written their own *brakhot* to share them with the other members at a meeting. How have participants felt about writing a *brakhah*? Are their *brakhot* based upon established liturgy? If so, what have they altered? If not, why? Does the personal *brakhah* fill a specific need that traditional prayers fail to address?

❖ Invite a rabbi or scholar to discuss the meaning of Jewish blessings. What is the purpose of reciting a blessing? What do blessings teach us? Which blessings are obligatory? How should we say them? How are blessings related to praying? If your speaker is a feminist rabbi or scholar, also include a discussion of recent trends toward gender-neutral language in Jewish prayer. (If your speaker is knowledgeable, a brief discussion of blessings in different religious traditions would also be fascinating. How does Judaism differ from Catholicism, from various Protestant denominations, from Buddhism, etc.?)

❖ Invite a rabbi or Jewish scholar to discuss *tekhines*, Yiddish prayers written specifically for women, and sometimes by women, during the middle ages and early modern era. Read several selections out loud in English translation, and discuss. Many of the *tekhines* were written to address parts of women's lives that the standard liturgy ignored, such as childbirth or weaning.

ANNUAL EVENTS

Refer to the "Annual Events" section of "The Future for Jewish Women" by Vanessa L. Ochs, page 238.

HANDS-ON

❖ Create your own *tallit* (prayer shawl), *tallit* bag, and/or *kippah* (yarmulke, skull cap). The Women's League for Conservative Judaism has instructions for making crochet, knitted, woven, or sewn *tallit*, a huck *tallit*, a knit *tallit* bag, crochet and knit *kippah*, as well as many embroidery patterns for a *tallit* and *kippah*. For information on ordering, write to 48 East 74th Street, New York, NY 10021.

❖ If you are a member of a Conservative or Reconstructionist congregation, learn how to *daven* (pray) with *tefillin* (phylacteries) through attending the daily *minyan* (quorum for prayer). (Most Reform Jews do not pray with *tefillin*. Orthodox men put on *tefillin* daily, but only a handful of Orthodox feminist women do. The overwhelming majority of Orthodox women do not.)

❖ If you are a member of a participatory synagogue, begin leading a portion of the daily or Shabbat service. (Most participatory synagogues offer opportunities to learn how.) Incorporate personal *brakhot* and alternative prayers, such as Marcia Falk's, as appropriate for your community.

❖ Learn Hebrew, the language of Jewish spiritual expression for four thousand years. Join or start an *Ivrit la Hadassah* class in your community. Call the National Hebrew Studies Department of Hadassah for details, 212-303-8164.

❖ Print the prayers which members have composed (see "Additional At-Home Activities," page 254) in your unit's bulletin. Also print members' descriptions of their experience in writing their own prayers and in reciting their own prayers.

---

1. *Piyyutim* are lyrical compositions that were used throughout history to embellish obligatory prayers and religious ceremonies. Some payyetanic material became part of the set pattern of prayer.

ON SORROW AND SOLACE

Nessa Rapoport

Undo it, take it back

Undo it, take it back, make every day the previous one until
I am returned to the day before the one that made you gone.
Or set me on an airplane traveling west, crossing the date line
again and again, losing this day, then that, until the day of
loss still lies ahead, and you are here instead of sorrow.

The message on my answering machine was brief: D.'s mother had died unexpectedly. Would I come to a morning *minyan* during the week of *shiva*?

When I reached D.'s apartment, the sun was brilliant in the east. I stood in a patch of hot light and opened the prayer book to a familiar page. The words were radiant with meaning as I thought of D. and her sister, their sober faces before me, and of my own three sisters and the grief that—years hence, I hoped—inevitably awaited us.

On a table were several books about mourning, waiting for our outstretched hands. There was a guide to Jewish practice and an anthology of essays about grief. There was a well-thumbed best-seller about goodness and suffering. And there were D. and her sister, standing as one body, comforting each other, and suddenly I thought: No book about women. No book for women. That moment was the start of *A Woman's Book of Grieving*.

Why did I respond so strongly? It had been a year of losses for me, my first such losses in an unusually stable life. In less than a year, the aunt with whom my sisters and I had shared our childhood was dead at 57; an uncle died; and then my grandmother, the matriarch at 92, was gone. Although she was old and rich in love, her death was shattering. Without my grandmother, the edifice of the family shifted at its foundation. My childhood, far longer than I'd had the right to expect, was over.

My grandmother, my mother, and my aunt knew what to do when sorrow struck: they sat, talked, wept, and said the traditional words they had heard their parents say. What do we do? Some of us are allied with Jewish communities whose members are able, because of birth and education, to avail themselves of the ancient salves of ritual and language. But for others, such resources are no longer theirs.

Like anyone intoxicated by the power of words, I began to read. During the next year, in which my mentor and a friend died—too young, of cancer—I read scores of narratives about the stages of grief and how to prevail in the face of them. I read books about predicaments unique to women—breast cancer, widowhood—and memoirs by siblings, parents, and husbands, describing the losses they had endured. Each kept me company in its way, and yet no one was quite what I needed.

Sorrow exposed feelings I had not encountered so powerfully since adolescence, as if I were hurled into a primal cauldron.

I was looking for a book that was not a story but a spiritual companion, a book that could be read again and again, passed from hand to hand—a kind of liturgy. Although all mourners make their way painstakingly along the same continuum, women have developed their own modes of feeling, imagery, and spiritual vocabulary; I wanted a book that drew on those distinctive modes. I began to think I would write that book, one that was ruthless about the rage of grief—the howls of outrage, as I thought of them.

A Grief Observed, C. S. Lewis's book about the death of his wife (portrayed in the movie *Shadowlands*), opens with his declaration that no one had ever told him grief felt so much like fear. I could have said: No one told me grief felt so much like fury.

In the days and weeks immediately after a death, most mourners do not have the stamina to read a sustained piece of descriptive prose. And so, my first reflections were short evocations of anger's force.

All day I dream of sleep

All day I dream of sleep, its lakes of sheets, pillows in undulating heaps. I want to mate my body to my bed, float in languor, infused, etherous. But when at last the night makes its descent, my body is a stranger, resisting all blandishment, and your face, your face, the only living thing.

Howl

*I am the lost baby, howling in night, annihilated by longing
I cannot moderate or excise, needing you without being able to
speak, before words, their tempering lies, tales of meeting in
another life or hackneyed reassurances: Life will go on. It will,
I know, go on and on and on, relentless, no reprieve from
consciousness.*

Sorrow exposed feelings I had not encountered so powerfully since
adolescence, as if I were hurled into a primal cauldron.

I want

*I want this one's hair and that one's father, this one's face and
that one's lover, this one's house and that one's toy, this one's
youth and that one's child. Before, I envied no living thing. Now
everyone has something that I covet.*

I was determined to be faithful to the brutality of pain, but also to offer
the comfort of other women's presence and consciousness, to distill the
wisdom of the remarkable women I knew who had endured.

Soliloquy

*I never held her hand. I never called the last week of her life. I
meant to make the trip and then postponed it. I said some words
I never can take back.*

*If only I had known.
         (Ah, but you didn't.)
If only I had thought.
         (But you could not.)
Why didn't I once tell you?
         (But I knew it.)
Why didn't I invite you?
         (Never mind.)
I hated you for growing weak, for dying.
         (I absolve you.)
I lie awake remembering how I failed you.
         (How I love you.)
For the rest of my life, I never—
         (Only love.)
How could I—
         (Don't you know you are forgiven?)
If only—
         (Would you want your child to live with such*

259

reproaches?)
No, I say reluctantly, I would not.
(Then forgive yourself. If only I could ask you, that is
what I'd ask.)

I had watched several friends undergo sorrows not imaginable to the uninitiated—in two families, the loss of a child. I witnessed, with something approaching awe, the fortitude my friends displayed. Their courage enabled them to soothe me when my lesser turn came.

When I began to work on the book I could not imagine solace; by the end I knew the consolations of love, particularly the love between women friends.

Woman Friend

Now, when the sea and sky die quietly, deepen to black before my eye, now when my thoughts are stilled and I can dream, remembering your strong arms, the words you floated to me, the flaring light they made while I was sinking, now until true night descends, and I descend into my bed and terror of the sleep that will not come, now, until that time I am alone and, robed in you, my dress of stars, am not afraid.

These reflections were not written specifically for Jews, and yet they are suffused with my identity. There is a section of portraits that conjures up the Jewish history of family and friends, from the pogroms of the early twentieth century to the Sabbath peace. There is the commitment to dailiness as an antidote to tragedy, and to the place of ritual in healing: both deeply Jewish strategies.

Last, there is a liturgical cadence to the language that only could have come from the pen of a woman raised to believe that words and books can be holy vehicles, through which suffering can be rendered useful—perhaps even alchemized into a gift.

In writing this book, I came to understand the truth of an old tale:

The woman grieving by the road was given this consolation: Go to every house that has known no sorrow and plead for flour. If from that flour you bake a cake before night comes, the one you mourn will be returned.

She ran from house to house, but each refused her. One door, then another, closed to her. The sky whitened and grew dark, an empty bowl.

"Alas," the woman cried, "I am undone. Not one would help me bring my lost one home."

Then she felt a hand upon her head. "My child," a voice said.

She saw the compassionate face and understood. No house is immune from sorrow, and no woman from a time of solitude.

From Textures, Hadassah National Jewish Studies Bulletin, *December 1994, vol. 13, no. 1.*

NESSA RAPOPORT is the author of a novel, Preparing for Sabbath, *and of* A Woman's Book of Grieving. *She is editor with Ted Solotaroff of* Writing Our Way Home: Contemporary Stories by American Jewish Writers. *She is a founder of the National Center for Jewish Healing.*

PROGRAMMING IDEAS

AT HOME

Torah Table Talk #1   A discussion of Jewish thought and values with your family and/or friends. Jewish mourning laws and customs are divided into five stages, as Maurice Lamm explains (in *The Jewish Way in Death and Mourning* [New York: Jonathan David, 1969], pages 78-79). The wording has been altered to achieve gender neutrality.

Maurice Lamm, "Five Stages of Mourning"

The first period is that between death and burial (*aninut*), during which time despair is most intense. At this time, not only the social amenities, but even major positive religious requirements, [are] canceled in recognition of the mourner's troubled mind.

The second stage consists of the first three days following burial, days devoted to weeping and lamentation. During this time, the mourner does not even respond to greetings, and remains at home (except under certain special circumstances). It is a time when even visiting the mourner is usually somewhat discouraged, for it is too early to comfort mourners when the wound is so fresh.

Third is the period of *shiva*, the seven days following burial. (This longer period includes the first three days.) During this time mourners emerge from the stage of intense grief to a new state of mind in which they are prepared to talk about their loss and to accept comfort from friends and neighbors. The world now enlarges for the mourners. While they remain within the house, expressing their grief through the observances of *avelut*—the wearing of the rent garment, the sitting on the low stool, the wearing of slippers, the refraining from shaving and grooming, the recital of the *Kaddish*—their acquaintances come to their home to express sympathy in the mourners' distress. The inner freezing that came with the death of the relative now begins to thaw. The isolation from the world of people and the retreat inward now relaxes somewhat, and normalcy begins to return.

Fourth is the stage of *sheloshim*, the thirty days following burial (which includes the *shiva*). The mourner is encouraged to leave the house after *shiva* and to slowly rejoin society, always recognizing that enough time has not yet elapsed to assume full, normal social relations. The rent clothing may customarily still be worn for deceased parents, and haircutting for male mourners is still generally prohibited.

The fifth and last stage is the twelve-month period (which includes the *sheloshim*) during which things return to normal, and business once again becomes routine, but the inner feelings of the mourner are still wounded by the rupture of the relationship with a parent. The pursuit of entertainment and amusement is curtailed. At the close of this last stage, the twelve-month period, the bereaved is not expected to continue mourning, except for brief moments when *yizkor* or *yahrzeit* is observed. In fact, our tradition rebukes a Jew for mourning more than this prescribed period.

In this magnificently conceived, graduated process of mourning an ancient faith raises up the mourner from the abyss of despair to the undulating hills and valleys of normal daily life.

Questions for Thought and Discussion

1. Based on your own knowledge of the stages of grief, do the five Jewish mourning stages fulfill the mourner's psychological needs? Consider the guilt and anger felt by many of the bereaved. How do the Jewish mourning periods deal with these emotions? How do they deal with other strong emotions of grieving?

2. Jewish mourning laws make no distinction between grieving for a beloved relation and grieving for a relation from whom we are completely estranged—provided that we know of the estranged relation's death. Why might this be?

3. Maurice Lamm states: "Our tradition rebukes a Jew for mourning more than this prescribed period" of one year. How can every mourner reach closure within the same time period? What might account for the traditional Jewish attitude?

4. Compare the Jewish stages of mourning to the rituals observed in America generally.

Torah Table Talk #2 During the fifth stage of grieving—the first year after a death—children who have lost a father or mother are required to recite *Kaddish*, a sanctification of God, each day during synagogue services. Until recent times, only sons fulfilled this duty, and when no son was alive, another man recited *Kaddish* on behalf of the family. Today, however, many women recite *Kaddish* when their parents die (even when the woman's brother also recites *Kaddish*). One of the first women to say *Kaddish* was Henrietta Szold, and she explains why in a letter written on September 16, 1916.

Letter of Henrietta Szold to Haym Peretz

It is impossible for me to find words in which to tell you how deeply I was touched by your offer to act as *"Kaddish"* for my dear mother. I cannot even thank you— it is something that goes beyond thanks. It is beautiful, what you have offered to do—I shall never forget it.

You will wonder, then, that I cannot accept your offer. Perhaps it would be best for me not to try to explain to you in writing, but to wait until I see you to tell you why it is so. I know well, and appreciate what you say about, the Jewish custom; and Jewish custom is very dear and sacred to me. And yet I cannot ask you to say *Kaddish* after my mother. The *Kaddish* means to me that the survivor publicly and markedly manifests his wish and intention to assume the relation to the Jewish community which his parent had, and that so the chain of tradition remains unbroken from generation to generation, each adding its own link. You can do that for the generations of your family, I must do that for the generations of my family.

I believe that the elimination of women from such duties was never intended by our law and custom—women were freed from positive duties when they could not perform them, but not when they could. It was never intended that, if they could perform them, their performance of them should not be considered as valuable and valid as when one of the male sex performed them. And of the *Kaddish* I feel sure this is particularly true.

My mother had eight daughters and no son; and yet never did I hear a word of regret pass the lips of either my mother or my father that one of us was not a son. When my father died, my mother would not permit others to take her daughters' place in saying the *Kaddish*, and so I am sure I am acting in her spirit when I am moved to decline your offer. But beautiful your offer remains nevertheless, and, I repeat, I know full well that it is much more in consonance with the generally accepted Jewish tradition than is my or my family's conception. You understand me, don't you?

Questions for Thought and Discussion

1. Henrietta Szold believes that the performance of positive duties by women should be "considered as valuable and valid as when one of the male sex performed them." ("Positive duties" are the time-bound commandments that only Jewish men are required to perform. These include praying three times daily; wearing *tefillin*; making up a *minyan*.) However, many Orthodox legal interpreters take the opposite position, that women are actually forbidden to perform the positive duties—particularly reciting the *Kaddish*. Comment.

2. Henrietta Szold did not consider herself a feminist, nor did she particularly advocate for the rights of women, yet her letter is a revolutionary feminist document. Discuss. (Also note the warm, touching, and apologetic language that Henrietta Szold uses in writing this letter of refusal!)

3. In saying the *Kaddish* herself, Henrietta Szold follows her mother's wishes. What options are open to women who seek to say *Kaddish* themselves

but are fairly certain that their deceased parent would have preferred a man to do so?

Additional At-Home Activities

❖   Writing provides a catharsis for the complexity of emotion that accompanies extremely sorrowful experiences. Think about the most difficult period of your life, and write down words and phrases that come to mind. To create one section in *A Woman's Book of Grieving*, Nessa Rapoport asked several women friends what sentences most console them. Write down these sentences as well, and later compare with your friends' or fellow Hadassah members' writings.

INTEREST/STUDY GROUPS

Hold a discussion based on the following questions:

1.   Do women and men cope with loss differently? Do you think that a man would be capable of providing the consolation found in "Woman Friend"? (See page 260.) If not, why?

2.   The Jewish mourner's prayer, the *Kaddish*, abundantly praises God, and expresses hope for peace and the speedy establishment of God's kingdom on earth. Nessa Rapoport's poem deals with the anguish of the living. Discuss how each of these approaches offers solace.

3.   In the past, women did not recite the mourner's *Kaddish*. Today, no rituals exist to mourn events such as miscarriage. If you could, what mourning rituals and prayers would you add to Jewish practice?

4.   Nessa Rapoport says that her book on grieving was "not written specifically for Jews," yet it is suffused with her Jewish identity. In what ways is Judaism apparent in the poems? She believes that "words and books can be holy vehicles, through which suffering can be rendered useful—perhaps even alchemized into a gift." Why is this a Jewish statement?

❖   Start a study group on coping with death and bereavement. Lynn Wachtel organized such a study group for the Champaign-Urbana (Illinois) chapter of Hadassah. Following the study group, Lynn Wachtel, together with Alice Scheeline Berkson, wrote "A Guide to Death and Mourning Traditions," which was printed by Champaign-Urbana Jewish Federation in 1993. This booklet was distributed to everyone in the Champaign-Urbana Jewish community, and is still given to all newcomers to the community. For a copy, write to the Champaign-Urbana Jewish Federation at 503 East John Street, Champaign, IL 61820. The cost is $5.00.

MEETINGS

❖   Invite a rabbi to discuss the Jewish laws of mourning and his or her work with mourners.

❖ In conjunction with discussing "On Sorrow and Solace," read some of the poetry aloud. Ask members to share their reactions and their own experiences of mourning.

ANNUAL EVENTS

❖ Organize a forum on death and bereavement. Invite a Jewish funeral director to discuss the laws of mourning (including *shiva* and commemorating *yahrzeit* as well as funeral procedures), another speaker to discuss current Jewish women's mourning practices (perhaps including poetry reading, a description of new rituals, and/or a discussion of saying *Kaddish* over the course of a year), and one or two widows to speak about their own grieving processes.

HANDS-ON

❖ Compile a pamphlet or book of your Hadassah members' thoughts on grieving. (See "Additional At-Home Activities," page 264.) Have everyone write down the words that come to mind as they reflect on the most difficult period of their lives, and compare the results. Also encourage group members to think of the phrases in which they have found the most comfort. Compare these writings as well. Do they find each other's ideas comforting as well?

❖ Learn about the *Hevrah Kaddishah* (Jewish burial society) in your community. If possible, join.

Recommended Reading

Adelman, Penina. *Miriam's Well: Rituals for Jewish Women Around the Year,* 2nd edition. New York: Biblio, 1990.

Berrin, Susan, ed. *Celebrating the New Month: A Rosh Chodesh Anthology.* Northvale, NJ: Jason Aronson, 1996.

Brin, Ruth. *Harvest: Collected Poems and Prayers.* New York: Reconstructionist Press, 1986.

Broner, E. M. *Mornings and Mourning: A Kaddish Journal.* San Francisco: HarperSanFrancisco, 1994.

Broner, E. M., and Nimrod, Naomi. *The Telling: The Story of a Group of Jewish Women Who Journey to Spirituality Through Community and Ceremony.* San Francisco: HarperSanFrancisco, 1993.

Broner, E. M. *A Weave of Women.* New York: Holt Rinehart, 1978.

Elbogen, Ismar. *Jewish Liturgy: A Comprehensive History.* Translated by Raymond P. Scheindlin. Philadelphia: Jewish Publication Society, 1993.

Falk, Marcia. *The Book of Blessings: A Feminist-Jewish Reconstruction of Prayer.* San Francisco: HarperSanFrancisco, 1992.

Falk, Marcia. *The Book of Blessings: A Re-Creation of Jewish Prayer for the Weekdays, the Sabbath, and the New Moon Festival.* San Francisco: HarperSanFrancisco, 1995.

Falk, Marcia, translator. *The Song of Songs: A New Translation and Interpretation.* San Francisco: HarperSanFrancisco, 1990.

Falk, Marcia, translator. *With Teeth in the Earth: Selected Poems of Malka Heifetz Tussman.* Detroit: Wayne State University Press, 1992.

Frankiel, Tamar. *The Voice of Sarah: Feminine Spirituality and Traditional Judaism.* San Francisco: HarperSanFrancisco, 1990.

Gold, Doris B., and Stein, Lisa, eds. *From the Wise Women of Israel: Folklore and Memoirs.* New York: Biblio, 1996.

Goldstein, Rabbi Elyse. "Take Back the Waters: A Feminist Re-Appropriation of *Mikvah,*" *Lilith Magazine*, Summer 1986, pages 15-16.

Grossman, Susan, and Haut, Rivka. *Daughters of the King: Women and the Synagogue.* Philadelphia: Jewish Publication Society, 1993.

Heschel, Susannah, ed. *On Being a Jewish Feminist.* New York: Schocken, 1995.

Kaye/Kantrowitz, Melanie, and Klepfisz, Irene, eds. *The Tribe of Dina: A Jewish Women's Anthology.* Boston: Beacon, 1989.

Koltun, Elizabeth, ed. *The Jewish Woman: New Perspectives.* New York: Schocken, 1976.

Margolis, Daniel and Patty. "Birth Ceremonies." In *The Second Jewish Catalogue,* Strassfeld, Sharon and Michael, eds. Philadelphia: Jewish Publication Society, 1976.

Moffat, Mary Jane, ed. *In the Midst of Winter: Selections from the Literature of Mourning.* New York: Vintage, Random House, 1982.

New Woman Collective. *The Jewish Women's Awareness Guide: Connections for the Second Wave of Jewish Feminism.* New York: Biblio, 1996.

Newman, Leslea, ed. *Bubbe Meisehs by Shayneh Maidelehs: Poetry by Jewish Granddaughters About Our Grandmothers.* Santa Cruz, CA: HerBooks, 1989.

Ochs, Vanessa L. *Words on Fire: One Woman's Journey into the Sacred.* New York: Harcourt Brace Jovanovich, 1990.

Orenstein, Debra, ed. *Lifecycles: Jewish Women on Life Passages and Personal Milestones.* Woodstock, VT: Jewish Lights, 1994.

Piercy, Marge. *Mars & Her Children.* New York: Knopf, 1982.

Piercy, Marge. *My Mother's Body.* New York: Knopf, 1985.

Plaskow, Judith. *Standing Again at Sinai: Judaism from a Feminist Perspective.* San Francisco: HarperSanFrancisco, 1990.

Rapoport, Nessa. *A Woman's Book of Grieving.* New York: William Morrow, 1994.

Ruether, Rosemary, and McLaughlin, Eleanor, eds. *Women of Spirit: Female Leadership in the Jewish and Christian Traditions.* New York: Simon and Schuster, 1979.

Schwartz, Howard, and Rudolph, Anthony, eds. *Voices Within the Ark: The Modern Jewish Poets.* New York: Avon, 1980.

Siegel, Danny. *Where Heaven & Earth Touch: An Anthology of Midrash and Halachah.* Northvale, NJ: Jason Aronson, 1989.

Solomon, Judith Y. *The Rosh Hodesh Table: Foods at the New Moon.* New York: Biblio, 1995.

Umansky, Ellen M., and Ashton, Dianne, eds. *Four Centuries of Jewish Women's Spirituality: A Sourcebook.* Boston: Beacon, 1992.

Wenkart, Henny, ed. *Sarah's Daughters Sing: A Sampler of Poems by Jewish Women.* Hoboken, NJ: Ktav, 1990.

GLOSSARY

Abba • father.

Adonai • literally "my Lord." God. *Adonai* is said when the tetragrammaton (the Hebrew letters corresponding to YHVH) is printed in a Hebrew prayer.

Agunah • literally "chained one." According to Jewish law, a wife is unable to divorce her husband. He must divorce her, and does so by handing her a Jewish divorce document. A woman whose husband leaves her but refuses to give her the divorce document is an *agunah*. Plural: *agunot*.

Aliyot • plural of *aliyah*, literally "ascension." Refers to (1) immigration to Israel, and (2) reciting blessings before and after the Torah reading during synagogue service.

Amidah • literally "standing." A prayer that is the heart of every synagogue service.

Aninut • burial.

Arayot • forbidden sexual relations.

Attah • you.

Avelut • mourning.

Ba'alat teshuvah • literally "mistress of repentance (or return)." The term usually refers to a woman who becomes an observant Orthodox Jew after having been raised in a less observant or non-observant home. (The term for a man is *ba'al teshuvah*—literally "master of repentance.")

Baba Kama • literally "the first gate." The name of one of the tractates of the Talmud.

Bar mitzvah • a Jewish male who takes on the responsibilities of an adult and who becomes a full member of the community. Also refers to the ceremony (held at age 13) that marks this transition.

Barukh • praised.

Bat mitzvah • in Conservative, Reform, and Reconstructionist Jewish practice, a Jewish female who takes on the responsibilities of an adult and who becomes a full member of the community. Also refers to the ceremony (held at age 12 or 13) that marks this transition. In Orthodox practice, the significance of a girl reaching adulthood and the type of ceremony held—if any—varies widely. Among the Modern Orthodox, bat mitzvah ceremonies have recently become commonplace.

Berakhot • literally "blessings." The name of one of the tractates of the Talmud.

Beit din • literally "house of law." Court of Jewish law.

Beit midrash • place of Torah study.

Bet Hillel · literally "house of Hillel." The term is used for those who followed the teachings of Hillel. In most cases, Jewish law follows the rulings of Hillel, as opposed to Shammai. Hillel is considered the more lenient and humane of these two rabbis. (*Beit* is an alternate spelling of "house.")

Bet Shammai · literally "house of Shammai." The term is used for those who followed the teachings of Shammai. (*Beit* is an alternate spelling of "house.")

Bikkur holim · literally "visiting the sick." *Bikkur Holim* societies arrange for community members to visit hospital patients or ill people at home.

Birkat halevanah · blessing of the moon.

Borei · creator.

Brakhah · blessing. Plural: *brakhot* (*berakhot* is an alternate spelling).

Brit bat tzion · Hebrew naming and covenant ceremony for a newborn girl. (The ceremony is also called *simhat bat.*)

Brit milah · circumcision and covenant ceremony for eight-day-old boy. The *brit* (covenant) and *milah* (circumcision) mark the initiation of the boy into the Jewish people.

Daven (Yiddish) · pray.

Dinar · ancient monetary denomination.

Ein hahayyim · the wellspring, fountain, or source of life.

Eishet hayil · woman of valor. This phrase comes from Proverbs 31:10-31.

Eloheinu · our God.

Eruvim · plural of *eruv,* literally "mixing." The *eruv* is a set of poles linked across the top by wires; it surrounds a public area and symbolically transforms the public domain into a private domain. According to Jewish law, carrying objects (including babies) is forbidden in a public area on Shabbat, but is permitted in a private area. By symbolically "mixing" the two areas, the public domain becomes a private domain, so that carrying objects—and pushing strollers—is legally acceptable.

Gedolim · literally "giants." The esteemed, historic commentators of Jewish law.

Gemara · a compendium of rabbinic discussions based on the Mishnah. The rabbis of Babylonia edited and compiled their discussion around the year 500. Together with the Mishnah, their work is known as the Babylonian Talmud. The *Gemara* is written in Aramaic.

Gemilut hasadim · acts of kindness. Also translated as loving-kindness.

Ger · stranger. Synonyms: *nokhri, zar.*

Get · Jewish divorce document.

Goyim · (1) nations; (2) gentiles.

Hai · literally "life." The word is frequently used to refer to eighteen dollars.

Halakhah · Jewish law. Adjective: halakhic.

Halitzah · a ceremony that nullifies the obligation of a man to marry his brother's childless widow.

Hallah · loaf of bread, usually egg bread, from which a small piece of dough was removed before baking.

Hashem · literally "the name." God. Orthodox Jews do not say the word God (or any Hebrew words meaning God) except when reciting prayers. *Hashem* is one common way in which traditional, observant Jews refer to God in everyday speech.

Havdalah · literally "separation." The ritual performed after Shabbat ends on Saturday evening; it distinguishes between the sacred day that has just ended and the regular, non-sacred weekday to come.

Havurah · literally "group." A group of Jews who pray and observe Jewish rituals together, usually holding egalitarian, peer-led, and rabbi-less services.

Herem · excommunication from the Jewish people. Used also to mean a ban.

Heter · permission obtained from a rabbinic authority.

Hillel · rabbi of the Second Temple period. See "Bet Hillel" above.

Hukkah · a law we obey even though we don't understand the reason for it.

Huppah · wedding canopy. The bridegroom and bride stand under a *huppah* during the wedding ceremony.

Ima · mother.

Issar · ancient monetary denomination.

Kaddish · a prayer sanctifying God, recited by mourners. (The same prayer is also recited aloud several times during every synagogue service by both mourners and non-mourners.)

Kallah · bride.

Kedoshim tihyu · "You shall be holy." God commands the people of Israel to be holy in Leviticus 19:2.

Kedushah · holiness.

Ketubah · marriage contract. Plural: *ketubot.*

Ketubot · literally "marriage contracts." The name of one of the tractates of the Talmud.

Kiddush · blessing recited over wine.

Kiddush Hashem · a holy act that sanctifies the name of God. Jews are obligated to die in sanctification of God's name rather than commit the sins of idolatry, licentiousness, or murder. (Jews must commit any other sin if they are forced to do so at pain of death.)

Kiddushin · marriage according to Jewish religious law. Also, the name of one of the tractates of the Talmud.

Kinyan · symbolic transfer of ownership.

Kippah · skull cap or *yarmulke* (Yiddish).

Latkes (Yiddish) · potato pancakes traditionally eaten during Hanukkah.

Lulav · palm, myrtle, and willow leaves bound together and sanctified (together with an *etrog,* a citron) during Sukkot.

Maariv · evening prayers.

Maimonides (1135-1204) · a Spanish scholar, legal commentator, philosopher, and physician. He wrote *Guide of the Perplexed* and the legal code, *Mishneh Torah.* He was born in Spain, and lived mostly in Egypt. The acronym Rambam (for Rabbi Moses Ben Maimon) is commonly used.

Mamzerim • children born out of wedlock. Singular: *mamzer*.

Matzmihat • nurtures.

Mayim hayim • living waters. Refers to any body of water that is not stagnant, such as a river or ocean.

Mazal tov • good fortune. Used colloquially as "congratulations."

Megillat Esther • Scroll of Esther.

Melekh • sovereign or king. (*Melekh ha'olam* • sovereign of the universe.)

Menorah • candelabrum. The seven-branched *menorah* (with seven candles) is a frequent Jewish symbol. A Hanukkah *menorah,* also known as a *hanukkiyah,* holds nine candles (or wicks).

Mezuzah • small box posted on the door frame of a home or a room. Inside is a small parchment scroll containing the *Shema* prayer.

Mi shebeirakh • prayer said on behalf of those in need of healing. It is recited in synagogue during the Torah reading on Shabbat and holidays.

Midrash—(1) A particular genre of rabbinic literature, written in Hebrew, that includes sermons, homilies, biblical exegesis, exegetical material on later Jewish texts, legends, tales, as well as some legal rulings. (2) A modern-day exegetical composition on the Bible or other Jewish texts, particularly one in the form of a tale or legend (when used in this sense, *midrash* is not capitalized).

Mikvah • ritual bath. Plural: *mikva'ot.*

Minyan • quorum of ten required for a prayer service. In Orthodox Judaism all ten must be men. Used colloquially to mean prayer group or prayer service.

Mishnah • the name for the sixty-three Hebrew tractates in which Rabbi Judah the Prince recorded the Oral Law around the year 200.

Mishneh Torah • 14-volume legal code written by Maimonides. The *Mishneh Torah* is the first complete, systematic, and rational arrangement of Jewish law.

Mishpahah • family.

Mitzvah • commandment. Plural: *mitzvot.*

Motzi • blessing recited before eating bread.

Naches (Yiddish) • joy.

Nefesh • soul, living person.

Nehalel • let us praise or celebrate.

Nekeivah • female.

Nevakesh • let us seek.

Nevareikh • let us bless.

Niddah • Jewish woman's untouchability during and immediately after menstruation.

Nishmat kol hai • the soul or breath of all living things.

Nitzonot hanefesh • the sparks or the spirit of the soul.

Oholot • literally "tents." The name of one of the tractates of the Talmud.

Parnoseh (Yiddish) • livelihood.

Perutah • ancient monetary denomination.

Pesak • determination on a point of Jewish law that seems unclear.

Piku'ah nefesh • saving a life.

Pilagshut • the taking of a concubine, or half-marriage.

Pirkei Avot • *Ethics of the Fathers*. A compendium of moral advice and insights, it is one of the tractates of the Mishnah.

Rabbanut • rabbinate.

Rashi (1040-1105) • great commentator on the Bible and Talmud. The name Rashi is a Hebrew acronym for Rabbi Shlomo Yitzhaki.

Rodef • pursuer.

Rosh Hodesh • the New Moon and New Month.

Sanhedrin • (1) The name given to an assembly of Jewish leaders convened by Napoleon Bonaparte in 1807. (2) The supreme political, religious, and judicial body in Judea during the Roman period, both before and after the destruction of the Temple.

Semahot hokhmah • celebrations of wisdom that come with age, usually held on the sixtieth birthday.

Shalom • peace, wholeness; hello; good-bye.

Shalom bayit • peace in the home.

Shammai • rabbi of the Second Temple period. See *"Bet Shammai"* above.

Sheheheyanu • literally "Who has kept us alive." The blessing that is recited upon reaching a new season (and upon other new experiences).

Shekhinah • God. Specifically used to refer to the feminine aspects of God.

Sheloshim • literally "thirty." The thirty-day mourning period following the death of a close relative.

Shema • the prayer "Hear O Israel the Lord our God the Lord is One" and its accompanying biblical passages.

Sheva brakhot • the seven blessings recited during a Jewish wedding. Also refers to the seven dinners or parties given for the newlyweds over the next seven days.

Shiva • the seven initial days of mourning following the death of an immediate relative.

Shofar • ram's horn that is blown in the month preceding Rosh Hashanah, on Rosh Hashanah, and at the conclusion of Yom Kippur.

Shulhan Arukh • authoritative code of Jewish law, written by Joseph Caro (1488-1575).

Siddur • prayer book.

Simhah • happiness. Also used colloquially to refer to happy occasions, such as weddings or bar mitzvah parties.

Simhat bat • Hebrew naming and covenant ceremony for a newborn girl.

Sofer • scribe.

Sukkah • booth (hut, tabernacle) reminiscent of the dwellings used by the Jews in the desert after the exodus from Egypt. During the holiday of Sukkot ("booths"), we eat in a *sukkah* for eight days.

Taharat hamishpahah • family purity.

Takkanah • legislative amendment. Plural: *takkanot*.

Tallit · prayer shawl.

Talmud · Mishnah and *Gemara*. The Talmud is the work of Jewish law from which all other legal writings are derived. In addition to legal rulings, the Talmud includes parables, stories of the rabbis' lives, commentary and explanation of the Bible, legends, and homilies. Adjective: talmudic.

Tanakh · the Hebrew Bible. The word *Tanakh* is an acrostic: T stands for Torah (the Five Books of Moses); N stands for *Nevi'im* (Prophets); and K stands for *Ketuvim* (Writings).

Tefillah · prayer.

Tefillin · leather straps and a small box, worn around one's arm and forehead during weekday morning prayer service. The box contains the *Shema* prayer.

Tekhines (Yiddish) · Yiddish prayers written specifically for women and sometimes by women during the Middle Ages and early modern era.

Tekiah teru'ah · one of the rhythmic patterns of shofar notes. *Tekiah* is one long note; it is followed by *teru'ah,* three intermediate-length notes.

Tikkun olam · the Jewish injunction to mend and repair the world.

Toharah · purification.

Torah · (1) The first five books of the Bible, also called the Five Books of Moses and the Pentateuch. (2) Parchment scrolls on which the first five books of the Bible are written. (3) All of Jewish learning, including the Bible, the Mishnah and *Gemara,* the Midrash, and the writings of great rabbis until the present day.

Tzedakah · charity.

Tzitzit · literally, "fringes." An Orthodox man wears a *tallit katan,* small prayer shawl, under his shirt. *Tzitzit* are the fringes of this garment, and the word also refers to the garment itself.

Tzva'ot · hosts.

Yalkut Shimoni · comprehensive anthology of Midrash, compiled approximately thirteenth century.

Yahrzeit · anniversary of a death. The commemoration of the *yahrzeit* includes reciting *Kaddish* in synagogue and lighting a 24-hour memorial candle. *Yahrzeit* is observed for parents, and in some cases for brothers and sisters, daughters and sons, and spouses.

Yevamot · literally "sisters-in-law." The name of one of the tractates of the Talmud.

Yeshivah · Jewish religious school for teenage boys and young men.

Yizkor · prayer of remembrance for deceased loved ones. *Yizkor* is said in synagogue four times a year: on Passover, Shavuot, Yom Kippur, and Shemini Atzeret (the eighth day of Sukkot).

Yom tov · festival.

Yoma · literally "day." The name of one of the tractates of the Talmud.

Zakhar · male.

Zenut · promiscuity.

Zuzim · ancient monetary units.

Acknowledgment of Sources

We gratefully acknowledge permission to use the following copyrighted material:

Unit 1: SELF

Sue Mizrahi, "The Beauty Myth—or the Mind/Body Problem, Revisited." Copyright © 1994 by Sue Mizrahi. Reprinted by permission of the author.

Edie Diament Gurewitsch, M.D., "Your Body Is a Jewish Responsibility." Copyright © 1994 by Edie Gurewitsch. Reprinted by permission of the author.

Sylvia Barack Fishman, "The Way of Women: Finding Jewish Models of Aging." Copyright © 1994 by Sylvia Barack Fishman. Reprinted by permission of the author.

Gail Katz Meller, "A Time to Mourn, A Time to Dance: An Unfinished Work in Progress." Copyright © 1989, 1997 by Gail Katz Meller. Reprinted by permission of the author.

Unit 2: FAMILY AND HOME

Yeroham Tsuriel, "The *Kedushah* of Monogamy: A Personal Perspective," and Ellen M. Umansky, "The Liberal Jew and Sex," from *Response, A Contemporary Jewish Review*, Winter 1996-97. Copyright © 1977 by Response. Reprinted with permission of Response, A Contemporary Jewish Review, 114 West 26th

Unit 3: WOMEN AND THE WORKPLACE

Unit 4: SOCIAL ACTION

David Epstein and Suzanne Singer Stutman, "The Story of Zelophehad's Daughters," from *Torah With Love: A Guide for Strengthening Jewish Values Within the Family*, published by Prentice Hall. Copyright © 1986. Reprinted by permission of the authors.

Rachel Biale, "Abortion in Jewish Law." Copyright © 1990 by Rachel Biale. Reprinted by permission of the author.

Alice Shalvi, "Women and Society in Israel." Copyright © 1989 by Alice Shalvi. Reprinted by permission of the author.

Unit 5: SPIRITUALITY

Vanessa L. Ochs, "The Future for Jewish Women." Copyright © 1992 by Vanessa L. Ochs. Reprinted by permission of the author.

Tamara Cohen, "Contemporary Jewish Women's Rituals." Copyright © 1994 by Tamara Cohen. Reprinted by permission of the author.

Marcia Falk, "On Blessing." Copyright © 1994 by Marcia Lee Falk. Used by permission of the author.

Nessa Rapoport, "On Sorrow and Solace." Copyright © 1994 by Nessa Rapoport. Reprinted by permission of the author. Excerpts from *A Woman's Book of Grieving* by Nessa Rapoport, published by William Morrow and Company, copyright © 1994 by Nessa Rapoport, are reprinted by permission of the author.

PROGRAMMING

All selections from the Bible are reprinted from the *Tanakh: A New Translation of the Holy Scriptures According to the Traditional Jewish Text*, published by the Jewish Publication Society, unless otherwise noted. Copyright © 1985. Reprinted by permission of the publisher.

Dahlia Ravikovitch, "Clockwork Doll," from *The Modern Hebrew Poem Itself*, edited by Stanley Burnshaw, T. Carmi, and Ezra Spicehandler (Cambridge, MA: Harvard University Press). Translation copyright © 1989. All rights for the original Hebrew poem are reserved by the author, c/o ACUM, Israel. English translation by Arieh Sachs reprinted by permission of Ezra Spicehandler and Stanley Burnshaw.

Lea Goldberg, "From My Mother's Home," from *The Modern Hebrew Poem Itself*, edited by Stanley Burnshaw, T. Carmi, and Ezra Spicehandler (Cambridge, MA: Harvard University Press, 1989). Translation copyright © 1977, 1989. All rights for the original Hebrew poem are reserved by Yair Landau. English translation by Ezra Spicehandler reprinted by permission of Ezra Spicehandler and Stanley Burnshaw.

ADDITIONAL PUBLICATIONS

True to its roots as a study circle, Hadassah encourages its members to explore the many facets of Jewish history and culture. To purchase any of the following study guides and resources, created by the National Jewish Education Department, please contact the National Hadassah Order Department at 1-800-880-9455.

An American Zionist Tapestry

Study guide on the leaders of American Zionism. Order #R252. $2 members, $3 non-members.

Around the Year With the Jewish Calendar

Summary of the important events of the Jewish year, including suggestions for programming.
Volume I: Tishrei to Adar (September-February). Order #R208. $2 members, $3 non-members.
Volume II: Nisan to Elul (March-August). Order #R209. $2 members, $3 non-members.

Images of Jerusalem: City of David in Modern Hebrew Literature

Study guide in honor of the 3000th anniversary of Jerusalem as the capital of the Jewish people. Order #R613. $10 members, $13 non-members.

Israeli and American Jews: Understanding and Misunderstanding

Study guide addresses the seemingly irreconcilable differences between the two leading Jewish populations of the world. Order #R222. $8 members, $12 non-members.

Jewish Marital Status

Anthology of essays offering Jewish viewpoints on dating, sex, intimate relationships, marriage, and the end of marriage. Special price $25. Call 1-212-303-8167 to order.

A Companion Guide to the Book Jewish Marital Status

Programming and activities on *Jewish Marital Status*. Order #R226. $3 members, $5 non-members.

Judaism and Ecology

Study guide on Jewish environmental values. Order #R229. $7 members, $11 non-members.

Leader's Guide to the Book of Jeremiah

Study the prophetic tradition in Judaism. Order #R197. $3 members, $5 non-members.

Leader's Guide to the Book of Psalms

Study one of Judaism's most beloved texts. Order #R198. $3 members, $5 non-members.

Leader's Guide to the Book of Samuel

The first study guide in Hadassah's Bible series. Order #R199. $3 members, $5 non-members.

Reflections on Jerusalem: City of David in Classical Texts

Study guide in honor of the 3000th anniversary of Jerusalem as the capital of the Jewish people. Order #R614. $6 members, $9 non-members.

Ribcage: Israeli Women's Fiction

Study guide contains short stories in English translation. Order #R492. $10 members, $15 non-members.

The Talmud and You

Units I and II (Book 1), III and IV (Book 2). Study series on the Talmud's relevance to daily life. Order #R232 for Book 1 and #R233 for Book 2. Each book $2 members, $3 non-members.

Understanding the Holocaust: How It Happened

Study unit focuses on the Holocaust itself and on the factors that permitted this tragedy to occur. Order #R221. $2 members, $3 non-members.

A Zionist Tapestry

Study guide presents the major thinkers and ideas of Zionism and their implications for contemporary Zionist thought and action. Order #R251. $2 members, $4 non-members.